GOODBYE, BUTTERFLY

GOODBYE, BUTTERFLY

Murder, faith and forgiveness
in a small Kansas town

ERNIE W. WEBB III

Clovercroft Publishing

For the Kellers and my Dad

Goodbye, Butterfly: Murder, faith and forgiveness in a small Kansas town
©2024 Ernie Webb

Published by Clovercroft Publishing, Franklin, Tennessee

Clovercroftpublishinggroup.com

Edited by Shana Curtis Webb and Heidi Koger

Interior Design by Suzanne Lawing

Printed in the United States of America

ISBN: 978-1-956370-46-1 (print)

Contents

CHAPTER ONE:

THE VOLLEYBALL TOURNAMENT

In the summer of 1991, 12-year-old Brenda Michelle Keller decided she was going to be a better athlete. At 5-foot-5 and 112 pounds, she had powerful legs from riding her bike miles across the hilly, winding country roads in the southwest corner of Shawnee County, 15 minutes from Topeka, Kansas.

The owner of an 18-speed Schwinn with shiny green paint and tires fit for rough gravel roads, Brenda pedaled for hours on the outskirts of Dover, the small town where she lived, reveling in the beauty of land marked by aging trees and an abundance of wildlife.

"Brenda just loved nature, loved animals," her father, Bob, said. "That bike was her prized possession. She'd ride that thing 10, 20 miles a day."

Logging thousands of miles on her bike gave Brenda an advantage in sports against some of her schoolmates. What she might have lacked in skill, she made up for in fitness, especially speed and endurance. She also knew natural ability wasn't enough and leaned on her older brother, John, a football and basketball player at Mission Valley

High School, for help. Almost daily, the siblings shot on a goal behind the family's home.

"When Brenda decided she wanted to do something, she worked at it," her mother, Tracy, said.

Volleyball bridged the gap between Brenda's summer of hoop dreams and her first season of basketball at Dover Junior High. A seventh grader, she didn't play much on the varsity volleyball team in September and October of 1991. But, like many young girls, being a part of the team meant spending time with her friends. And sports, like in many small towns, were vital in Dover.

Toward the end of the volleyball season, the Tigers had a tournament on Saturday, Oct. 19, at Mission Valley, where kids from Dover and several other small towns in the area traveled for the ninth through 12th grade. On a cool, crisp autumn morning, Brenda, her teammates, coaches, and Terri Anderson, the principal of the junior high and grade school, climbed onto a bus and headed southwest to the tournament.

Three hours and several matches later, the Tigers were on their way back to Dover. Brenda's teammates and others on the bus remember little about the tournament, but they do recall the 10-minute trip home. During that time, Brenda asked her friends to hang out that afternoon.

"She asked me if I wanted to go on a bike ride, and I said, 'I'm tired,'" said Jill Wilson, Brenda's best friend. "We'd been playing all day, and I said, 'No.'"

Brenda didn't stop with Wilson. She asked several other teammates, including Misty Lange, a close friend who lived across the street from the Kellers and often went with Brenda on her long bike rides. She also asked Crystal Sievers, Brooklynd Thomas, and Jana Blodgett. Exhausted from a long morning of volleyball, each passed.

The trip home had a profound impact on several of the people on the bus. As sunlight shined through the back and side windows, Allen Zordel, a teacher and coach, and Kristi Osburn, a teammate and eighth-grader, saw a light tracing Brenda's body. Anderson can still see Brenda sitting on the bus.

"I remember her turning around, looking at me," Anderson said. "Our eyes locked, and she smiled. That was the last time I saw her."

Arriving at the junior high school early in the afternoon on a sunny, uncharacteristically warm day for mid-October, members of the team went separate ways. Brenda came home at about 2 p.m., grabbed a snack, and watched TV for an hour before changing for her bike ride. In the few hours before leaving, she asked her mother, John, and younger brother, Pat, if they wanted to tag along. Each said no, and she climbed on her bike at 4 p.m.

"I remember looking out the window and seeing her get on her bike and getting ready to head out," Lange said. "She went out of town, to the east, and off she went."

Brenda had several routes. Sometimes, she rode west from her house along 57th Street, the main road running east and west through the heart of Dover, turned right on K-4 Highway, which zigged and zagged northeast to Auburn Road, just outside of Topeka, before heading back to the south along the gravel of Davis Road. On another route, she headed west for miles on 57th, picked one of many dirt roads, and rode between farmland dotted with greenery.

On this day, Brenda picked her favorite route, heading east on 57th Street up the steep hill leading out of Dover. About a mile from her house, she turned right onto Davis Road, a sparsely populated dirt road just outside of the community. On any other day, Brenda might be gone for three or four hours taking in the beauty of nature, admiring butterflies, squirrels, and other critters. On this day, she had a little more than an hour to travel six miles. At 5:30 p.m., the Kellers planned to drive to the junior high for the annual Ladies Aid banquet, a charity event held by a women's group at the Dover Federated Church.

Brenda rode south on Davis, which had only a handful of houses surrounded by large open pastures and hills. Though few people lived on this section of the ride, longtime Dover resident Roger Lambotte,

11

whose house was a mile south of 57th Street, spotted Brenda before 5 p.m. Brenda pedaled on to the south, turning right on 79th Street and heading west toward Douglas Road. About a mile later, she turned north onto Douglas to finish the final two miles of her trip. At some point between 79th Street and 69th Street, Brenda had to stop riding her bike due to a mechanical issue – either the chain came off or the rear tire went flat – and that left her pushing it along the east side of Douglas a little after 5 p.m.

Before Brenda turned north onto Douglas, friend Aimee Grubb drove toward the junior high with her father, Don. A 13-year-old, Aimee Grubb was on a driving lesson as they delivered pies for the Ladies Aid dinner. Moments before pulling into the parking lot, the Grubbs met a red Camaro with the license plate "TAMSTOY," which pulled into the driveway of the house on Douglas Road owned by Gene and Tammy Blake. The Grubbs dropped off the pies at the grade school and traveled back on Douglas toward their home in Harveyville, a small town 15 miles south of Dover. Less than a half mile from school, the Grubbs drove past Brenda as she pushed her bike directly south of the Blake home.

"She was right by the Rileys' driveway because we could have pulled in there," Aimee Grubb said. "I wondered why she was pushing her bike, and I thought maybe we should ask her if she wants a ride."

Don Grubb, who grew up in Dover, said, "She rode her bike lots of times around that square. I'd never given (stopping to pick her up) a thought. I just thought maybe she's tired. You get tired and you get off and push sometimes. I never paid any attention if she had a flat tire. It goes through my mind quite often. I lay awake at night at times wondering why in the hell I didn't stop and ask her if she needed any assistance."

As the Grubbs drove back to Harveyville, they crossed paths with Penny and Francy Lister, who lived a little more than a mile south of Dover. The Listers, including husband and father Larry, are lifelong residents. Their daughter Francy was one year ahead of Brenda in school and knew her well from the Dover Federated Church and its popular youth group.

"Brenda and Francy were really good friends," Penny Lister said. "They were close. Her and Crystal and Jill ... those kids were just close."

Like the Grubbs, the Listers were dropping off pies that evening for the banquet and left their home a few minutes before 5:30 p.m. Penny hosted a family gathering that evening, so she and Francy were gone no more than 15 minutes before returning home. Less than five minutes into their drive, they passed the Blakes' house, a two-story, blue home on the west side of the road. Resting on several acres of property covered in thick timber, the Blake house has four bedrooms, two bathrooms, and a cellar.

In 1991, the property had several buildings, including multiple red barns, an open field directly north of the barns, a large pond with a makeshift diving board, and a creek running through the woods. A dilapidated small building, which the family and others referred to as a boatshed, rested on the west side of the pond atop a small hill. As the Listers approached the driveway leading to the house, Penny Lister spotted three men sitting at a picnic table in the front yard.

Moments later, the Listers passed Brenda as she pushed her bike north on the east side of the paved road. When the Listers drove by her, Brenda was 50 yards north of the Blake home and crossing a small bridge at the section of the Blake property that opened to a pasture.

"I was like, 'That's not too good.' She was pushing her bike past their house and they were just sitting there," Penny Lister said.

She considered stopping and asking if Brenda wanted a ride, but decided not to because they were hosting a family birthday party that night. The Listers arrived at the grade school at about 5:30 p.m., and Francy Lister dropped off the pies, which took no more than 5 minutes. They were back on Douglas Road by 5:35 p.m., heading south toward their house.

"We came directly back, and Brenda wasn't anywhere," Penny Lister said. "I thought, 'Well, that's kind of strange.' But Brenda was notorious for, if a squirrel would have gone across the street, she would have been checking out where it went, so I really thought that she could have got through the fence line and taken a little jaunt back. I really was not that concerned."

As the Listers drove by the Blake house, Penny also noticed something else: The three men sitting at the picnic table minutes earlier were not there and out of sight. That memory haunts Penny more than 30 years later. She and her daughter were the last people to see Brenda alive, other than her killer.

CHAPTER TWO:

MOVING TO DOVER

To know the Kellers is to know their faith. The son of a pastor, Bob is well-versed in God's word, and church is the center of the Kellers' being. Brenda embraced God from an early age, but her devotion grew drastically in the summer of 1990 while she was doing something else she loved.

"I always thought I was a Christian when I was little, but I think I really became one last year," Brenda wrote on a Bible camp questionnaire in 1990. "I had been going to a lot of youth group things, and they started making me feel guilty. So, one time when I was on a long bike ride, I asked Jesus into my heart, and ever since then have been growing more and more in Him every day."

Brenda finished the survey with the following answer to "What can we pray for you this year?": "That I will learn to be a good witness and have a perfect heart for God."

The change in Brenda afterward was profound. She started reading the Bible daily, became more tender-hearted, and displayed more willingness to learn. Brenda regularly wore shirts praising Jesus and featuring biblical messages, but her faith was not something she pressed on others.

"She was about God," Jill Wilson said. "But she never judged anybody. She did her own thing. She was kind to everybody."

Brenda sang all the time, just like her mother, who often treated large congregations at the Federated Church to hymns with her beautiful soprano voice. If Tracy and Brenda weren't talking, they were humming or singing. Crystal Sievers loved her voice so much that she begged Brenda to sing tunes from the "The Little Mermaid," Brenda's favorite movie.

"There's a scene in the movie, and it was like she had perfect pitch and it was so spot on, we wanted her to sing that over and over again," she said.

BOB'S STRAWBERRY

Brenda's welcoming nature stemmed from the fact that she was the new kid in town in 1984. The family moved from Hutchinson, a city of 40,000 people near the center of the state, and lived in Wichita for several years before Bob felt a calling to work in ministry.

John was born in November 1976 just as Bob and Tracy began their work lives. Before John came along, the plan was for Tracy to work as a licensed practical nurse while Bob worked toward a degree to become a pastor.

"She had John, so the idea of her working while I went to school went down the tubes," Bob said. "So, I worked different jobs and went to Friends University in Wichita at the same time. I worked a funeral home, then I worked at a Kwik Shop, then worked at a bank, where I got robbed!"

Pining for something a little less dangerous, Bob returned to his original plan to pursue a career in the church. In 1979, the family moved to Portland, Oregon, where he attended Western Evangelical

Seminary, a small college 10 miles from the Columbia River and Portland International Airport.

"It was dreary," Tracy said referring to the rain-logged Northwest city. "I didn't like Oregon."

The Kellers moved back to Kansas before Bob finished school, but Brenda was born during their short stay in Portland on March 8, 1979. Much to Tracy's relief, the pregnancy and rearing were seamless after a difficult time with John, who was colicky, defiant, and suffered through numerous ear infections. It was such an ordeal that a second pregnancy made Tracy nervous, but her daughter was much easier to handle.

"Brenda was 4 pounds when she was born, really small. But she slept all through the night, never woke up. I remember I would go in to check to see if she was alive because I'd never seen other babies do that," she said. "She was still that way as a toddler. She'd wake up and be happy and not bother you until you came to find her. She was such a good little baby."

Beyond her faith and good nature, one thing about her stood out: her shoulder-length, bright-red hair and freckles. To her father, she was simply "My Strawberry."

"She was gorgeous. She had the prettiest red hair and striking blue eyes," Brooklynd Thomas said. "Her look was really topped with her hair."

BACK TO THE PULPIT

When the Kellers left Oregon behind for the familiarity of Kansas, Bob pastored a church in Hutchinson for five years. Two years after Brenda's birth, Pat was born in 1981 as the family grew to five. By 1984, Bob was taking a break from the ministry and working in insurance. That career change didn't last long, and at age 30, he was ready to return to the pulpit.

"I hated it, selling insurance," Bob said. "I'd met a professor at Manhattan Christian College who was filling in here (Dover), and he suggested the church. They (church board) asked me to come and preach, to fill in one time."

Bob delivered the message at the Federated Church on two Sundays, and the congregation's board asked him to come back the following weekend as a candidate. During that trip, the church offered him the full-time position of pastor. The decision was an easy one because Bob's sense of humor and contemporary approach were a perfect fit.

"We liked his style. He usually opened up his message telling some kind of a story or joke, and how he could relate modern day stuff to the biblical lesson," said Nancy Fewell, a Dover native who has attended the church her entire life and still plays the organ during Sunday services. "I liked how he could connect all of that, which was very similar to a previous minister that was well-liked. He was very similar in style."

Bob and Dover flowed as easily as Mission Creek drifted through town. A big man with a big heart, his kind, gregarious personality and quick wit made him a beloved person. Dover had a year-round Santa Claus as a pastor, with the exception of Bob's red hair, a trait his children inherited.

"Bob Keller is the best minister and person in the whole wide world," said Dottie Wendland, a resident of Dover and member of the church for 70 years. "He is just top-notch."

Brenda inherited the best of her parents. She was a gifted writer and artist and loved reading and history. She loved to work out and be outdoors. She had a sneaky quick sense of humor, laid-back personality, wonderful voice, and devotion to God. Brenda had a special bond with her mother and father.

"Have you ever loved somebody, and it was like seeing through their eyes? That's the kind of relationship Brenda and I had," Tracy said. "It was like she was a blend of Rob and I together."

Brenda also adored animals, just as Tracy did. The Kellers had a small zoo at their house, including lizards, ferrets, spiders, bugs, and a pet rat. Brenda loved God and her family above all, but animals were a close second. A neighbor, Janet Baldwin, remembered Brenda owning a pet chameleon, which she almost lost when she brought the lizard over to show it off.

"We had bushes in front of the porch, and that chameleon jumped into those bushes. She was just squealing," Baldwin said. "She would just shriek and squeal if she got upset or excited about something. She was in a panic. Tracy and Brenda both loved animals so much."

Brenda had such a soft spot for animals that it broke her heart to see any creature suffer. Her grandmother, Jean Keller, recalled a moment in her kitchen in which Brenda pleaded with her not to swat any bothersome flies, and Bob remembered tears running down her cheeks when he smashed a spider crawling across a book she was carrying. One of Sievers' memories of Brenda is her despair when Brenda's rat bit the head off of her minuscule pet turtle.

"She was just so distraught," Sievers said. "I was just laughing because it was kind of funny, but she was so upset."

It was one of the many times Brenda suffered a broken heart over an animal. In another instance, she and friend Amy Best found an abandoned mouse in a nest near the Kellers' house. Brenda wanted to warm it up, so the girls put it in the microwave.

"Obviously, a poor choice," Best said. "We found another small rodent of some kind and tried a heating pad. That didn't work either. She was hysterical and in tears. I was kind of shocked, but she was just devastated."

Among the kingdom of animals and wildlife Brenda kept, cared for, or tried to nurture to health, Charlemange is the one almost all of her friends and family remember. An aging white rat, Charlemange lived in a piano in the Kellers' home. When it wasn't hiding behind the hammers and strings inside the instrument, it was often with Brenda, either crawling on her or resting on her shoulder as she played with her friends.

"She had birds and rodents, and she'd let them crawl all over her," Jana Blodgett said. "And that freaked me out!"

Brenda treated Charlemange like she would any of her best friends and had the rat for several years before it died of old age. Seeing her care for a pet that would make most people queasy impacted her friends.

"I remember the day it died … it was so sad," said Amber McGhee, who moved to Dover as a second grader in 1988 and had numerous sleepovers with Brenda. "She had the coolest animals. Because of Brenda, I actually own two rats as an adult."

BROTHERLY LOVE

Brenda loved her brothers, but as is often the case with siblings, it wasn't always easy. Like many older brothers, John teased Brenda and pushed her around. Years before he offered to help her with basketball, he was mean to his sister, including a time he convinced Brenda to put her finger in their mom's sewing machine and stitched a needle through it.

"Well, I was a (jerk) as a child," John said. "Brenda and I were friendly, actually getting friendly, I think. I think we would have been close, but we were just starting to get there."

John was your typical high school freshman boy trying to find his way. While he was standoffish with his sister at times, he also was a good student, played several sports, and stayed out of trouble. Though Brenda and John were getting closer, she struggled with Pat, who was as rambunctious as any little boy in Dover.

"Her and Pat fought a lot, like cats and dogs," Tracy said. "He antagonized her. I told her he'd stop if she would ignore him and realize that he was doing it to get a rise out of her."

Pat was a rough-and-tumble child. Like many of the kids in Dover, he was all over the neighborhood, riding his bike down the roadways and hanging out with the dozens of children who lived within a few blocks. His best friend growing up was Tyrel Buchmeier, whose family lived less than a half mile from the Kellers.

The Buchmeiers moved from Emporia, Kansas, to Dover in 1987 before Tyrel started first grade. He and Pat were friends from the start, and Pat was like a second son to Lavella and Jerry Buchmeier, who grew up in the nearby town of Burlingame.

"Basically, Tracy and I were the newbies. She was the imperfect preacher's wife," Lavella Buchmeier said. "She always said she didn't do all the cooking things. She was outdoors and animals. She was the perfect friend because she was not from there, either."

Pat was also fearless. He led a group of kids down to Mission Creek, which runs west of K-4 and Douglas Road as it snakes out of Shawnee County and into Wabaunsee County, and was the first to jump into untested waters.

"He was probably the worst of us (about getting into trouble)," said Autumn Buchmeier, Tyrel's younger sister. "He was a daredevil. You think, 'That's a bad idea,' and he's five steps ahead of you. Whether fishing or jumping off something on the creek. Pat jumped … and he lived!"

Brenda tagged along on many of the adventures, often because she was babysitting Tyrel and Autumn. In fact, she was the only babysitter the Buchmeiers ever had. She came home with the kids for an hour after school and watched them while Jerry slept before working the night shift at his job in Topeka.

"She was there every day. She was good with our kids," Lavella Buchmeier said. "She played with them. We just kind of let them run wild. As long as we hollered and rang the bell, they'd come home."

For Tyrel Buchmeier, Dover was utopia.

"You couldn't have grown up in a better place," he said. "Hell, we played in the highway. Everybody from 7, 8 years old until you had a driver's license, you rode your bike around Dover. When we moved to Dover, life became life."

It was the perfect place for so many children, including Brenda, until Oct. 19, 1991.

CHAPTER THREE:

THE KELLERS

Jean Keller had a special bond with her grandchildren until the day she died. In her late 80s, she could tell you how many grandkids she had, including great-grandchildren, and the names and ages of every one. As the first granddaughter, Brenda had a special place in her heart. When Brenda was at her Grandma and Grandpa's house, they had one stop to make.

"Brenda would come and spend a weekend with me, or a day, and we always had to go to the pet store," Jean said. "We went one time, and they had little cages of miniature hamsters. I reached in to pet one of the little bitty things and it bit my finger, and when I jerked my finger back, the hamster flew into the next cage, and I just said, 'Well, you can stay there.' Brenda said, 'Oh, Grandma, you hurt him,' and I said, 'Well, he hurt me.'"

Born at home on Nov. 28, 1931, Jean grew up in a small family with her younger sister, Beverly, and parents, Charles and Belva Everett. Charles worked as a mechanic while his wife took care of the home and their children attended school in Wichita. The Everetts were deeply invested in church. Jean had perfect attendance for years at Sunday

School and dedicated her life to Jesus during a concert held by Stuart Hamblen, one of the first singing cowboys during the Golden Age of Radio.

Jean graduated from Wichita North High School and met Robert Roy Keller when he moved back to Wichita. Roy was born on a farm in 1929, one of 11 siblings. Roy came back to Wichita after being injured in a fall while working on the construction crew that built the county hospital in Pratt, Kansas.

"My aunt was married to Roy's dad's cousin, and Roy came back to find a job in Wichita," Jean said. "She kept trying to get him in with a cousin of hers. One night, my aunt thought he was going to call her (the cousin), and she could tell he was really nervous. He kept going downstairs and coming back up and he said, 'What's Jean's phone number?' It just went from there."

The courtship was a short one. Just a few months later, Roy, 20, and Jean, 18, married on Sept. 3, 1950. Nine months later, the Army drafted Roy, and the couple moved to Columbia, South Carolina. Jean later returned to Wichita while Roy served in the Korean War until January 1953.

LOSING BELVA

Belva Everett died of cancer in 1954, just six weeks after Jean gave birth to Bob. The loss of his wife was too much for Charles Everett, who died less than a year later, though he did enjoy his first grandson in the months before his death.

"My dad would sit in the yard with his overalls on," said Jean's sister Beverly, known to the family as Aunt B. "Robert was on his lap and chewing on his watch. I remember somebody said, 'He's going to ruin it,' and Dad said, 'Let him ruin it.'

For several years in Wichita, Roy and Jean lived typical American lives in the 1950s and early 1960s. Roy worked for The Coleman Company, a cornerstone business in Wichita known for selling camping gear and other outdoor recreation products, while Jean cared for their growing family, with help from Aunt B.

Aunt B was 16 when Bob was born and more of a sister than an aunt. When Jean needed help looking after him as a toddler, Aunt B was there.

"I bought him the world," she said. "Whatever he wanted to do, I figured that was the thing to do. He was just like the cream of the crop. Him and I had a good time. We bonded. We were really close."

ROY'S CALLING

As the family grew to include daughters Janice and Beverly, born in 1957 and 1962, Roy began to feel that The Coleman Company wasn't where he was meant to be. In the early 1960s, the Kellers were members of the Calvary Mission Church, one of the oldest in Wichita. During one Sunday service, the pastor was out of town and the church needed somebody to preach. Roy volunteered and delivered the sermon on a few Sundays in the upcoming weeks.

"I noticed there was something about him, but he wouldn't say what was wrong," Jean said. "He was feeling God calling him into the ministry, but he felt like he was too old and didn't have his schooling. He wrote to his brother in California, who was a minister, and he said, 'Don't question God. If you feel He's calling you into the ministry, follow His calling, and He will lead.'"

Roy cut his teeth as "sort of an apprentice" in his words at Riverside Christian Church in Wichita. He also attended Friends University and took correspondence courses through the Free Methodist Church. As he studied and worked to become a pastor, Jean took care of their children, babysat two other boys, and did all of Roy's typing for sermons. A couple of years later, Roy took his first gig in Kingman, Kansas, a small town an hour west of Wichita. The Kellers continued to live in Wichita, traveling west to their church on the weekends.

Kingman was a far cry from the hustle and bustle of Wichita. The church was a vintage small-town congregation. Roy repainted the inside and outside of the one-room building, and the family cleaned until it was spotless.

"We were in Kingman for one year, and I preached two sermons on Sundays ... those poor people," Roy joked.

"He was trying to build it up," Jean said. "It was great; it was an experience. Roy was a good caller."

After Bob finished his sixth grade year, the family moved from Wichita to Minneapolis, Kansas, for Roy's first stint as a full-time pastor. Located in north central Kansas and more than 100 miles from their hometown, Minneapolis is a small town of 2,000.

Though leaving Wichita was difficult for the Keller children, they settled in Minneapolis as the quintessential pastor's family, excelling in school while spending much of their free time in the church. Roy drove a school bus part time for extra money, Jean was a housewife and helped Roy attend to the church, and Bob was heavily involved in high school, participating in football, band, and a Christian student organization.

"I remember we were always at church ... Sunday morning, Sunday night, Wednesday, and in between," Janice said. "We enjoyed it. We liked being there. None of us rebelled. It was a good childhood."

Though active, the Keller children were also quiet, spending much of their time reading and listening to music in their rooms. The holidays were their favorite times of the year. Jean took Christmas seriously, choosing a color scheme every year for decorating their tree and house.

"My mother always did holidays up big," Beverly said. "We got pretty good presents, and they weren't very wealthy. We also had the Easter Bunny, and on Halloween, she would decorate the garage behind the house in Minneapolis into a haunted house."

Beverly and Janice said Bob could be a bit of a "pest," constantly teasing them. During one choir practice, Bob waited until a quiet moment in the middle of singing to play a device that made a laughing noise.

"He turned that thing on in the middle of choir, and it was funny at first, but then the choir director got pretty upset," Janice said.

A ROUGH BEGINNING

The Kellers' childhood was paradise compared to Tracy's. Born at Fort Riley, an Army base 75 miles east of Minneapolis, on Feb. 6, 1954, to Weston and Vernita Comfort, she was in survival mode during the first several years of her life. Her father was a career military man who served in Vietnam and Korea and was rarely home. At age 7, her mother left her and her siblings, then 5 and 3, to fend for themselves in a trailer home in Oklahoma. After missing class for an extended period, Tracy's school investigated.

"She (her mom) took off with a boyfriend," Tracy said. "I took care of them (her brother and sister) the best I could. I fed them whatever I could find in the house. That might be why I hate peanut butter. I really don't like peanut butter because that's all we had. All of a sudden, people I didn't know showed up, and my mom's parents and my dad's parents showed up."

Tracy and her siblings moved back to Kansas, where they lived together with an aunt on a farm near Minneapolis. Even with the structure her aunt and uncle provided for the first time in her life, Tracy was a handful for her new family. She cussed, often sneaked out at night to hang out with friends or boyfriends, and drank as a young woman.

"I just was not an easy teenager, and I didn't connect with my family," she said. "I was really searching for the Lord, even then. I'd tried other things, but I didn't feel like I was a whole person in high school."

That changed when she met new friends, including her future husband. A small group of students began a Christian movement and had a regular Bible study. Bob, who had his eyes on Tracy for a while, was one of the members of the group. The two met in seventh grade and became friends as freshmen in high school, during which time Bob developed a crush.

"We had some kind of concert, and Mom asked who the redhead was with that pretty smile, and I said, 'Oh, that's Tracy,'" he said.

The attraction wasn't mutual at first. A beautiful, skinny redhead, Tracy was a bit wild and had plenty of boys interested in her. In fact, one of her boyfriends proposed to her in high school.

"The guy that I was engaged to told me, 'Well, God told me I was to marry you,'" Tracy said. "Well, God hadn't told me that, and that was the approach I was taking. I wanted somebody who loved the Lord and wanted to serve the Lord. So, I gave him his ring back."

Bob waited patiently, remaining his future wife's friend as she tried to find herself. During a bookkeeping class that had tables for two students, Bob and Tracy sat together and got to know each other.

"We didn't learn anything about bookkeeping," Bob said jokingly. "She'd talk about her boyfriend problems, and I'd talk about my lack of girlfriend problems. At one point, she told me she broke up with this boy, and I thought to myself, 'I better hurry.'"

TAKING THE NEXT STEP

By 1972, when they graduated from high school, Bob and Tracy were a couple. A few months later, Bob began attending Central Christian College, a private two-year college an hour south of Minneapolis in McPherson, Kansas. As he was starting college, Bob realized just how serious Tracy was about their relationship.

"They had some kind of get-together for the new students, and I walk in and there's Tracy," he said. "And I said, 'Tracy, what are you doing here?' She said, 'I'm going to college here.' I said, 'I didn't know that!' We'd been seeing each other all summer, so she hadn't admitted until not too long ago that she was there because I was there. For years, she didn't tell me that."

Bob and Tracy attended Central Christian together for a year before Tracy decided she would rather work. As Bob finished his second year, Tracy worked in Kansas City at Life Line Children's Home, helping abandoned infants and homeless children. The couple stayed together despite living two hours apart. During the first two years of their relationship, Bob gave Tracy a "pre-engagement" ring before the official proposal ... which neither remembers.

"I don't think there was a proposal. We just started talking about it," Bob said.

"I don't remember how he asked me. I might have asked him," Tracy said while laughing.

After the "proposal" in 1973, Tracy lived with the Keller family in Wichita while Bob finished his last semester at Central Christian. As Bob worked toward an associate's degree and held a job, Tracy worked and planned the couple's wedding. Tracy even made her own wedding gown, with help from Jean. One day, as the wedding approached, Tracy came down the stairs, crying, and hugged her future mother-in-law.

"I thought, 'Oh, no, she's decided she doesn't want to get married,'" Jean said. "I said, 'Tracy, what's wrong?' And she said, 'Oh, mother, I don't want to leave you. This is the first time I've ever felt like I had a mother.'"

ON THEIR OWN

Though they lived close to Portland during their two years in Oregon and experienced city life in Wichita, Bob, Tracy, and their kids were more comfortable in smaller communities. In 1984, the family left Hutchinson for one of the smallest towns in the state.

"I remember driving into Dover the first time," Tracy said. "We came up over the hill, and it was just ... it was awesome. It was so beautiful."

In addition to pastoring the Federated Church, Bob drove a school bus for supplemental income, just as his father did for years while he preached. Tracy was heavily involved in the schools, working in the cafeteria, and managed the home. The family lived in the church's parsonage, an old two-story house less than 100 yards away from the church and sitting just to the north of 57th Street.

The Kellers lived in a quiet neighborhood consisting of several young families and children the same age as John, Brenda, and Pat. The sons of Greg and Janet Baldwin were close to the Keller boys, spending summers playing in or around their house located a few doors to the east. Bob and Tracy often had a television that didn't work, so Brenda, John, and Pat regularly visited the Baldwins on Saturday mornings.

"Our kids weren't particularly early risers on Saturdays, but we'd have John and Patrick wanting to watch cartoons with the boys, and Brenda would come in, too," said Greg Baldwin, a teacher at the Dover schools for several years. "We loved them. They were good friends."

Dover was a sparsely populated community with little to no crime, so kids ran wild and free. When they weren't riding their bikes up and down Douglas Road or swimming in Mission Creek, they were in a neighbor's backyard or living room.

"We'd take walks in the evening, particularly with Tracy. She was a health nut and loved to walk," Greg Baldwin said. "When the kids were older, they played baseball, and we all traveled together to Paxico, Eskridge, and Maple Hill to watch games. That was always fun."

Tracy also bonded with the Buchmeiers, especially Lavella. They moved to Dover three years apart and were still relatively new to the tight-knit community that included several families whose ancestors settled there as founding members of Dover in the 1850s. Young and different than most of the straight-laced women in town, Lavella Buchmeier warmed up to the preacher's wife quickly.

"Tracy and I hung out," she said. "She would drink wine coolers. She made me feel better about my faith because you don't have to be perfect."

'YOU WORRY TOO MUCH'

When Brenda didn't babysit the Buchmeier kids or watch "Scooby Doo" with her brothers at the Baldwins', she played with several girl-friends. Jill Wilson's parents drove her from the minuscule town of Keene, about five miles west of Dover on K-4, to the Kellers' home, where she and Brenda spent long summer days together. The best friends rode their bikes to the Sommerset Café every afternoon for soda.

"I'd leave Jill there at the Kellers' when I worked during the summer, and they did everything together," Judy Wilson said. "I remember Brenda loved dolls. Jill couldn't care less about dolls, but Brenda always took her Barbies with her and Jill would play along. The kid next door had a trampoline, and they'd jump on that."

By the late 1980s, Brenda's group of closest friends also included Misty Lange, Amy Best, and Amber McGhee, who lived two doors to the east of the parsonage. Living directly across the street, the Langes and Kellers were close. Misty Lange's grandparents, Glenn and Ruth, moved to Dover from Corning, Kansas, a small town in the northeast corner of the state near the Nebraska and Missouri border.

The Langes came to Dover in 1969 when the principal's position at the junior high and grade school opened. Glenn Lange served in that role for 20 years, while Ruth worked as a school librarian for several years and in other jobs in the district for more than 30 years.

"God sent Brenda to us for Misty to have a playmate," Ruth Lange said. "Brenda would lie down and watch TV with Glenn. We had a nice neighborhood. One of them across the street had a swimming pool, and we'd have some memorable summer evenings."

The Langes took their granddaughter in during the late 1970s. By 1984, Misty Lange and Brenda were the only girls living in the neighborhood, and they were together virtually every day. Within a few years, Brenda, Misty Lange, Jill Wilson, and Best spent many of their days playing in the Kellers' old Victorian house. As they approached their teen years, riding bikes was their mode of transportation.

"She didn't used to ride a bike, then in the sixth grade, she had gotten kind of chubby and decided that she was going to lose weight," Misty Lange said. "That's why she started riding a bike, and she rode all the time, miles."

By the time Roy and Jean moved to Topeka, where Roy pastored the First Free Methodist Church from the late 1980s to mid-1990s, Brenda was addicted to cycling. She routinely rode 20 miles a day, especially during the summers, and enjoyed exploring nature with her friends and by herself.

A few days before the volleyball tournament, Jean drove to Dover and picked up Tracy, Brenda, and Pat to take them to a football game. On the way home, Brenda sat next to her grandmother in the front seat.

"Brenda always had to hold Grandma's hand, and she was holding my hand," Jean said with tears welling in her eyes. "We were coming back, and she's talking about going bike riding. And I said, 'Oh Brenda, Grandma doesn't want you going by yourself. You be sure there's always somebody with you.' She just patted my hand and said, 'Grandma, you worry too much.'"

CHAPTER FOUR:

DOVER SCHOOL DAYS

Sam Bays grew up on a farm closer to schools in Wabaunsee County than the Dover schools he attended, riding a bus for 30 minutes just to get to class. The lack of exposure to fellow students, combined with a personality that was vastly different from his classmates, made life difficult.

"It was tough. I didn't grow up close to them. I just didn't fit in well," Bays said. "I think it was that I thought I was smart and had a chip on my shoulder. I had several fights. I got kicked off the bus one time and spent the entire day in the library. It was just bad."

Bays was part of a small class of 11 who progressed through grade school, middle school, and high school together. The class included Brenda, several of her girlfriends, and five boys. Though he didn't connect with his classmates for several years, Bays thought highly of Brenda, whom he met in kindergarten. Years later, during a dance, Bays didn't know where to place his hands on the girls during slow songs. That made them uncomfortable, and they wouldn't dance with him.

"I was upset, but Brenda would dance with me and she said, 'You're supposed to put your hands here,'" he said. "It just made me feel … that was special to me."

PRINCIPAL OF THE MATTER

When Bob and Tracy moved their family from Hutchinson to Dover, John was about to enter the second grade and Brenda was a kindergartener. The siblings enrolled at the grade school more than 30 years after it opened, but the building looked much the same.

Located less than 50 yards to the east of Douglas Road and a quarter mile north of the community's cemetery, the rectangular facility had a circle drive for school buses and parents to pick up and drop off their children and a small parking lot on the northwest side. The building had a large, open field to the south, a football/baseball field to the north, and a small grassy area with a playground to the east.

A short sidewalk led from the parking lot and circle drive to heavy metal doors opening to a small lobby. As one entered the lobby, to the right was a front office where the school secretary worked. To the east of the lobby was the boys' bathroom and a hallway leading to the school's kitchen. To the left of the lobby was the entrance to the auditorium, a room about 100 feet long and 200 feet wide.

The auditorium was an important part of the school and town. The stage on the west end of the space contains the original gold curtain to this day, 70 years after the school opened. Families packed the auditorium to watch Brenda and others in plays, the school's band, and dozens of other events. When it wasn't used as the lunch room or for a school function, the hall hosted a plethora of town gatherings, including the annual Ladies Aid banquet.

The entire south end beyond the lobby housed the principal's office and classrooms for every grade from kindergarten through sixth before the latter moved to the junior high after consolidation. Several educators occupied the principal's office, including Glenn Lange, a former helicopter pilot with the Marines who became a fixture. Though strict, Lange, a short and stocky man with glasses and gray hair, surrounded himself with a staff of teachers revered by students and parents.

"To this day, I call him Mr. Lange," said Pam Leptich, who began teaching at the junior high in 1986. "He was such a great teacher and such a great mentor."

HOT ROLLS

The south end of the grade school was the longest part of the building, stretching 200 feet from the lobby. The narrow hallway rested between cinder block walls painted tan with brown trim and had a floor with red tile. The walls on both sides were decorated with cartoons painted by longtime custodian Sonny VanCleave.

VanCleave, a gifted artist who also served as an assistant coach in several sports, painted characters ranging from Wile E. Coyote, to Dopey of the Seven Dwarfs, to Darth Vader on the walls in the hallways. It was one of the many things the highly regarded man, who excelled despite missing several fingers on his right hand, did to connect with children.

"What I remember the most about physically being there was the awesome cartoons," Bays said. "(Sonny) was so nice and funny. He always smiled. He always had jokes. He always listened to you. I loved that man."

Organized chronologically, the first classroom just south of the principal's office was for kindergarten. Across the hall was first grade, and about 40 feet to the south came the next classroom, second grade, down to the end of the building, where the fifth grade was the last room before two doors opened to a long field separating the building from the cemetery.

Each classroom was similar, including dark green chalkboards, small desks for students, and large desks for teachers. A set of four rectangular windows rested above the radiator heating system, but none of the classrooms had air conditioning.

"It was horrible with no AC," Crystal Sievers said. "It got so hot in the grade school. They'd cancel school if it got too hot."

During the bitterly cold Kansas winters, the students rested their coats and shoes below the radiators to dry them off and ensure that they were warm when it was time to go home. Late in the morning, the mouth-watering aroma of lunch drifted down the hallways and into the classrooms.

"Those rolls ... so good," Bays said. "My Aunt Helen (head cook of both schools) made the best whole wheat rolls. You could smell those rolls all morning."

A STARBIRD IS BORN

The Dover schools were small, but the staff was mighty. When a new class started every year, a seasoned group of teachers welcomed the students. Most of the teachers at the grade school worked there for decades, including several who started and finished their careers in the same building.

Earlnor Starbird was the most well-known teacher in the district. She was born in Dover in 1921, raised on a farm outside of town, and graduated from Dover High in 1938. Starbird, who was Brenda's favorite teacher, began her career right out of high school and taught for 48 years, including 43 at the grade school.

"When Ms. Starbird retired, she'd taught a third generation," Penny Lister said. "There were several third-generation families that attended the retirement party, so she taught grandparents, parents, and kids."

Though no one matched the half-century Ms. Starbird taught, a number of her colleagues worked at the grade school for years, including Dottie Wendland. After working as a stay-at-home mom, Wendland returned to college in the 1970s and became a teacher at

Dover Grade School in 1979. She taught the fourth grade for 20 years before retiring.

"When I first saw Dover, I thought it was kind of a strange little place, and I hardly knew what to think of it," she said. "It wasn't long before I just loved the people. It's a wonderful place."

Brenda's fifth grade teacher also spent the majority of his career teaching in Dover, with all but one year in the same classroom at the end of the building. Jim Ediger began teaching in Harveyville for four years, then moved to Dover Grade School in 1976 and taught there until 2001. He taught his last year before retirement in the junior high. The following year, Dover and the surrounding schools consolidated, and the junior high moved to Harveyville.

"I really enjoyed the small-town school," he said. "The community was so supportive. The teachers would always comment when it came to parent-teacher conferences, we had almost 100 percent turnout."

'EVERYBODY KNEW EVERYBODY'

Brenda and Jill Wilson bonded the moment they saw each other during kindergarten. Though Wilson lived in nearby Keene (the children in Keene traveled to Dover for school) and knew many of the children in Dover, she was painfully shy. Brenda was new to town and connected immediately with Wilson. They were best friends from that point, hanging out in school, the youth group and church, and when Jill Wilson's parents were at work.

"Every day after school, every summer, every day of my life ..." Wilson said. "Since I didn't live in Dover, we'd always go to their house after school."

While Brenda and Wilson were best friends, there were no strangers in their class. A core group of 10 students who graduated from Dover Junior High also graduated from Mission Valley. Eight of the 10 were together from kindergarten through their senior year.

"Everyone knew everyone's parents, and everyone knew everyone's kids," Amy Best said. "There was just a feeling like you belong somewhere. I can't imagine being anywhere else."

That feeling of security existed largely because the parents, many of whom grew up in and stayed in Dover, were so deeply connected to the schools. They were there at potlucks, basketball games, plays, band nights, and parent-teacher conferences. When the school needed money, members of the community pulled up their sleeves.

Pat, who started kindergarten in 1987, remembered playground equipment that could be dangerous, notably a merry-go-round that you could climb inside and push. Standing inside the apparatus was against the rules because of the potential of getting trapped and breaking an ankle. Once it became apparent that the playground needed an overhaul, parents and other community members went to work, and the school had new slides, jungle gyms, and other equipment.

"They just dug into that like crazy," Leptich said. "Before you knew it, we had the equipment and all the dads putting it up. They were totally invested in what the kids needed."

Several of the teachers said that devotion to the schools and their children showed in the classroom. Rarely did they have to discipline their students, and if there was a problem, a phone call to the parents took care of it. The biggest grade school controversy anybody can remember is one teacher catching a couple of fifth graders holding hands.

"It was pretty peaceful," Sievers said. "You had your little best friend wars; hate you one day, love you the next, but that was it. It was very innocent."

A PERSONAL EXPERIENCE

Everyone knew Brenda loved all of God's creatures, enough so that Allen Zordel worried how she would react when his seventh grade science class had to dissect dead animals. Like any of her schoolwork,

Brenda took it seriously, did the assignment, and moved on with the rest of her day. She also exhibited composure during a situation that unnerved many of her classmates. For a while, Zordel had a large black snake in his class that the students had to feed, as well as clean its cage.

"The only person who would really touch the snake was Brenda," Brooklynd Thomas said.

One time as the class attended to the snake, she held its head while another student held the tail. The apprehensive classmate lost control of the tail, and the snake began to go up Brenda's shorts. She calmly managed to help the snake and get it back into the cage.

"I remember her saying that was the weirdest feeling she'd ever had," Thomas said. "I don't know how she did it. I want to say a week before she died, that snake went missing, and we never found it."

Worrisome moments like that were few and far between for Brenda and her classmates in an evocative setting. As they walked through the short hallways of the red brick building, they passed dozens of class photos honoring the students who graduated from the former Dover High School. Many of the alumni immortalized in those shots were the parents, grandparents, aunts, and uncles of the kids in Brenda's class.

"The schools were very personal," Autumn Buchmeier said. "I don't think a lot of people get that experience."

The junior high sat a few hundred feet east of Douglas Road about a half mile behind the Federated Church and northeast of the grade school. To get to the front of the building, which faced the west side, students either walked from the parking lot to the north, or up a long sidewalk running from the road to a small set of stairs, which led to the first floor and a classroom to the left and right. To get to the science and math classrooms, they walked a flight of stairs inside the facility. The basement had just enough space for a home economics room, computer lab, and a handful of lockers.

Each classroom was small, but the school rarely had more than 50 students. The rooms had large chalkboards, small student desks, a large desk for the teacher, and large windows with frosted glass sections at the top. The wooden floors had a layer of tiled concrete, and the interior walls were white cinder blocks.

A set of radiators below the windows kept the building warm, but there wasn't much relief if it was hot, aside from opening the windows, as only one room had a window-unit air conditioner. The building was small enough that the students ate lunch at the grade school, walking along a sidewalk that ran from the east end of the football/baseball field to the auditorium.

The entryway had a white wooden frame from the ground to nearly the top of the building, with a circle top window resting above a "HIGH SCHOOL" sign. That window gazed out to the front of the school from the principal's office, which was only 10 feet wide by 10 feet long and had an opening to the east allowing the principal to see who was walking into the office.

The junior high also had a small basketball gym that was the envy of many schools. The stained wood basketball court doubled as a volleyball court and floor seating for athletes. The basketball court was so narrow that the modern-day 3-point line was right up against the set of white bleachers with black tops that looked like they came from the set of the 1986 movie "Hoosiers."

"Our gym was so tiny, and you had everybody packed in there," Zordel said. "There was barely enough room for kids to sit on the bench. It was an advantage for us to have such a small gym."

TEACHING CORE

Like the grade school, the junior high had a veteran staff, including Leptich, one of Brenda's favorite teachers. Born in Louisville, Kentucky, Leptich attended Topeka West High School before going to Kansas State University, where she was a member of the first women's basketball team in the 1960s.

Leptich taught in Topeka for a few years before coaching basketball and earning a master's degree at the University of South Carolina. She worked as a sports information director and coach at Washburn University, then briefly for the Kansas State Board of Education.

"I was totally bored out of my mind, because after being SID, having a radio show, and traveling with the team, it was such a high-profile job," she said. "The Department of Education job was three times the money, but I couldn't stand it that I didn't have enough to do."

Leptich came across a job listing in Dover and interviewed with Lange, who offered her a position at the junior high as a basketball coach and English teacher. She started there in 1986 and didn't leave until she retired in 1999.

Zordel ended up in Dover largely because he needed a first job out of college. A native of Ransom, a small town in western Kansas, he was a star athlete in high school before attending Dodge City Community College and Fort Hays State University. After not landing a job out of college, he went to graduate school before interviewing in Dover.

"I'd never heard of Eskridge, Mission Valley, or Dover, but I had the interview and fell in love with the place," he said.

Zordel joined the staff in 1983-84, the year before Brenda started school, and taught science, social studies, health, and physical education until the doors of the junior high closed 17 years later. He also worked as head coach or assistant coach in several sports, including volleyball, basketball, football, and baseball.

"I loved it," he said. "It was kind of hard to get all the practice time you wanted, but we had a blast, and the kids were great. We had a lot of success."

THE CHURCH AS A CENTERPIECE

When the Kellers weren't at work, home, or school, they were at church. Built in 1931 and a decade after three churches consolidated, the Federated Church was a heartbeat of the community, much like the schools. The building is a long, narrow facility less than 100 yards east of the town's intersection and surrounded by several houses, a small parking lot, and a fellowship hall built in 2006.

Longtime music teacher Ted Lassen taught all three Keller children and worked in Dover for 19 years. At the request of Lange, Lassen performed a short three-person play with Brenda and Tracy at the church in 1990 during Dover Heritage Day, which is held on the third Saturday in June every summer and celebrates the history of the community.

"Glenn Lange was such a good, kind man, and every time he asked me to do anything, I did it," Lassen said. "Well, they should have let me use the script, because I can't remember text to save my soul."

Performing in front of a large audience in the church, Lassen lost his composure, forgetting lines or saying them in the wrong place. Every time, Tracy patiently tried to bring him back to the script.

"Brenda just looked at me like, 'What are you doing?'" he said while laughing. "It was one of the funniest experiences I remember with Brenda."

THE BEGINNING

Native Americans inhabited the Dover area for hundreds of years before settlers came along in the mid-1800s. The first settlers arrived in 1855, and the Sage and Bassett families officially established the Dover Township in 1867. The Sages and Bassetts named the town after the area where the families immigrated from in England, Sommerset Shire, which is close to Dover, England.

The community thrived after its founding and had a blacksmith shop, two large cheese factories, a grist mill, two hotels, a post office, and a bank by 1880. During the late 1800s and early 1900s, there were general stores, two restaurants, a hardware store, a furniture store, a machine shop, and a creamery. Dover continued to flourish until the Great Depression, an era during which the town struggled mightily.

It didn't recover until a second world war resulted in an influx of jobs and resurgence in crop prices.

Through the years, the Dover area maintained a population of a little more than 1,000 people. Many of the families, such as the Sages, Bassetts, and Todds, have lived there for more than 150 years now. By the time the Kellers arrived in 1984, there were only a handful of businesses in Dover. While a number of families relied on agriculture as an income, the vast majority of people living there worked in Topeka or other small towns nearby.

"It wasn't a rich community," Leptich said. "Dover had kind of grown into a little bedroom community for Topeka. For such a small town, what's unique about Dover is they refused to die after the schools went out. It's still a vibrant, vital community. Dover seems to get stronger and stronger."

FOUNDATION OF FAITH

Faith has been an integral part of Dover for going on 200 years. The first church service in the settlement dates back to the 1850s, during which time many people living in the area attended Sunday school at the first log schoolhouse built in town.

"A chapter of scripture was read, prayer offered, and hymns sung the same as now," Elizabeth Berryman Eddy, an early resident, wrote in the early 1900s. "All this was before the time of automobiles or buggies or spring wagons. The road were just trails, and often it was so muddy that it was hard to get a wagon over these roads, and people would come on horseback or walk."

Without an official church, Dover didn't have a pastor or minister. As such, it relied on a man named Elder Reymond to travel to the township and lead revival meetings, the beginning of the Baptist Church of Dover. A few years after the dedication of the Baptist Church, a group of Methodists began meeting in the building every other Sunday for three years until they finished their own church. Within a few years, a third patronage, the First Congregational Church of Mission Creek Valley, opened in 1874.

Maintaining three churches in town was a constant struggle, enough so that the parishioners at each decided to unite in 1920 and form one fellowship: the Dover Federated Church. More than 100 years later, it still bears that name.

In 1931, churchgoers broke ground on a physical church. Though the early years were difficult without a regular minister and the devastation of the Great Depression, the congregation survived and became wildly successful, prompting Topeka reporter Milton Tabor to write, "one church can grow where three barely existed."

WHAT ABOUT BOB?

As it had for decades, the church had a core group of members, many of whom attended services their entire lives. Wendland, who had a hand in selecting Bob, began attending the church when her family moved to Dover in the 1950s.

"You cannot go to Topeka or any place and hear a better service than Bob Keller's," Wendland said.

Bob's delivery, in particular, resonated with the congregation, which shared his laid-back personality and humility. He wasn't afraid to tell a joke at his own expense and wove stories from his personal life into his messages. It also helped that Bob wasn't obtrusive about faith.

"Bob makes being a Christian a realistic plan," Lavella Buchmeier said.

In addition to being kind and welcoming, Bob also had political savvy. He knew better than to focus on any denomination, which he learned while researching the church's history. He discovered that a pastor tried to evangelize the Federated Church years before he came along.

"You know if you have a pastor who insists that emersion is the only way to do baptism, you can have trouble because Baptists, Congregationalists, and Methodists all do it a different way," Bob said.

What mattered to Bob is people showed up. He treated those who sat in the back row the same as those who sat in the front. Before every service, he walked around and greeted the patrons. When it ended, he rushed to the front door, shaking hands and helping elderly patrons down the stairs leading out of the church.

A SPIRITUAL WARFARE

For many years, the church often was full, including a stretch during which an impressive throng of youth lined much of the first three pews. Most of the youngsters were in the youth group, which had an inauspicious beginning. Though a number of children, including Brenda and many of her schoolmates, regularly attended Sunday school and the service that followed, the group didn't take off until Paul Todd and Frog May led the charge in the late 1980s and early 1990s. By the time Brenda started junior high, the youth group was flourishing.

"It was GODS posse: Going Out and Destroying Satan," said Caleb May, the son of Frog and Bonnie May, who have been members of the church for decades. "It really was spiritual warfare. We were trying to make things better out of our goodness."

Brenda was a driving force for the youth group, recruiting her friends to join. She was deeply concerned about their faith and actively worked to get them to participate without being obtrusive.

"Our family wasn't overly religious, and she never held it against us," Amber McGhee said. "I went to youth group, we did Bible study. Pretty much everything I did there was because of Brenda. She would let you be you and accepted you for you."

Through the years, many of Brenda's friends experienced pivotal moments in faith, including Thomas, who was baptized with Brenda in early 1991. Even though Jill Wilson and her family attended a different church, she spent hours hanging out with her best friend in the group.

"Brenda was about God, and it was refreshing," Wilson said. "I did what she wanted, and that was youth group. She really lived by it."

Several of Brenda's friends who didn't attend church often were regulars at youth group. Todd and the Mays kept the children engaged, taking them on trips to Colorado and Arkansas, as well as several Bible camps. At weekly meetings, the basement of the church was full of young people.

"There was so much excitement and energy," Caleb May said. "It totally energized the church."

'ONE OF A KIND'

Autumn Buchmeier wasn't so sure about communion. As Bob explained the members of the Bible school would be drinking the blood and eating the flesh of Jesus, she looked skeptically at him, thinking, "There's no way I'm putting somebody's body in my mouth." Bob noticed her hesitation and kindly told her that she was drinking grape juice and eating a small piece of bread.

"Tracy and Bob are the only two people I ever trusted with my children," Lavella Buchmeier said. "They were just perfect for our church."

One of the talents Bob and his family brought to the congregation was music. The children didn't serenade the church by themselves often, but Bob and Tracy sang songs of the gospel almost weekly.

"Bob and Tracy singing was a constant presence," Autumn Buchmeier said. "They both have amazing voices."

Pat wasn't as invested in the church as a child, though he was there every Sunday. While his parents and siblings were always in the front few pews, Pat was hanging out with friends in the balcony seats and nursery, or crawling underneath the pews at people's feet.

"I have a lot of good memories," he said. "We'd whisper and color on pamphlets, and Dad would let me bang away on the piano and organ when we weren't at a service."

Bob's impact extended beyond the church. When he wasn't driving a school bus, working on a sermon, attending school functions, or meeting with patrons, he was officiating weddings and funerals. Through the years, he officiated the weddings for a number of Brenda's schoolmates, including Best, Thomas, Kristi Osburn, and Misty Lange.

Leading a funeral, however, is where many believe Bob does his best work because of his kind, genuine, and caring nature.

"I have never heard Bob give a bad speech," Ruth Lange said. "One of my older friends passed away, and we were there for the funeral, and Misty and I were talking about how when I died, I want to have Bob preach my funeral. He's one of a kind."

His response was vintage Bob: "I'd be glad to ... if I'm still here."

CHAPTER FIVE:

JON BOY

"We drank, smoked weed, and chased (women). We were in high school just partying as teenagers."

That is Fred Howell's description of life during the mid-1980s as a kid living in the Brookside neighborhood of Tulsa, Oklahoma. Howell, now in his late 50s, was one of several teens hanging out with Jon Mareska Jr. as he grew up.

Jon Jr. moved to Tulsa with his mother LaDonna, stepfather Stephen Davis, and stepsister Teresa in the early 1980s after living in Arkansas for several years. For a while, Jon Jr. stayed out of trouble, forming a close bond with his sister, who was the same age. A little more worldly than Teresa, he looked after her when they moved from rural Arkansas to Tulsa.

"It was like the hillbilly moved to the city," Teresa Davis said. "QuikTrip was a whole new trip for me. I'd never even had a fountain drink. He showed me the ropes."

Teresa Davis was her stepbrother's best friend for years until she moved back to Arkansas in 1985 to live with her mother. Though she loved Jon Jr., she had had enough of living with her father, who was so strict that he asked his children's teachers to provide him with a weekly report.

"My daddy was 'Do as I say, not as I do,'" she said. "My mom instilled enough fear in me that I did not test him. He had a tight hold on me, and I just left. Maybe if I had stayed, things would have been different."

THE BLACK SHEEP

Lucille Hersh grew up in a well-to-do family with roots stretching all the way back to the founding fathers. Her father was a savings and loan executive in Topeka, and her mother was a great-granddaughter of John Marshall, the fourth chief justice of the United States.

Lucille Hersh didn't quite fit in the straight-laced family, which included three sisters and one brother. Born in 1919, she married three times, including as a young woman to a man named John Lamm. That partnership produced two children—Tamra, born in 1940, and Jon, who came along in 1945—but ended shortly after Lamm returned from serving overseas in the military.

Lucille Hersh then married Charles Mareska Sr., and he adopted Tammy and Jon, who took his last name. According to Tamra (now Tammy Blake), this did not sit well with the Hersh family.

"Mom, I guess, was the black sheep of the family," she said. "Because she married a couple of times."

Marrying Mareska didn't help matters. Tammy Blake said he treated her mother poorly, and abused Tammy and her brother. On one occasion, he made Tammy lie on the floor of the family car while watching a movie at a drive-in as punishment for not coming straight home from school. On another, he made Tammy, then 11, and Jon, 7, stand by the mailbox while shooting a BB gun at them.

"He turned around one day and said he was going to do me in because I was such a sassy little girl," Tammy said. "I really wasn't. I just didn't like him treating my mom mean."

Lucille and Mareska Sr. had one child, a boy named Charles Jr., known to family and friends as Chip, who was born in 1952. Unlike his older brother, Chip was laid-back and easygoing. Jon was rambunctious, enough so that his mother sent him to the Missouri Military Academy in Mexico, Missouri, as a seventh grader in the late 1950s, and then to a boys' home in the early 1960s.

"(Lucille) had boyfriends, and she didn't want him around," said LaDonna Thomas, Jon Sr.'s ex-wife.

By the mid-1950s, the family split, with Tammy moving in with her grandmother during high school and Jon and Chip staying with their mother and, for a while, her third husband, Glenn Johnson. Tammy went to Washburn Rural High School, on the outskirts of Topeka, before transferring to Topeka High, located in the middle of the city. Living with her grandma provided a more stable environment for Tammy, who graduated in the late 1950s, married a military man, and lived in several states and Scotland over the next few years.

Meanwhile, Jon Sr. stayed with his mother when he wasn't at the military academy or boys' home. He returned for a few years in the early 1960s, when he attended Topeka West High School and ran with a rough crowd.

"He was a handful," Chip Mareska said. "Then, he went into the service, and again, he was gone for a long time."

Tammy and her brothers weren't close for many years, but Jon Sr. moved to New Mexico to live with his sister after serving in the Navy. During his short stay there, Jon Sr. met Thomas, and the couple moved back to Topeka in the late 1960s.

'THE GORILLA CAME OUT'

Jon Sr. might have been rough around the edges, but he also had an amiable side that appealed to many women. He married several times and had six children with several women, including Thomas, who he met while they both were in beauty school in 1968.

"It was interesting. He was rough," Tammy Blake said of her brother cutting hair.

It was a whirlwind romance for Thomas and Jon Sr. A friend introduced them, and they were married soon after in 1968. Their only son, Jon Jr., was born a year later on March 30. Thomas said the honeymoon phase ended rather quickly after they tied the knot.

"He was like a chameleon," she said. "He could be nice, a sweet-talking man, and then the gorilla came out."

According to court transcripts and presentence investigation reports (PSI), abuse and addiction marred the seven-year marriage. In a PSI from a case in Wabaunsee County in 1990, Jon Jr. told an investigator that his parents abused alcohol and drugs throughout his childhood, a claim Thomas denies. During a sentencing hearing in 1992, Jon Jr.'s attorney said an unidentified relative sexually abused him at ages 3 and 4, and "there was nothing but sheer violence in that household from his mother and father fighting all the time."

Thomas, however, said the couple fought just once when Jon Sr. wrecked her car. That fight led her to leave him in 1974. For several months, she stayed in the Topeka area with Jon Jr. Ultimately, Thomas and Jon Jr. bolted for Arkansas in 1975 because Jon Sr. continued to harass her after the separation.

"He wouldn't leave me alone," she said. "I had my uncle and mother come and get me and Jon. I was afraid of what he would do if he knew we were leaving the state."

Thomas and Jon Jr. moved to Atkins, Arkansas, a small town in the north central region of the state and a few miles southeast of Russellville. Thomas struggled at first, but met Stephen Davis in a bar in Russellville. Davis had two daughters, including one, Teresa, who lived with him. Like Jon Sr., Stephen Davis had a history of violence.

"My father was not a good husband," Teresa Davis said. "He did abuse my mom in his young adult life and was in prison. He straightened his life up after that, but was still strict."

Jon Jr. and Teresa Davis became best friends immediately, forming the bond of a brother and sister. They rode bikes together, traveled with their parents on vacations to the World's Fair in Tennessee and Six Flags, played video games, and listened to music. They behaved like twins, and Jon Jr. was protective of her from an early age. That bond got even stronger when the family moved from the quiet, rural life of Atkins to the hustle and bustle of Tulsa, the second-largest city in Oklahoma.

FAIR BROOKSIDE

The Brookside neighborhood of Tulsa long had a friendly reputation, dating back to the 1940s when pharmacy owner Guy Scroggs gave successful students from Eliot Elementary School free ice cream. According to city historians, the area got its name from Scroggs' business, Brookside Drug Store. For years, Brookside was a must-see destination in Tulsa because of its strong school district, number of places to shop, and array of churches.

By the 1950s, the neighborhood was a hub for local teens, and thousands cruised Peoria Avenue, which ran through Brookside. The main drag became known as the "Restless Ribbon" in the 1960s, featuring locally famous hangouts like Pennington's Drive-In, Weber's Superior Root Beer, Van's Hamburgers, and the Brook Theatre.

"On the east side of Peoria, especially, is a pleasant little middle class neighborhood," said Randy Krehbiel, a reporter at the Tulsa World for more than 40 years and a former resident of Brookside. "It would not have been unusual in the 1980s where one street was pretty tidy and one that was not so good."

Jon Jr.'s family moved to Tulsa at an opportune time, as the city was in the midst of an oil and gas boom. According to the Oklahoma City Oklahoman, the economic surge began in the late 1970s when industry investors poured billions of dollars into drilling rigs on the Anadarko Basin, located in the western part of Oklahoma and the

Texas Panhandle. From 1978 through 1982, companies invested more than $2 billion in the region, believing the boom would stretch through the end of the century. By 1982, however, the explosion burned out.

The downfall of Penn Square Bank, in particular, crippled the region. That institution dumped millions into energy loans, gambling that the boom would last for decades. When the industry collapsed, those in debt could not cover their loans, and thousands of uninsured depositors, including other financial companies, suffered major losses.

"Everything collapsed," Krehbiel said. "All of that was reflected in Brookside, where places were popular, then gone almost overnight."

LaDonna and Stephen Davis, however, were hard workers and in fields that didn't suffer during a recession that lasted for several years. She worked as a hairdresser at Woodland Hills Mall while attending college to prepare for a job in computers, and he owned a small extermination company. That allowed the family to make a comfortable living with a nice home on Rockford Avenue.

Like virtually every street in Brookside, trees blanketed Rockford Avenue on both sides. The homes were a mix of modern designs and older houses, many of which were updated after a major flood hit the neighborhood during the 1980s. Teresa Davis and Jon Jr. lived just a few blocks from several teenagers who bonded with the brother and sister to form a tight group of friends, many of whom attended Thomas Edison Preparatory School.

Edison, which housed grades six through 12, was an eclectic school with students from all walks of life. The large facility in midtown Tulsa is located on a city block with multiple buildings connected by winding sidewalks on the outside and long, narrow hallways on the inside.

Jon Jr.'s experience early on at the school was a good one. He competed in talent shows and connected with several kids in Brookside, largely because his sister made friends quickly. Among those was Sharron Jenkins, who met Teresa Davis at Henthorne Park in the summer after seventh grade. A year older than the brother and sister, Jenkins noticed Jon Jr. immediately.

"He was just a good guy, just like your average guy," Jenkins said. "I met him and thought he was so cute."

Before long, Jenkins and Jon Jr. were boyfriend and girlfriend, hanging out at Henthorne Park, walking to the local McDonald's together, watching movies, or strolling around the neighborhood. Though they only dated for a few months during the summer, Jenkins said Jon Jr. was a gentleman, holding hands and never arguing or making an inappropriate move.

"I don't think I even kissed the guy; we just hung out," she said. "He never pushed me to do anything."

THE BROOKSIDE BREAKERS

In an era before smartphones and Netflix, teenagers in Brookside spent most of their time hanging out in a park. Then a go-to spot for hundreds of families in the area, Henthorne Park encompassed an entire block and had a swimming pool, indoor facility with multiple rooms, basketball courts, tennis courts, playground equipment, and numerous open, green spaces.

Henthorne is where Jon Jr. and Teresa Davis met up with a large group of fellow teenagers who spent hours swimming, playing basketball, listening to music, and, eventually, partying. But before the group really got into partying, a trio of boys dove into something a little different: breakdancing.

Breakdancing's popularity exploded in the 1980s, and Jon Jr. and friends Mike Goodenough and Tim Livermore were hooked on the craze. Forming the Brookside Breakers, they honed their craft while listening to Michael Jackson, Prince, early rap, and rock 'n' roll.

"(Jon Jr.) liked to dance, I liked to dance, and our buddy Mike liked to dance," Livermore said. "The lady that ran Henthorne Park would let us go in the back and dance in our own little studio. The room had all these mirrors, so she'd let us go back there and practice our dance."

The Breakers took their craft seriously, entering competitions and taking a bodyguard, Howell, with them to the events. Howell was a few years older and an imposing figure.

"I was kind of the big boy out of the bunch," Howell said. "I went to make sure they weren't in a situation where it was four on three."

The Breakers didn't last long, but many of their friends said the group was entertaining and dressed the part, complete with parachute pants and tank tops.

"They were actually really good, which kind of surprised me," said Di'Anna Dentis, a member of the Brookside crew and the same age as Jon Jr. and Teresa Davis. "They used to go out a lot to the Caravan Club (a popular night spot in Tulsa)."

Life away from the Breakers and Henthorne appeared to be normal for Jon Jr. and Teresa Davis, though their parents were stern. Friends and family knew Stephen and LaDonna Davis as regular people, including Debbie Davis, Teresa's sister who lived with her mother in Arkansas but spent summers in Tulsa.

"It was a normal life," Debbie Davis said. "They had day jobs, would come home in the evenings and have dinner. On Friday night, we went and saw a movie or went out for pizza. There was really nothing out of the ordinary."

That began to change for Jon Jr. when Teresa Davis left Tulsa to live with her mother at age 15 in 1985. The loss of his best friend proved to be a turning point for Jon Jr., one from which he never recovered.

"He said one time, 'Why didn't you take me with you?'" Teresa Davis said as her voice trailed off.

AN EARLY ADDICTION

Constantly dancing and happy. Those were the words Teresa Davis used to describe the brother she knew up until he was 15 years old. In addition to breakdancing, Jon Jr. seemed to be getting along fine at school and relished the life he had with his friends in Brookside.

When he wasn't practicing with his Brookside Breakers teammates or riding his BMX Mongoose, he was at Henthorne Park, playing basketball, swimming, and listening to old-time rock 'n' roll like Led Zepplin and Black Sabbath.

But life was beginning to change as the group grew older and delved deeper into the party life. According to a Douglas County PSI report, Jon Jr. long battled addiction. A parole officer wrote that he began drinking at age 8 and was exposed to alcohol and drugs when he was even younger. His mother pointed to Jon Sr. as the culprit.

"Before his father and I divorced, his father was a drug dealer, and he used to take my son, who was 4, 5 years old, with him," LaDonna Thomas said. "I got pissed, and I found a babysitter. He was around drugs at a very young age because of his dad. He was piddling with drugs for a long time. My sister told me when he started he was 7."

If Jon Jr. was using drugs during the first part of his time in Tulsa, he hid it well. Jenkins and Teresa Davis said they never saw him consume them. Drinking, however, was common among the Brookside crew. They sat in the grass at the park, drinking Bacardi and Wild Turkey while listening to KMOD FM 97.5, Tulsa's go-to rock station.

By 1985, Jon Jr. had lost two important figures in his life. As if not having a relationship with his father wasn't enough to handle emotionally, his girlfriend, Jenkins, moved nearly five hours away to Locust Grove, Arkansas, and Teresa Davis moved in with her mother, leaving Jon Jr. alone with his mother and stepfather. He had little interest in hanging around a house with firm rules, spending more and more time with his friends and more and more time partying.

Jon Jr. also struggled at school after his sister left, often fighting. Dentis said Jon Jr. was always in trouble and referred to him as a "rule-breaker." Livermore, who also attended Edison, said he wasn't afraid to stand up for himself.

"I never saw a mean side of him, but he would get into fights," Livermore said. "If you said something the wrong way or he took it the wrong way, he'd fight."

Some of that had to do with the composition of the high school, which Livermore described as "preppies vs. greasers."

"Jon did not fit in at school," Dentis said. "He was vocal, had a temper. We called him Jon Boy or Jon Jon."

LIFE WITH LOIS

Lois Dentis fought the good fight for a long time to maintain a level of normalcy for her three daughters. A 6-foot-2, broad-shouldered woman, she married her first husband, Larry Dentis, as a teen and gave birth to Di'Anna in 1970, followed by Shellie and Stephanie a few years later. Maintaining that stability wasn't easy in a home funded largely by burglaries, Stephanie Dentis said.

"It was a wild household," she said. "I have fond memories of growing up. We'd wake up on Christmas to a room full of presents. Of course, my dad was stealing to get us those presents."

Larry Dentis spent a number of years in prison on burglary convictions, and Lois Dentis had to support the family. The Dentises moved in with Lois' father on 50th Street in Brookside and survived on her work as a hairstylist. They even converted the garage attached to the small, three-bedroom home into a salon. That worked out for a while until she was struck by lightning, then years of chaos followed.

"Mom couldn't stand long enough to do hair after that," Stephanie Dentis said. "There was never a dull moment in that house."

To make ends meet, Lois Dentis became a bail bondswoman. That was the public face of her work life. Behind the scenes, she was a drug dealer, selling anything from marijuana to psilocybin (mushrooms) to dozens of customers.

"She literally made money either way she went," Stephanie Dentis said. "If somebody went to jail for drugs, she would bond them out and sell them more."

After her father died, Lois Dentis took over the home on 50th Street, and it quickly became a hangout for many of the kids in Brookside.

The family converted the living room into a bedroom, used the garage as a makeshift bedroom, and sectioned off parts of the attic to create more living spaces. The modest home served as a boarding house where nearly 20 people, almost entirely teenagers, lived. Howell said the home was somewhat dilapidated, with trash strewn about, clothes scattered, and food left out to rot.

"It was nasty. That place was nasty," he said. "I'm talking QT cups that still had pop in them full of cigarette butts, mold, roaches. You think the slums ... this was worse than the slums. It was the pig sty from hell. After you left, you felt like you had to take a shower because you felt like you had something on you."

It might have been disgusting, but the Dentis house was a refuge for many. A few kids moved into the house when Lois Dentis took guardianship of them, and numerous others stayed there night after night. It also was a place where they could feed their addictions, be it alcohol or drugs.

"A lot of drugs, mostly smoking weed. Every now and again, we'd be doing some cocaine," Howell said. "It was a party house. We had to have a place to party."

As Jon Jr. fell deeper into addiction, life at his house, especially without his sister, worsened. He got into more trouble at school and with his parents, notably his stepfather, according to those who grew up with him. Though Thomas and Teresa Davis said Stephen Davis never got physical with Jon Jr., others say their deteriorating relationship pushed him to leave his house and stay elsewhere in Brookside.

"I know he laid into Jon a couple of times," Howell said. "Jon would be staying at Tim's house, or Lois' house, or wherever he could stay. There were times he stayed at my house. I felt bad for the guy."

FIRST SIGNS OF TROUBLE

At 16, Mike Goodenough didn't seem like the prototypical hell-raiser. The same age as Jon Jr., Livermore, and others in the Brookside crowd, he was the son of a police detective father and pastor mother. Perhaps that pedigree is what led Goodenough, who later served as a Marine, to become the leader of the pack in the neighborhood.

"Mike and Ray (Johnson, another friend of Jon Jr. in Brookside) were the life of the party," Stephanie Dentis said. "They knew everybody. They were always showing up at our house with a car full of people. It just seemed like once those two guys came around, it got really busy really fast."

Although she was three years younger, Stephanie Dentis fell hard for Goodenough when she was 13 years old. They started dating just as the havoc ensued at the Dentis household, where Stephanie Dentis said her mother provided drugs to any of her friends who wanted them. Among those was Jon Jr., who moved into the home when he no longer wanted to stay with his mother and stepfather. Di'Anna Dentis said that Thomas asked if Jon Jr. could stay there after he and his stepfather "had gotten into it pretty bad." Thomas, however, said that she did not ask if her son could move in, but did say she gave him the option of going to rehab or moving out.

"I told him he couldn't live with me anymore because he stole my wedding ring and my class ring for drugs," she said.

Regardless of how it happened, Jon Jr. did move into the Dentis home, and it didn't take long before he wore out his welcome. First, he made a move on Stephanie Dentis, going into her room and trying to force his body onto her. She said he attempted to rip her clothes off and told her she might as well mess around with him since she was hooking up with Goodenough.

"When I started screaming for help, he burned me with a cigarette on my hand. I still have the scar from that," she said. "He traumatized the living daylight out of me. I really thought he was going to rape me."

Goodenough and several other boys were in another room in the house when they heard Stephanie Dentis screaming. They pulled Jon Jr. off her before pummeling him. A few weeks later, Di'Anna Dentis said Jon Jr. assaulted her, too, pinning her down on the couch and clawing at her clothes. When she told him she had a boyfriend, he responded in the same manner he did to Stephanie about Goodenough.

"He left this huge scratch down my leg from his toenails, and I'm bleeding," Di'Anna Dentis said. "I was going to scream, and he got off of me and said, 'I was just kidding.'"

Di'Anna Dentis told her mother about the incident, and Lois Dentis started taking a closer look at Jon Jr. It didn't take long before she caught him violating the family's trust again. When he wasn't hanging out with friends in the house, Jon Jr. spent much of his time in a small cubby he organized in the attic, including running a phone line through the ceiling, which no one in the home knew about. He ran the line to a rotary phone that he removed the mouthpiece from and listened in on calls coming into the house.

"That really upset my mom a lot," Di'Anna Dentis said. "That was his exit out of our home."

RETURNING TO KANSAS

Jon Jr.'s expulsion was one of several from the Dentis house, including that of one of the sisters, in a short period of time. Barely a teen, Stephanie Dentis left the home after a falling out with her mother.

For several months, Goodenough was a fixture at the home, partly because it was the go-to place for partying and access to drugs, and because he was dating Stephanie Dentis. Despite that fact and that she was 20 years older, Stephanie said, Lois Dentis took a liking to Goodenough beyond a surrogate mother-son relationship.

"My mother very much liked Mike," Stephanie Dentis said. "At one point, she professed her love for him."

Goodenough responded that Lois Dentis was more like his mother and that he planned to marry Stephanie and build a life together when they were old enough to do so. Stephanie said that conversation infuriated her mom, who dragged her by the hair out of the house, beat her in the front yard, and told her to leave.

"Mike's mom came and got me, and I stayed with her," she said. "I got to stay in the house, and Mike got the garage apartment because we weren't married, and we weren't old enough."

Meanwhile, Jon Jr. bounced around from house to house, staying with his friends in Brookside. Things began to spiral out of control when he was arrested for stealing and wrecking Livermore's car in 1985. Livermore said Jon Jr. grabbed his keys one night and took off in his 1977 Cutlass. In LaDonna Thomas' version of the event, Livermore allowed Jon Jr. to borrow his car.

"We were all at a party one night, and I got ahold of my family and told them I was at a friend's house," Livermore said. "I wake up in the middle of the night, and my car's gone, and my keys are gone. Jon stole it."

Livermore said police officers attempted to pull Jon Jr. over, and he took off before totaling the vehicle. According to a PSI in 1991, Jon Jr. was placed in a boys' home. When he returned from the home to visit his mother and stepfather, he said Stephen Davis hit him in the face and kicked him in the ribs. Jon Jr. immediately went back to the boys' home and never returned to Brookside.

Thomas and Stephen Davis tried to help their son, offering to enter him into rehabilitation when, upon completion, he could return home. They also gave Jon Jr. another option: Return to Kansas and live with his father. In 1986, at age 17, he left Oklahoma for good. He did not speak to his mother for more than five years and had no contact with the Brookside crew he grew up with until the 1990s.

"My daddy was tough, so I'm wondering if he might have been a little hard on Jon," Teresa Davis said.

OUT OF BROOKSIDE

Life moved on in Brookside after Jon Jr. left for Lawrence, Kansas, in 1986. Livermore played football at Edison High and Metro Christian before his sister died in an accident on Interstate Highway 44. His focus shifted from sports to drinking heavily, and he left Tulsa not long after Jon Jr. for California.

Several of the boys in the close group of friends went into the military, including Goodenough in the Marines. He and Stephanie Dentis eventually broke up, and she began dating another Brookside kid not long after. Like she did with Goodenough, Lois Dentis took an interest in this boy, too. Years later, after Stephanie moved on to another relationship, her mother married the boy she dated after Goodenough.

"My mom was a troubled person," Stephanie Dentis said. "When we were small kids, she didn't seem troubled. She got up every morning, made us breakfast, fixed our hair, got us off to school. She seemed pretty normal. As teenagers, that's when everything changed, and it never got better for me."

Struggle was a common theme for many of the kids who frequented the Dentis house. Several battled addiction for years. Howell eventually left Oklahoma for the East Coast when he realized he was "having too much fun with the needle." Goodenough battled an addiction to alcohol for more than 30 years before dying at age 49. A number of them went to prison, including one who killed a man in a drinking and driving accident. Some of them lived on the streets. Two of the Dentis sisters did manage to survive and live productive lives. Di'Anna and Stephanie both live and work in the Tulsa area.

"It was crazy. We did crazy stuff," Di'Anna Dentis said. "A lot of rough lives."

At least for a while, moving to Kansas appeared to help Jon Jr. He connected with new friends at Lawrence High School, including a girlfriend who calmed him down for a while. Jon Jr. and Becky Taylor dated for more than a year after he arrived.

"He was extremely nice and caring," Taylor said. "He didn't look at me crossways. He never raised his voice. He was just always a gentleman."

Old habits die hard, though. Jon Jr. got by on weed and alcohol for a while, then started using more heavily. Not long after he and Taylor broke up, trouble resurfaced. By the late 1980s, his life was out of control.

CHAPTER SIX:

THE TROUBLE WITH JON

By the fall of 1988, Jon Jr. was deep into addiction. According to Douglas County Court documents, he began drinking at age 8 and by 19 was consuming enough—two cases of beer and a bottle of hard liquor every day—that he experienced blackouts. A partier for several years at that point, he also was using amphetamines, cocaine, LSD, mushrooms, and marijuana.

Jon Jr. dropped out of high school when he was 18, just two years after moving to Lawrence, Kansas, where he lived with his father. He passed a high school equivalency exam in February 1988, but struggled to maintain a steady job, working as a laborer and for his father as a painter. Jon Sr., who had connections to motorcycle gangs, also provided Jon Jr. with access to alcohol and drugs.

"His dad was a One-Percenter (an outlaw motorcycle group), and those guys could get us anything we wanted—liquor, drugs, you name it," an acquaintance of the Mareskas who asked not to be identified said. "Now, it always came with a price if they got it for you, but they would get it."

But Becky Taylor, who dated Jon Jr. during her sophomore and junior years at Lawrence High, saw a different side of Jon Sr.

"Big Jon ... he was just the greatest guy to me," she said. "He looked out for Jon. He worked hard on keeping Jon on the straight and narrow."

What efforts Big Jon took to keep his son out of trouble went for naught. Shortly after midnight on Sept. 15, 1988, Lawrence Police Department officer Tony Garcia spotted Jon Jr. as he carried a white box through a breezeway near the Ernst and Son Hardware store on Massachusetts Street, the main street running through the central business district of downtown.

Realizing Garcia saw him, Jon Jr. turned around and walked in the opposite direction, setting the box against a wall. Garcia ordered Jon Jr., who was drinking that night, to stop and realized that he had blood on his finger and palm. The officer discovered that the display window of the hardware store was broken and contained blood. In the box, Garcia found a knife, pair of binoculars, fishing pole, first aid kit, and several other stolen items. Jon also stuffed a fishing knife down the front of his pants. Officers arrested him and took him to the Douglas County Jail.

After being charged with several crimes, he pleaded guilty to attempted burglary, theft, criminal damage to property, and unlawful use of weapons. That offense was the beginning of a three-year run of crime.

OCTOBER 1988

"Massive. Excessive. ... Ten hits of acid, and he robbed a liquor store," Taylor said. "When we dated, I didn't consider him a druggie. He did smoke pot, but it wasn't like every time I saw him, he was smoking pot."

By the time Becky and Jon Jr. were dating at Lawrence High in 1986 and 1987, he had tried a little bit of everything. He told Becky he was on an acid trip in October 1988 when he broke into a liquor store and stole several bottles of booze. In a statement to Douglas County law enforcement officials, Jon Jr. said he was drinking, but did not mention drugs.

"I did it. I was getting drunk. I left the party," he said. "Me and (a friend) went to the liquor store to get some beer. I said, 'I'm gonna go get some more.' I grabbed a board and broke the window. I took a few bottles of stuff out of the window."

According to a Lawrence Police Department report, Jon Jr. and two friends drove to Patterson Liquor on Illinois Street, just a few blocks from Massachusetts Street, moments before the store closed at 11 p.m. As the clerk left after closing the store for the night, he noticed Jon Jr. lingering outside. The clerk drove around the block several times until Jon Jr. left. Moments later, the store's alarm sounded, and police arrived to find the front window of the store shattered, with a two-by-eight board, about three feet long, lying on the ground. One officer detained Jon Jr. within minutes.

The officer who stopped Jon Jr. also found a trail of broken bottles and busted cans of beer from two 12-packs in a parking lot leading away from Patterson. Alongside the lot were several unbroken bottles of liquor lying in the grass, matching the brand and description of the bottles taken from the store. A witness told one of the officers the name of a friend who was with Jon Jr. in the store. After interviewing the friend, police arrested Jon Jr. for burglary, theft, and damage to property and placed him in the Douglas County Jail.

"I was somebody he could be around and not necessarily have to explain what was going on with him," Taylor said. "His dad would call and say, 'He's in jail.' I'd said, 'OK,' I'm going up to talk to him.' I was like, 'Why are you here? What part of this do you like?' And he'd say, 'I don't like any of it.'"

Like it or not, Jon Jr. was in Douglas County Jail from Oct. 5 to Oct. 27, released for five weeks, then remanded to custody on Jan. 3, 1989. Two months later, on March 15, 1989, he was convicted on misdemeanor counts of criminal damage to property, unlawful use of a weapon, and two thefts, all tied to felony charges, according to the Topeka Capital-Journal. Jon Jr. went to an intensive supervised probation program, and for more than a year, he was in multiple alcohol and drug rehabilitation programs in Wichita.

WINTER 1989-90

Jon Jr. caught a break after he was convicted of burglarizing two downtown Lawrence businesses in 1988. He spent only three months in jail and completed a 60-day program before moving to the Alumni House, a halfway house program, where he spent the next two months, before relapsing in the summer. During that relapse, he took an undetermined amount of Dilaudid and Demorel, both powerful opioid pain medications, and nearly overdosed.

Jon Jr. went to Parallax, where he detoxed, before going to the Dodge House, another halfway house in Wichita. He was clean for three months before relapsing again, this time drinking a case and a half of beer and a bottle of tequila, resulting in a month of restrictions at the facility. Jon Jr. managed to stay on the wagon for a while, from the end of 1989 into early 1990, even working as a shift manager at the Dodge House for two months. During this time, he began dating Kim Hardesty, another addict who endured her share of struggles.

"I went in there (Parallax) when I was 30, and that's how we got to know each other," Hardesty said. "My drug of choice at the time was cocaine, but we never did drugs together because we were sober then. During the whole time we were together, we were clean and sober."

At 5-foot-1, a trim 100 pounds, and with long, blonde hair, Hardesty fit the mold of the girl Jon Jr. typically liked. And like the other girls he dated, she liked to have a good time.

"We had some things in common. He was just fun," she said. "He was very soft as far as being affectionate, and he didn't have a bad attitude. We never had any big arguments, or knock-down, drag-out fights."

Being confined to a halfway house meant growing close to those around you. The residents replaced drugs and alcohol with AA meetings, dancing, and playing pool. Hardesty said Jon Jr. worked hard at the program.

"He was really involved," she said. "Everything we did was sober. I never saw him high."

They became an item quickly, even traveling to Topeka in early 1990 so Hardesty could meet his father, who was recovering from a motorcycle accident. Getting closer to Jon Jr. meant she learned quite a bit about his parents, a topic that provided insight to his struggles.

"He told me his parents, and he didn't say specifically who, shot him up with dope when he was 9 years old," Kim said. "You hear a lot of stories when you go to treatment and you're around all those people, and I'm telling you I heard a lot of shocking stuff over the years. I can't even fathom a parent shooting a child up with drugs at 9 years old. But that's when his addiction started."

Jon Jr.'s addiction may very well have started when he was a child, but by age 9 he was living with his mother in Arkansas and hadn't seen his father for several years. When he was a teen, however, Jon Jr. and his mother often were at odds.

"He did talk about his mother, and he hated her," Hardesty said. "All I can think is eventually, because of the way he was growing up, that he grew to hate women."

If he did hate women, Hardesty never experienced it. After years of being in and out of recovery and dating abusive men, Jon Jr., 10 years younger than her, was a breath of fresh air. He and Hardesty talked about their pasts, confiding in one another about their difficult upbringings. For a while, they were inseparable. Eventually, though, Jon Jr. wanted to be around her too much.

"The immaturity started coming and driving me crazy," she said. "I wanted space."

Jon Jr.'s attention became smothering in the spring of 1990 when Hardesty asked him not to attend a clean and sober dance so that she could spend some time with her friends. She arrived at the party to find that he was there and broke up with him.

"It really made me mad, and I told him, 'Look, I can't do this,'" she said.

In the following days, Jon Jr. called her dozens of times. He never threatened her. He didn't stalk her. But he did lose her.

"He begged me to come back and said how he would change," Hardesty said. "It's always been said that women mature faster than men, and I started seeing the reality of that, and I couldn't stand it. The further things went on, the more I felt like a mom to him more than anything else."

Jon Jr. left the Dodge House in May 1990, falling back into old habits almost immediately with a relapse. He moved back to Lawrence, spending several weeks with a girlfriend while trying to find steady work. According to a Douglas County Department of Community Corrections report on his supervised probation, Jon Jr. was close to securing a full-time job at a company specializing in molded plastic products. He also worked off nearly $500 in community service work and a small portion of the amount he owed in restitution for burglarizing the liquor store.

That report, written in June 1990, also noted that Jon Jr. had several negative drug tests and regular attendance in aftercare counseling. Within a matter of weeks, though, he left Lawrence, moved in with his father in a trailer behind his aunt and uncle's hair salon in south Topeka, and began dating a new girl.

SEPTEMBER 1990

After moving in with his father for a second time in 1990, Jon Jr. met Cheryl Reeb in Topeka at her cousin's party, during which a dog bit him in the face. Reeb, then 32 and a striking, small blonde at

5-foot-4 and 100 pounds, felt sorry for Jon Jr. and took him into her home in Harveyville while he recovered.

"My mom introduced us to this guy she met, and he was a lot younger than her, and I remember thinking it was kind of strange," said Ashley Reeb, Cheryl's daughter, then 7. "He was very nice. He kind of played around with us kids when he was around. He was a very kind person. I remember thinking I wish she would date him."

Jon Jr. left Cheryl Reeb's house after a few days, but returned, begging to stay the night. According to a police report by Wabaunsee County deputy Harry Carpenter, Cheryl Reeb said she could not get Jon Jr. to leave the house: "She took her son, and they went to bed together. She said in the middle of the night, he (Jon Jr.) came upstairs and sexually assaulted her, and she was afraid to resist or say anything for fear he would hurt the kids."

A few days later, on Sept. 9, a Wabaunsee County Sheriff's Department dispatcher sent Carpenter and fellow deputy Dickie Forkner to Harveyville, where they found Cheryl and Ashley Reeb standing outside of their house.

"(Cheryl Reeb) said that (Jon Jr.) had broken in the house and was probably still around," Carpenter said in his report. "Deputy Forkner and I searched around the house, the garage and the house, finding no one."

While Cheryl Reeb and her children were away from home earlier in the day, Jon Jr. climbed the back of the house, broke her son's bedroom window, moved a bunk bed, and opened the front door. He spent several hours in the house, drinking seven beers out of a 12-pack in the refrigerator. When the Reebs came home at 10 p.m., the front door was open. After entering their house, the mother and daughter heard a knock at the back door. Ashley Reeb opened the door to find Jon Jr. standing there.

He forced his way into the house when Cheryl Reeb asked him to leave. Ashley Reeb immediately ran to neighbor Larry and Sherry Robertson's house as Jon Jr. grabbed a knife from the kitchen.

"Jon told Cheryl the only way she was going to get rid of him was to stab him," Carpenter said. "Cheryl took the knife, threw it in the sink and ordered him out of the house. He left, but then stuck his foot in the door until (Larry) got there, and then he left."

After spending 15 minutes at the neighbor's house, Cheryl Reeb returned with Larry Robertson to check and secure her home. Moments later, Jon Jr. was back on the roof, removing the storm window from Ashley's room.

"I heard him on the stairs and found him creeping down the stairs with his shoes in his hand," Cheryl Reeb said. "When he realized he was caught, he walked out the door."

Forkner patrolled the area after he and Carpenter arrived in Harveyville at 11:42 p.m. Despite a search of the home and the area, they couldn't find Jon Jr.

"I remember the cops looking for him and not finding him, even though he was right there. I remember that frustration," Ashley Reeb said. "He was looking at me sitting on the porch (at a house across the street) looking at him. He probably thought that was entertaining. That was creepy."

The deputies left after midnight when they finished taking a report. They weren't gone for long when another call came in from Harveyville.

"It was 80 and 90 miles an hour, maybe 100, back out there after another call," Carpenter said.

He and Forkner arrived at the home at 3:45 a.m. to find Cheryl Reeb moaning and gasping for air on the kitchen floor while holding her stomach. Carpenter radioed for an ambulance, and the paramedics recommended that she be taken by Life Star to Stormont-Vail Hospital in Topeka.

"By the time I got there, he was gone, nowhere near the house," Carpenter said. "I did as much as I could, went out and looked for him. I hollered, 'If you don't come, I'm going in.' I went in, and he wasn't hiding in there (a nearby field)."

Carpenter, Forkner, and fellow deputy Michael Watson spent the next two hours searching Harveyville. Hiding in a town of about 275 people with a land area of 83 acres, Jon Jr. was still on the loose when Carpenter left for Topeka to check on Cheryl Reeb, who had multiple contusions.

"Cheryl said that she and her daughter had gone to bed together in Cheryl's bedroom after I left from the first call," Carpenter said. "At around 1:45 a.m., she saw the bedroom door open. Jon crawled in and started looking through the jewelry and coins on the dresser using Cheryl's cigarette lighter. He held the lighter over her on the bed and lit it, and she pretended she was asleep."

According to Carpenter's report, Jon Jr. walked to the closet to pick through it, giving Cheryl Reeb the opportunity to jump out of bed, run out of the room, and race down the stairs. Jon Jr. caught up to her when she reached the phone, yanking the line out of the wall.

"You're not going to call the cops back," Jon Jr. said. "I could have blown up your house, the cop up and robbed the bank. I could have shot you all while you were talking, and I heard you tell him about me breaking parole."

Cheryl managed to grab a baseball bat and hit Jon Jr. with it, but he took the bat, threw her down, then kicked her in the stomach several times as she lay on the floor. At that point, Ashley came down the stairs to find Jon Jr. attacking her mother.

"I heard a noise, screaming I'm assuming, so I wake up and come down the stairs and he's in the kitchen," Ashley said. "I didn't know that he had a knife behind his back, and he said, 'Oh, did I wake you up? Come here and let me give you a hug.' The next thing I know, I'm on the floor, and she's an obvious mess. She somehow managed to grab me and pull me to her, and he's laughing."

Cheryl Reeb pushed her daughter out of the back door, and she ran to a house next door, where a neighbor called 911.

"I don't think she would have made it much longer," Ashley said. "It was like he needed to torture her. She somehow managed to push me out, or we might not have made it. I could tell she was in trouble. He was so sweet and chuckling. He wanted to comfort me, and I believed him until she grabbed me."

Jon Jr. hid in and around Harveyville for several hours before Watson spotted him just west of the small post office on the northeast side of town. The officer arrested Jon Jr. for battery before transporting him to and booking him into the Wabaunsee County Jail.

As Jon Jr. emptied his pockets, Watson noticed two plastic baggies containing marijuana and marijuana debris. He had 88 cents in change, three hair ties, two Bic lighters, two key rings with six keys, a small screwdriver and a wallet, which contained Zig-Zag rolling papers, and the Wabaunsee County Sheriff's business card that Carpenter left with Cheryl several hours earlier.

After Jon Jr. went to the county jail, he and Carpenter, who also worked as a jailer, saw each other almost daily. Carpenter recalled an incident during which one of Jon Jr.'s fellow detainees stole batteries and put them in a sock to use as a makeshift weapon. Carpenter carried a shotgun into a cell Jon Jr. and the inmate shared.

"Jon said, 'You would have shot him, wouldn't you?' And I said, 'Hell, yes, I would have shot him. The guy had a weapon,'" Carpenter said. "'I'm not supposed to bring a gun in here, but how am I supposed to protect myself and you guys?' Jon, from then on, had some respect for me."

OCTOBER 1990

By the time officers arrested Jon Jr. for attacking Cheryl Reeb, he had a long rap sheet accumulated in a short period of time. The charges in Wabaunsee County were among more than a dozen he faced in three years and ranged from burglary to battery, though they resulted in only a few months in jail. Even though the break-in and beating of Reeb fueled by beer and drugs was the third incident in two years, Jon was about to get another chance.

"I didn't have a sense of how I do today that prosecution is sort of a no-win game," said Rob Matthews, then the Wabaunsee County attorney. "As a prosecutor, if you look at my record, I tried to avoid putting people in prison. If you look at the charges I file against people, I'd file appropriate charges. But I'd almost always recommend probation. I did not put people in jail for long periods of time."

That's not to say Matthews didn't consider stiffer charges against Jon Jr. Ultimately, the attorney's decision hinged on a critical distinction: Was the assault on Reeb simple battery or aggravated battery? Simple battery is the least serious form of battery, typically resulting in minor injuries, and usually a misdemeanor. Aggravated battery involves circumstances that make the crime more serious and can include hitting a person with a weapon, shooting them, or beating someone into disfigurement.

"As I recall, she did not suffer a whole lot of injuries," Matthews said. "If I see that she escalated with a bat, and he responded, that might have had something to do with my decision."

Reeb indeed grabbed a bat and hit Jon with it, but that was after he chased her down the stairs and threw her over a dishwasher. He proceeded to take the bat away, kick her in the stomach several times, and choke her. More than 30 years later, Matthews struggles with the decision he made to charge Jon Jr. with the lesser battery.

"This case ... it has always sat in my mind as an awful thing that I was a part of," he said. "I don't know if sitting him in a pretty empty Wabaunsee County Jail was the best thing. On the other hand, if I had been more aggressive as a prosecutor, I could have put him away for a really long time. Maybe it was a dumb mistake not pushing for aggravated battery. I've got an ambivalent feeling about it."

Matthews said Jon Jr. received one of the longer sentences given during his six years as the lead prosecutor in Wabaunsee County. He agreed to accept sentences on three counts of criminal trespass (90 days in jail), one count of criminal damage to property (180 days), one count of battery (180 days), and one count of possession of marijuana (60 days), all to be served consecutively. The court also gave him credit for the 51 days he spent in jail since his arrest in Harveyville, placed him on probation for two years, and ordered him to complete a treatment program.

The charges in Wabaunsee County, however, meant Jon violated his probation in Douglas County, and he was going to prison. After spending a little more than two months in the county jail, he moved to the Kansas Reception and Diagnostic Center in Topeka on Nov. 19, 1990, then the Norton Correctional Facility on Dec. 17. He was released on Feb. 21, 1991, after serving 164 days behind bars.

DECEMBER 1990

Jon Sr. never backed down from a challenge, and he wasn't afraid to fight, no matter the size of the opponent. That caught up with him on Dec. 7, 1990, when he pushed the wrong man at a bar in north Topeka.

A friend told the Topeka Police Department that Jon Sr. argued with a large white male who was 6-foot-3 and 300 pounds at Charlie Hall's, a strip club and pool hall located across the Kansas River and three miles north of the Capitol building on Topeka Boulevard. The friend forced Jon Sr. out of the bar before the situation escalated, but Jon Sr. broke free from him and stormed back into the establishment.

Jon Sr. confronted the man, Matt Fabry, again, and Fabry, who worked as a bouncer at other bars in Topeka, hit him in the face, causing him to fall backward and hit his head on the floor. Though his nose bled and he was inebriated, Jon Sr. refused help or medical treatment. He ended up sleeping in the back of the friend's van until the next day, at which time the man found Jon Sr. lying unconscious in the driveway.

"They think he fell out of the van when he got up and landed on his head again," Tammy Blake said.

According to a Topeka Police Department report, doctors diagnosed Jon Sr. with a closed head injury. Ten days later, he was still at Stormont-Vail Hospital and in critical condition. He eventually opened his eyes and began to respond. Jon Sr. was on a ventilator for nearly two weeks and couldn't engage in conversation.

He spent a few weeks at the Veterans Administration Hospital in Kansas City before being transferred to the VA in Topeka on Jan. 8, 1991. A month removed from the fight and hitting his head on the ground twice, he still couldn't talk. The Topeka Police investigated, but could not determine if Fabry's punch caused the brain damage Jon Sr. suffered and closed the case.

After several months in the hospital, Jon Sr. moved in with Tammy and Gene Blake in Dover. A doctor later diagnosed him with severe brain damage, and he relied on relatives and the staff at a nursing home in Topeka to care for him.

MAY 1991

Terri Morin had one simple rule for Jon Jr. when he moved into her modest home in Burlington, Kansas, a small town of 2,500 and the location of the only nuclear power plant in the state.

"I told him and my brother the same thing, that they could live there in my house as long as they had a job," she said.

A few months removed from a three-month stay in a county jail, Jon Jr., nearly 22 years old, didn't have many options when he moved in with Morin in March 1991. Up to that point, he stayed with Gene and Tammy in a small cabin they owned off the Neosho River in Burlington.

"He lived with us because his father couldn't take him in," Tammy Blake said. "We tried to help him out with a few things."

It was during a night on the town that Jon Jr. met Morin, a pretty and petite 27-year-old redhead with a warm personality.

"He was as sweet as he could be," she said. "He had black hair, down a little bit below his shoulders. He had a mustache and was really skinny. He was a good-looking guy. I basically worked all the time at the nuclear plant. I was working, my brother was working, and he was working. We'd either go out and party at the bars, or we'd stay here at the house and do nothing."

Jon Jr. didn't have much luck with jobs, a fact Morin wasn't aware of at the time. A few months into their relationship, though, he seemed to be getting his life on track, settling in as a member of the makeshift family.

That all changed on May 24. After a night of drinking and partying, Morin and Jon Jr. returned home from the local American Legion bar, leaving her brother behind. With her two sons, age 4 and 8, sound asleep, Jon Jr. came clean.

"Right on my birthday, he lost his job," she said. "And when he told me he lost his job, I told him he had to move out. That was my rule, as long as you work and help with the bills, you can stay. I just wasn't in the position to support anybody. That's when everything exploded."

When Morin told him to move out, his eyes went "totally black" and his face blank. Surprisingly strong for his slight build, Jon Jr. attacked her in full force, wrapping his fingers around her throat while attempting to squeeze the life out of her. He then dragged Morin from the kitchen to the living room, continuing to choke her while hitting her head on the floor before the police arrived.

Fortunately for Morin and her children, neighbor Angelina Roney, then just 18 years old and a police officer's daughter, heard screaming and called the Sheriff's Department. Deputies arrived a few minutes later, and Jon Jr. scrambled to hide.

"If they hadn't showed up, he would have killed me," Morin said. "All of sudden, he got very angry real fast, and I don't remember much because I passed out."

Officers Kenneth Roney and Kevin Bailey arrived to find Morin crying and beaten up with marks on her face and neck. They found

Jon Jr. hiding on the front porch, arrested him for assault and battery, and transported him to the Coffey County Jail.

JUNE 1991

It wasn't long before Morin saw Jon Jr. again. In fact, police released him the day after the attack.

"They let him out after 12 hours, and they called me and told me he was out," she said. "Well, I was sitting on my couch, talking to my sister on the phone, and he was standing in the window watching me."

Morin called the police, who escorted him away from the property. Despite the attack and the incident, Morin continued to try to help Jon Jr., offering the next day to drive him to Topeka, where he could stay while he waited for his court appointment in Coffey County. She came to regret that decision.

"Him and my brother were up front, and I was in the back with my kids, and we were all just talking," Morin said of the hourlong drive from Burlington to Topeka. "He was being a smart aleck because he didn't want us to take him over there, but I couldn't let him stay around me."

Just days before, Morin watched as Jon Jr.'s temper exploded, beginning with dark, cold eyes and a blank stare. When he turned around in the middle of the conversation and looked at her with the same expression, she was terrified.

"I told my brother to stop the car right now," she said. "We just happened to be by some apartments, and I jumped out with my kids and ran. I was knocking on everybody's door to let me in. My brother came and got me after Jon got out of the car."

Her brother stopped the car in Lyndon, the seat of Osage County and another small town of about 1,000 located 30 miles north of Burlington and 30 miles south of Topeka. Morin and her family drove home, while Jon Jr. roamed around Lyndon for several hours before he decided it was time to head back to Burlington.

Sometime between 11:30 p.m. on June 14 and 7 a.m. the following morning, Jon Jr. stole a brown/beige 1977 Chevy pickup truck from the driveway of a home located immediately south of the Lyndon city limits. A few hours later, he visited Morin one last time.

"He was looking in my windows at me again," she said. "I called the police again. To this day, I'm leery of men. I was actually ashamed to tell anybody that the man lived in my home. He's just crazy."

Coffey County Sheriff's deputies located and arrested Jon Jr. the same day. He admitted stealing the truck, which the Sheriff's Department found in the mud at John Redmond Lake on the outskirts of Burlington. Osage County deputy Eldon Croucher drove to Burlington to transport him back to Lyndon to be booked in the jail there.

"I remember (Jon Jr.) was weird," Croucher said. "When I got to the jail, I said, 'You guys better watch this guy.' He didn't say much. The look on his face, his eyes. When you're a cop, you get to the point where you notice stuff like that. He was just out of it. He had that look that, 'If I could do it, I'd kill you.' He didn't like cops, that's for sure."

Jon Jr. remained in the Osage County Jail through June and pleaded no contest to theft. On July 2, the court found him guilty, set his bond at $2,000, and scheduled sentencing for July 30. He stayed in jail until his sentencing date, when he received one year in the Osage County Jail, to run consecutively with any pending parole violations, from Judge James Smith.

A little more than a month later, Jon Jr appeared before the Coffey County Court, where the charge of assault for the attack on Morin was dismissed. He pleaded guilty to battery and received a six-month sentence, concurrent with his sentence in Osage County.

"So, this is early, almost pre-computer," then-Osage County attorney Cheryl Stewart said. "This was back before we did real pre-sentence investigations, and if we wanted somebody's criminal history, we sent a letter to the Kansas Bureau of Investigation, and they would send us back a packet with a copy of the journal entry from the court where the convictions had occurred. We didn't have access to incident information or information that we could get quickly.

"The information that we had on him was pretty minimal. (In the Osage County case), he did a burglary in a woman's garage. He went in and took something out of somebody's garage without any kind of contact with a human being. That is a nonviolent crime."

CHAPTER SEVEN:

THE SEARCH FOR BRENDA

The Ladies Aid dinner was an event for members of the Dover Federated Church featuring a chicken and noodle supper, auction of goods donated by churchgoers, and a raffle. One of the highlights of the banquet was local children waiting tables, a duty Brenda volunteered for, along with several of her friends, including Misty Lange and Amy Best.

Brenda planned to finish her bike ride at about 5:30 p.m., change her clothes, and attend the dinner with her family. Tracy left early to help set up at the event, and Bob, John, and Pat left their home together shortly after 5:30 p.m. Though Brenda wasn't home by then, the assumption was that she lost track of time, as she had on some of her rides, and would make the half-mile walk after she was finished.

Some of those attending the dinner noticed shortly after it began that Brenda wasn't there, including Best, who remembers Bob and Tracy asking her if she had seen their daughter.

"I knew something was wrong because that's not like her," Tracy said. "She's not irresponsible."

Still, this was Dover, a place where significant crime amounted to the occasional break-in, and there was no need to panic. Her parents figured Brenda might not be feeling well and decided to stay home. At a time when nobody carried a phone, there wasn't a way to contact her.

"There was not really a whole lot of concern because (when the dinner started) it was still daylight," Best said. "She would kind of get distracted on her rides."

A MOTHER'S INTUITION

By the time Tracy drove along Douglas Road at 9:30 p.m. on Oct. 19, her daughter had been missing for four hours. For more than an hour, she and Bob drove around Dover, traveling the routes Brenda typically took during her long, leisurely bike rides, before they returned home, frantic and deeply concerned.

After a series of phone calls to friends in the community, Tracy learned that Penny Lister saw Brenda on Douglas Road at about 5:30 p.m. Tracy didn't hesitate, driving directly to the house closest to that location, a large farm home a mile south of the main intersection in town and less than five minutes from the Kellers. Unlike the thousands of other times she drove on Douglas, though, Tracy sensed something for the first time.

"I felt danger. I just felt like something was wrong," she said. "I guess you'd call it a mother's intuition."

Tracy pulled into the driveway in the dark, with the moon, stars, and a few glowing windows from the house producing the only light in an area of town that didn't have street lights. In fact, there were no street lights in Dover until 1992.

When Tracy, a fit 5-foot-2 woman, knocked on the door, Jon Sr. answered it. A tall, burly, rough-looking man with dark brown, graying hair, a moustache, and brown eyes, he was known in the Dover community as the older brother of Tammy Blake who was staying there after suffering a head injury.

When Tracy asked Jon Sr. if he saw Brenda, he told her that he saw a girl walking south with a boy earlier in the evening. As Jon Sr. answered the question, Tracy noticed another man sleeping on the couch in the living room while she stood on the front porch. Jon Sr. hesitated when she asked if she could talk to the man on the couch, so Tracy cleverly asked if she could come in for a drink of water.

"I wasn't scared," Tracy said. "I just felt like that's where she was. I was calm and asked if they'd seen her. There was something inside of me that said that's where she was."

Tracy didn't ask to look around the house, but she did try to wake up the man on the couch, Jon Jr., who moved in Oct. 1, when a parole officer in Douglas County placed him in the custody of the Blakes. He was living in Dover while waiting to be admitted to the Osawatomie State Hospital, a psychiatric hospital 80 miles from Dover and an hour southeast of Lawrence. He didn't wake up, and Tracy left to return home and call the Shawnee County Sheriff's Department.

"I just remember him on the couch, sort of drugged out," she said. "Somehow, it's almost like I knew she was dead."

TAMSTOY

From time to time as she cruised around the countryside, Brenda had to stop and adjust the chain after it fell off the derailleur gear. This was an easy fix, one that took no more than a minute to make, and she was on her way again. On Oct. 19, her bike malfunctioned because of the chain or a flat tire somewhere during the second half of her trip.

Between the time she turned north onto Douglas Road and the Blakes' home about a mile south of the main street in Dover, she had to stop riding and start pushing the bike on the east side of the road. This path went by several houses on each side of the street, including a cluster of homes within a few hundred yards of the Blakes' place.

At least four people spotted Brenda as she headed north toward her family's home. Don and Aimee Grubb drove by her heading south, continuing on to Harveyville, where they arrived shortly before 6 p.m. A few minutes later, Penny and Francy Lister passed Brenda on their way to the grade school, which was less than a half mile north of the bridge she just crossed.

Less than a quarter mile to the north of Brenda on Douglas Road was a trio of homes, two on the right side of the road and one on the left, sitting on top of a small hill. Dover's cemetery was 300 yards further, and the grade school another 200 yards past that, one-half mile and less than a minute drive from the Blakes'. Despite the presence of several homes, the cemetery, and an open road, no one saw Brenda once she crossed the bridge, including the Listers when they drove home on the same road moments later.

"I did think it was strange that I didn't pass her, but I still didn't do anything about it," Penny Lister said. "It's just ... that's not like me."

Even though the area was fairly populated for a rural community, many of the people living in those homes weren't there at the time. Among those was the Sievers family, close friends of the Blakes who lived 100 yards to the south. Mary and Leon and daughters Marilee and Crystal left late in the afternoon for a picnic in nearby Burlingame, another small town 20 miles to the southeast in neighboring Osage County. Not long after the picnic, Mary drove her daughters to Topeka to watch a movie at West Ridge Mall before returning to Burlingame. The family didn't arrive back in Dover until after 6 p.m.

"I just remember feeling guilty later because I had a feeling that she (Brenda) was coming by or stopping by," Marilee Sievers said.

Many people did recognize a car they saw thousands of times through the years, a bright red Camaro with a personalized license plate reading "TAMSTOY." That car, which stood out among the pickup trucks and tractors typically seen on the roadways around the farming community, belonged to Tammy Blake.

Bob Marling, a lifelong Dover resident who lived on the property adjacent to the Blakes from the west, spent much of his day hunting around Mission Creek before returning home to a sick wife. He left town after 5 p.m. to drive to a pharmacy in Topeka to pick up a prescription. Driving through Dover on 57th Street at about 5:15 to 5:20 p.m., he crossed paths with the red Camaro heading westbound near Davis Road just outside of the community. Moments later, Aimee Grubb and her father met the Camaro while driving north toward the grade school on Douglas.

"We did pass a red Camaro before we passed Brenda (on the way home)," Aimee Grubb said. "I remember that because after it happened, my dad asked me if I remembered the red Camaro, and at the time I didn't. (It would have been) right around the Blakes' house."

Don Grubb couldn't recall all of the details of he and his daughter's fateful trip to Dover, but he remembers that two people were in the red Camaro.

COUSIN IVAN

By most accounts, Otis Wright Jr., who went by his middle name, Ivan, was a decent man. After growing up in Burlington and graduating from the high school there, he served in the National Guard before attending Emporia State University, where he earned a bachelor's degree. Born in 1944, he was close to Gene Blake, his cousin who also grew up in Burlington. Ivan was far closer to his mother, Gladys, who divorced Ivan's dad, Otis Sr., a tough, at times difficult man whose second wife was more than 20 years his junior.

"Ivan wasn't like his dad, not mean, anyway," said Terry Thoele, Ivan's stepbrother. "He'd say, 'I know he's a mean old man.' Ivan knew how his dad was."

Ivan Jr.'s stepsister, Anne Oram, said her stepfather was demanding.

"We were never good enough, us kids," she said. "We weren't abused physically, but mentally we were. There were comments and negative things."

Something Ivan struggled to move on from was his marriage to Linda Wright. The couple met after he finished serving in the Guard and as he worked as a surveyor for the State of Kansas. Ivan, a tall, slender man with reddish blond hair, later worked for several years at Santa Fe Railroad and as a real estate agent in Topeka. In 1976, the couple had their only child, a son.

One of Ivan's defining characteristics was his stubbornness. He lived life his way, with little regard for advice or risk. That attitude benefitted him at times.

"Ivan was pretty outgoing," said Terry Wright, a cousin who grew up with him. "He liked to play. And when he moved to Topeka, he played. He played a lot of big-stakes poker games where he'd come out $2,000 to $3,000 ahead playing with some of the legislators who liked to play poker. That was the kind of high stakes games he was in."

That throw-caution-to-the-wind attitude also came with conse-quences. Ivan liked to drink, and he didn't let a debilitating disease stop him. By 1991, an ailing foot from diabetes resulted in regular insulin treatments. He spent hours at St. Francis Hospital in Topeka to ease his pain.

"He didn't want to give up drinking. He wouldn't listen to the doc-tors," Terry Wright said. "He did his own thing when it came to that. He was going to go live his life the way he wanted to."

As Ivan's body began to shut down, his marriage began to do the same. By 1989, he and Linda Wright divorced and split custody of their son. In December 1990, according to court records, he lost his temper with his ex-wife in front of his son. He was charged with bat-tery on Dec. 5 and appeared before the court on Feb. 1, 1991. He was convicted of battery, placed on supervised probation for nine months, and ordered to participate in an intervention program.

"Just from talking to his wife, he was pretty abusive to her, mentally and physically," said Debbie Johnston, another stepsister of Ivan's. "It was mainly mental abuse. She said he would change from one person to another at the drop of a hat and just be mean and crazy. His dad, my stepdad, was kind of like that, too."

By the fall, and a few months from the end of probation, Ivan was trying to remodel his house on the outskirts of Topeka on Ratner Road, with the help of his son. The Blakes offered Ivan and his son a room in their house while they finished working on the home.

"(Ivan) had troubles off and on," Tammy Blake said. "We had room in here, and we just told him he could come stay here for a while. We thought that would be a good deal because he could help us during the time we were going to be on vacation. He could feed the horses, things like that."

By the beginning of September, Ivan was living with the Blakes, sleeping in Dover overnight and waking up early to drive to Topeka and remodel his house. He was there about a month when Jon Jr. moved in with the Blakes and Jon Sr.

On the morning of Oct. 19 and right around the time the Dover Junior High volleyball team was on the way to Mission Valley, Ivan and Jon Jr. were traveling to Topeka in Tammy Blake's Camaro. Ivan's plan that day was to drive to the house on Ratner Road, then head to St. Francis Hospital to receive an insulin treatment. Before he left the Blakes', Jon Jr. asked to tag along, and, according to Shawnee County Sheriff's Department detective Larry Baer's report, Ivan said he agreed because "he thought it would be good to get the boy away from the house and in town for a while."

Ivan and Jon. Jr. stopped at Banjo Belly's, a small restaurant on the south side of Topeka, to eat breakfast. They then drove 15 minutes east to Tecumseh, an unincorporated community bordering Topeka, and the location of Ivan's house. After showing Jon Jr. around the house and property, they returned to Topeka, stopping at St. Francis for Ivan's treatment. When Ivan told Jon Jr. that he would be at the hospital for a couple of hours, Jon Jr. decided to walk to the Full Moon Saloon, a bar a few blocks north in downtown Topeka, arriving at 1 p.m.

CONCERN TO REALITY

By the time the Ladies Aid banquet ended at 8 p.m., Bob and Tracy were anxious to return home and check on their daughter. But when they arrived moments later, Brenda was nowhere to be found, and panic began to set in. Though the weather was warmer than a typical fall day in mid-October, the temperature was beginning to drop as the night grew darker, and the Kellers were concerned that she was in an accident and needed help.

Tracy and Bob began making phone calls to neighbors and friends, asking if they saw Brenda or knew where she was. The Kellers – Bob, Tracy, and John – and several members of the community began searching. Bob and Tracy hit some of her favorite routes, including one leading north of town on K-4 Highway toward Maple Hill and winding back to Topeka, as well as the trek she traveled that day. Jim and Judy Wilson drove into Dover from their home in Keene.

"Bob called and wanted to know if Brenda was here with us, and, of course, she wasn't," Judy Wilson said. "I asked if there was anything we could do, and he asked us to come in and look for her, they needed people to look for her. We (Judy, Jim, Jill and Jana Blodgett) went out to the Gold Finch Road. We walked behind all the houses, stuck our heads in all the barns and all the buildings."

As the Wilsons and Blodgett searched along Gold Finch Road about a mile southwest of the Blakes' house, others branched out to various parts of the area. Best and her mother, the late Cathy Best, drove all the way out to Mission Valley, then back toward Dover and Echo Cliff, a park with folk art signs, picnic tables, and a scenic look-out onto 50-foot cliffs that Brenda often explored.

"I had a sense that it was bad," Amy Best said. "I remember driving in the car thinking it's not going to turn out well."

More friends began looking in as many places as they could. Some drove north of town and scoured the desolate dirt roads largely hidden by hills and spacious fields. Others looked behind barns, houses, and sheds. Members of the Dover Fire Department, a small unit staffed by volunteers, drove along Douglas Road, shining the lights of their fire truck into ditches.

The Kellers placed more phones calls, including to their families. In Topeka, Roy, preparing his sermon for the following morning's service at Topeka Free Methodist Church, immediately called Jean, who was out of town for the weekend at a Christian women's retreat.

"We listened to a speaker, and a bunch of us ladies went to my room, and we had a craft. We were all working on a craft, circled around two beds," Jean said. "I got a phone call, and it was Roy, and he told me they were searching for Brenda and she was missing. I remember just laying down and stretching out across the bed, and everything got so quiet. And, then I told them, and I had ridden up there with three ladies from Topeka. One of those ladies came to me and said, 'Let's have prayer,' and we all gathered for prayer, and then they said, 'Jean, we're going to take you back to Topeka.'"

As Jean began the two-hour ride from Salina, members of the family called Beverly, Janice, and Aunt B, beginning a prayer chain that stretched across eastern Kansas.

"Beverly called me and said, 'We need prayer, we can't find Brenda. We need that bad," Aunt B said. "I said, 'OK, you got it.'"

Despite all the prayers and people canvassing Dover looking for Brenda, she was nowhere to be found. On one side of town, John and Misty Lange rode in the back of a truck while looking for her and yelling her name. On the other side of town, Brooklynd Thomas was a bundle of emotion, namely fear.

"Somebody called and talked to my daughter, and she immediately went into a panic," said Kaiden Barraclough, Brooklynd's mother. "I was trying to tell Brooklynd that she'll show up, maybe she just took a longer bike ride. The phone was just a buzz. It was constantly ringing.

Once one person heard it, they call that person, and it goes round and round. My daughter was insistent that she wanted to get out and figure out what was going on because she knew something was wrong. I took her with me and we went into town. It was a hubbub of activity in town. There were people everywhere. It was confusing at first."

Confusing and terrifying. Finally, after dozens of phone calls, Tracy connected with Penny Lister and realized she was the last person who saw Brenda. Tracy immediately drove to the Blakes' house, desperate for any information on her daughter.

THE SEARCH KICKS INTO HIGH GEAR

As she stood in the Blake house, Tracy was convinced Brenda was somewhere on the property. But alone and with no proof of wrongdoing and little information from Jon Sr., she had no choice but to leave. Within minutes, she was on the phone with an emergency operator, who dispatched William Vaughn to Dover. Vaughn, a young detective new to the gig at the Shawnee County Sheriff's Department, left Topeka at 9:35 p.m., arriving at the Keller home at 9:59 p.m.

As Tracy filed a missing person report, she told Vaughn about Lister spotting Brenda near the Blakes' at 5:30 p.m. Vaughn relayed the information to dispatch, which assigned additional deputies to the scene.

In the meantime, community volunteers and members of the Dover Fire Department continued the search for Brenda. As Tracy met with Vaughn, a veteran law enforcement officer and chief of the Dover Fire Department was on his way home to nearby Maple Hill when his handheld radio suddenly buzzed with activity.

Bill Kilian grew up in Manhattan, Kansas, but spent most of his life living in Wabaunsee County while working in several roles for the Topeka Police Department and Shawnee County Sheriff's Office for more than 20 years. As the radio cackled for several minutes while fire department volunteers discussed the search for Brenda, something stood out to Kilian: the lack of cohesion.

"We started hearing individual firefighters were out, and I remember hearing they were on the fire engine driving some roads," Kilian said. "Even after I got to the scene, it became obvious that it was a lot of good people doing a lot of good things, but they were spinning their wheels."

Kilian's first stop in Dover was at the Keller's house. At 10:20 p.m., he learned from Tracy that Brenda was wearing a light-colored jacket and white tennis shoes. Kilian then called Penny Lister and learned that she saw Brenda just north of the bridge between the Blake and the Kemble house, less than a quarter mile to the north. Through various other calls and conversations, Kilian also learned that a man named Jon was at the Blake house and saw Brenda walking south on Douglas at 5:30 p.m.

"Pretty early on, I said, 'Let's meet,'" Kilian said. "It was a big plus with us being firefighters because of the communications (with the handheld radios). It needed to be more organized."

Nearing 11 p.m. and with the temperature dropping into the 30s, several units of community members and volunteer firefighters met on Douglas Road. The group formed a line on the east side of the road going north from the small bridge Brenda was on at around 5:30 p.m., covering from the road to 50 yards east.

As that search got under way, the Shawnee County Sheriff's Office contacted the Topeka Police Department for assistance from the latter's helicopter crew. A little after 10:30 p.m., pilot J.D. Moore and fellow officer Dana Ortiz were on their way to Dover, landing near Douglas Road at 11:15 p.m.

At about the time Moore and Ortiz were dispatched to Dover, Wabaunsee County deputy Harry Carpenter, Shawnee County Sheriff's Department corporal David Reser, and reserve captain Alvin Moran arrived in town, joining Vaughn in the parking lot of the small café and store on the southwest corner of the town's intersection. The

Shawnee County officers briefed the Wabaunsee County officers on the search and witness accounts of Brenda earlier in the day.

"We went to Dover, and I said, 'Well, what's going on?'" Carpenter said. "And they said the minister's daughter has disappeared. I asked who the person was down at the house where she disappeared, and they said, 'Jon Mareska.' I looked at Alvin, and Alvin looked at me, we both smiled, and I said, 'That's your suspect.'"

A GROWING SUSPICION

By the time Jon Sr. opened the door to four law enforcement officers at 10:45 p.m., Brenda had been missing for more than five hours. Two of the officers, Carpenter and Moran, knew Jon Sr. Carpenter served him a subpoena on another case years earlier when Senior lived in a trailer behind a car restoration shop on Kansas Avenue in Topeka. Moran, who grew up in Dover, graduated from the high school, and still lived in the community, knew him because he knew the Blakes.

"He didn't recognize me," Carpenter said. "I called him by name and he said, 'Do I know you?' I said, 'Yes, I met you at the trailer.'"

Because the Sheriff's Department didn't have a search warrant, the officers needed permission to look through the house and the out buildings surrounding it. Their visit had two objectives: get more information about Brenda and try to search the house. The officers spoke to Jon Sr. for several minutes. According to Moran's report, Jon Sr. said that he was working on the roof on the side of the house facing Douglas Road between 4:30 p.m. and 5 p.m. when he saw a girl with blue or red in her hair walking south with a male who was a foot taller. He told Vaughn that he attempted to start a conversation with the girl and male, but did not get a response. Both Reser and Carpenter noted that Jon Sr. wasn't completely coherent, a statement several other officers who worked the case echoed.

"I think his mind wasn't all there," Carpenter said. "He'd been an alcoholic and a drug addict. The old man was so burnt out."

Jon Sr. did give the officers permission to search the house and buildings near the home. As they entered the living room from the front porch, Jon Jr. slept on the couch. When they woke him up, he recognized Carpenter immediately from his recent stint in the Wabaunsee County Jail.

"So, he come up to me, and when he did, I shook hands with him," Carpenter said. "That's when I rolled his arm over, and he had them scratches on his arm."

The fresh cuts on Jon Jr.'s arms were a sign that the Sheriff's Department needed to take a closer look at the Mareskas and the property. The officers began by asking Jon Jr. about Brenda and his whereabouts earlier in the evening. Jon Jr. told them that he arrived home at 5:25 p.m. after Ivan dropped him off. He said he didn't expect Ivan, who drove back to Topeka in Tammy Blake's car and was staying the night in Topeka, to return until noon the following day.

As the officers spoke to Jon Jr., they scanned his clothes, looking for signs of mud, dirt, and blood. The clothes he had on, which included sweat pants and a T-shirt, were clean.

After speaking with the Mareskas, the officers searched the house from the cellar to the second floor, finding no trace of Brenda. As Vaughn, Moran, and Reser looked in the home, a handful of deputies looked in the barns and outbuildings closest to the house with their flashlights, finding no evidence that Brenda was on the property that night.

The Sheriff's Department left the house between 11 p.m. and 11:30 p.m., and Vaughn returned to Topeka to deliver the missing person report. In the meantime, as night began to shift to the early morning, the search for Brenda intensified.

IDENTIFYING THE FOCAL POINT

By 11 p.m., the Blake house and property were the focus of the ongoing search for Brenda. Leading up to that time, dozens of community members drove all over the southwest corner of rural Shawnee County and into the northeast corner of Wabaunsee County, blanketing the countryside. Despite looking in hundreds of barns and sheds, behind houses on dozens of properties, and the ditches of virtually every road in Dover, there was no sign of the 12-year-old.

"We were trying to figure out where we were going to look for her (early in the search)," said Paul Meek, a Dover resident at the time who served on the fire department. "We were trying to get in groups. The initial fear was that somebody had picked her up. We started just calling her name and walking to see what we could find."

Not long after Kilian organized the volunteers and community members, a small group of men offered to walk through the thick timber behind the field on the Blake property west of Douglas Road. Among them were Larry Lister, Leon Sievers, and Jim Wilson, all of whom were familiar with the property. With a significant amount of ground to cover, the group meticulously picked through the brush and navigated rugged terrain from the north end of the fence line 100 yards west of the road. They looked around trees, walked around the pond, covered several trails, and shined their lights into the makeshift boatshed northwest of the pond.

"We went through there," Larry Lister said. "She was not there (on the west side of the pond)."

What the group did find was evidence that a bike had been on at least one of the trails weaving through the woods.

"I've been on (Mission Creek) ever since I was born, and I can read track," Larry Lister said. "The first time we started looking, in the first search we did, I picked up the bicycle tracks as they went in, and they turned and went to the barn and toward the house. They didn't go down across the draw and to the pond."

By the time the search focused on one property, many of Brenda's classmates and schoolmates were together, spending the evening in the home of Rick and Lila Osburn, who had three daughters attending Dover schools or Mission Valley. Many of the children were at the

Osburns' house after the Ladies Aid event and after participating in the search of a field north of the grade school. Volunteers blanketed that part of town, but several parents organized the children because they knew they wanted and needed to help their missing friend.

"Later, I found out that field had been combed," Amy Best said, "so I thought that was amazing of my community to know that we needed to do something, but knowing that if we found something, it would be very traumatic."

Because of the location of the Osburns' home across the street from the Blakes, the children had a close look at the flurry of activity on Douglas Road that night. Many described it as similar to watching a movie, and several of them, along with their parents, still have vivid memories of that night.

"We took her (Jill) out there, and I'll never forget you could see them upstairs going through the Blakes' house, through the upstairs," Judy Wilson said.

MAYHEM ATTRACTS THE MEDIA

As dozens of volunteers from the fire department and community cast a wide net around Douglas Road, a young reporter at the Topeka Capital-Journal working the late shift heard a report about a missing girl in Dover on the newsroom police scanner. Tim Hrenchir, then a 27-year-old working the police beat, knew he had a big story on his hands.

"Hearing that is what really made it interesting," said Hrenchir, who began working at the Capital-Journal as a 16-year-old copy clerk in 1980. "You have a lot of girls that are 14, 15, 16, that are missing. Usually, they're runaways, usually with a boyfriend. Well, this one was 12; she was on a bike. The dispatcher was really forthcoming. It was a mystery. Why would this girl suddenly be gone? And what could have happened in this small community of Dover that could have caused her to be gone?"

Hrenchir was hooked on covering crime at an early age. He grew up in Topeka and was 10 years old when a neighbor across the street, 59-year-old Rosemary Ronnau, was murdered in 1974. The person who committed the crime cut through the screen of an open window, confronted her in a second-floor bedroom, stabbed her numerous times, and strangled her to death. Fifty years later, that case remains unsolved.

"I got to see as the Topeka police came over and interviewed my parents, and I got to see how a murder like this scares people," Hrenchir said. "I knew I wanted to cover crime then."

Working in an era where newspapers went to press much later than today, Hrenchir had time to track down additional information. The Dover school secretary opened the grade school so that it could be a command post. Hrenchir arrived with just enough time to gather the information he needed to get a story in the Sunday edition.

"(Bill Kilian) had been friends with my dad for years, so there was a familiarity," Hrenchir said. "There were a lot of people there. I was surprised how many were there. When I got there, it was at night, so searching had become more difficult, but people were out in the dark looking for her. I remember bafflement, just bafflement. They hadn't totally thrown out the idea that she'd run away, but it wasn't like her. So, they thought maybe there had been an accident. There was a sense of hope that maybe she was still out there, but needed help. Nobody seemed to think anything bad could happen in Dover."

Hrenchir returned to the newsroom in time to file a short story just before the midnight deadline that ran inside the A section. He finished his shift and left for home, going to bed without knowing if Brenda was still missing.

A VOICE IN THE WOODS

As Shawnee County Sheriff's Department deputies spoke to the Mareskas in the Blake house, more people in the community began to search around the property close to midnight. At least a dozen people were walking through the woods, searching in and around buildings not far from the house.

At 11:30 p.m., less than half an hour after law enforcement officers left the Blakes', longtime Dover residents Kenny and Sandy Mitchell were at the red barn behind the house and just east of the pond. As Kenny Mitchell looked inside the barn, his wife stood outside. While Sandy Mitchell waited on her husband to finish scanning the interior of the barn, she heard voices a short distance away. At first, she thought the voices were those of others searching, so she looked around, trying to spot lights or flashlights. When she couldn't see any equipment, she realized she wasn't sure who the people were. Sandy Mitchell later told deputies that she thought she heard one of the voices say, "Oh, God."

She also heard voices from the south of the barn, then again to the east, and told Sgt. Mark Wanamaker of the Sheriff Department's Criminal Investigation Division that she heard people moving in the brush. The Mitchells didn't see who the voices belonged to, and they didn't find any signs of Brenda in the barn. They reconvened with dozens of other volunteers at the grade school before midnight. Despite an extensive effort in a five-mile radius, all of the groups returned to the command post empty-handed, and Atkins and Ortiz did not see any sign of Brenda from the helicopter hovering above.

"It was at about that point that we gave more direction to (the search)," Kilian said. "A map of the surrounding area was used and marked to show what areas that we knew had been searched thoroughly. We then determined areas that needed to be searched based generally where Brenda could have gotten to in a short time span of the last sighting."

As midnight approached, Kilian formed groups of five community members and paired them with at least one firefighter and a radio. One group searched south of town around the Daisy Hindman Girl Scout Camp, starting on 67th Street about a half mile from the Blakes and going back to the south edge of the camp. Another went further south on Douglas to check an abandoned house on the far south end of Brenda's route close to a large curve on the road.

Other groups looked again in the cemetery and an open field east of the grade school and behind the houses around the Keller home, along with numerous people who drove several of the roads on Brenda's typical routes. But, by 1:30 a.m., groups began to return with no information or sign of Brenda.

"In the back of my mind, the cop was operating," Kilian said. "I never did say anything, but early on, I thought, 'This doesn't smell right,' but you keep hoping."

WHAT DREAMS MAY COME

Aimee Grubb was painfully shy, so much so that she didn't join the wildly popular youth group at the Dover Federated Church, which her family attended on Wednesdays and Sundays. That shyness made it difficult for her to meet new friends, but Brenda's kindness made her comfortable.

"My brother played football, and she and I hung out one night at a football game in Council Grove," she said. "We had talked about hanging out, and we had planned a time do so. Something came up for her, so that got canceled, and we never got the chance to hang out."

Hours before she went to bed on Oct. 19, Aimee Grubb hoped to see Brenda again as she drove by her on Douglas Road.

"I really just wanted to give her a ride to see her," she said. "I was just starting to become friends with Brenda."

Even though she had no way of knowing that Brenda was missing, she had a dream that night that seemed all too real.

"I knew something was wrong in my sleep," she said. "I dreamed that she was dead. I can see little snippets of it today. There was a play kitchen (in the dream), and I just remember knowing that she was dead."

Aimee Grubb was sound asleep as the final wave of the exhaustive search for Brenda began at about 1:30 a.m. Without a search warrant at the time, law enforcement's involvement had been somewhat limited. Vaughn filed a missing persons report when he returned to Topeka after midnight, four officers had spoken to the Mareskas, and the Topeka Police Department's helicopter crew explored Dover for two hours.

Another Shawnee County Sheriff's Department deputy, James Honn, relieved Vaughn at 12:30 a.m. After being briefed, he called dispatch and asked them to contact fellow deputy Michael Mulford, who was patrolling the Tecumseh area that night. Mulford drove to Ivan's home on Ratner and knocked on the door, but there was no answer. During this time, Reser called his supervisors, the department's lieutenant, captain, and major.

"I used to patrol Dover when I was a supervisor," Reser said. "It's a peaceful little town. It's the type of community you could live in and never lock your doors. But, in a way, you get that gut feeling."

THE SEARCH COMES TO AN END

By 1:30 a.m., Brenda had been missing for eight hours and a search team of 60 volunteers hadn't found any sign of her or her bike. Though one small group had already searched the area further west and deep into the woods on the Blakes' property, Kilian and other organizers determined that area should be looked at more closely.

"The search consisted of about 30 people, and they were lined close together so as not to miss any area," he said. "The group started at the south fence of the Kemble property, roughly in line with the bridge on Douglas, and proceeded south on the west side of Douglas for 200 to 300 yards."

Bob was among those searching, while Tracy stayed at home with Jean, other family members, and several of the women in Dover.

Though Bob had been involved since the end of the Ladies Aid event, he was not on the Blakes' land until this concerted effort.

"It seemed when everybody was looking, like those in the know said there's something there that's dangerous," Bob said. "They assigned guys to me to keep me from going over there and to protect me. I felt like they were trying to keep me from being the one that found her."

Others in the search were more concerned with running into someone other than Brenda, possibly the individual or individuals who might have been responsible for her disappearance. Barraclough volunteered to help, but by 2 a.m., she was scared.

"Brenda's dad was in our search party, and the lady next to me was a big woman, and I was grateful for that," she said. "I was afraid. It was frightening. We're out there in the middle of nowhere in the deep woods after dark, and something very bad had happened here. We were all pretty certain of that by then. I was worried there was somebody out there."

Kilian's son, Shawn, a Mission Valley graduate who was home from college that weekend, also participated in the search on the Blakes' property.

"It was kind of surreal," he said. "It was a line of people searching, a helicopter circling around overhead with a spotlight, dogs barking. Spooky would be a word you could use."

As the time passed 2 a.m., several volunteers, including Leon Sievers, Larry Lister, Jim Wilson, and lifelong Dover resident Clinton Lambotte, concentrated their search on the west side of the pond behind the Blake home.

As they made their way toward the pond on either side, searchers found several tracks that looked like they belonged to a bicycle and others that looked like they belonged to a car. Leon Sievers and Larry Lister said the tracks went from a barn to the creek and pond. In addition to tracks, the group found something even more chilling: a shovel lying near the creek.

"I remember the symbolism of the shovel. That was when it kind of hit me, that it sunk in," Shawn Kilian said. "It was the first realization that I had that it was something more sinister."

Moments after volunteers found the shovel, Lambotte, then 25, made his way up the bank of the pond toward the makeshift boatshed. The small shed-like structure was white, with a width of 12 feet and length of 18 feet and an opening of 8 feet at the front. Lambotte arrived at the shed at 2:38 a.m.

"I walked around to the front and shined my light into the building, and I said, 'There she is!'" Lambotte said in a written statement.

At first, he thought he made a mistake and was looking at one of the mannequins the Blakes used at their cosmetology school in Topeka. Then he saw a large pool of blood next to the body.

"She was crumpled up in the back of that barn," Leon Sievers said. "It's something you see that you never forget."

Brenda's nude, battered body was curled up in a semi-fetal position under a window along the west side of the shed. She was lying on her left side with the left arm next to her body and her right shoulder and arm against the wall. Brenda's knees were drawn up toward her waist, with her bloodied head and face resting on the concrete floor. Her body was covered with bruises and blood, and her clothes were in a pile on top of her.

"They called me when I was on the radio and they said, 'We got code, code blue,' so I went stomping through the water over there and into the shack," said Mary Sievers, a registered nurse for more than 50 years. "Leon pushed me back out and said I wouldn't want to see this."

Thomas Horn, an emergency medical technician with the Dover Fire Department, arrived moments later to check her vital signs. Brenda Michelle Keller, Bob and Tracy's "Strawberry," was dead at age 12.

CHAPTER EIGHT:

THE INVESTIGATION, PART I

Brenda didn't resemble the beautiful, blue-eyed girl she had grown into. She was laying on her left side with the left arm pressed against her side and the right arm resting behind her to the right side. Brenda's left leg was straight and the right leg bent at a 45-degree angle with her knee on top of the left hand. The left side of her face was on the floor, with her head facing slightly up.

Her body was covered with bruises and blood, and the top of her skull on the right side caved in. The signature red hair was matted with blood, dirt, and leaves. She was nude, with the exception of two items: a white sock on her right foot and the friendship bracelet Jill Wilson made for her months earlier on the right ankle. She had several wounds on her face and multiple dark bruises on the upper left side of her chest.

There was a large pool of blood on the floor around Brenda's head. Her tennis shoes, other sock, and underwear, drenched in blood, were near her shoulders. There were two blood spots to the right of her feet, and another on the outside of the sill of the west window. The large pool of blood under her head streamed to a pile of leaves behind her.

It appeared someone had hurriedly thrown her blue jeans, pink shirt, and jacket on her body.

The shirt stretched from her backside to just below her right shoulder, with one of the sleeves covering part of the stomach. The blue jeans were strewn across her right leg from the upper thigh to the ankle, with the white jacket partially underneath the denim and on the ground next to her. Brenda's bra, mostly clean and white, was a foot behind her head. She endured a brutal attack before dying.

"I've seen a lot of things being in emergency medical services for 30-some years, so I've dealt with a lot of bodies," said Paul Meek, a longtime EMT and healthcare executive. "But when there's violence against a child … it's just very difficult to have to witness. You want to think it doesn't happen."

As the news broke over police radio, it began to filter from the pond to Douglas Road and the grade school, where many of the volunteers waited anxiously. Bob heard the commotion and began to walk through the woods behind the Blake house. As he was heading west, Mary Sievers hiked up the hill behind the barn and ran into him.

"I was going back up to the highway when Brenda's dad came walking down," she said. "I got ahold of him and said, 'You don't want to go down there.' So, I argued with him, and finally somebody came along and convinced him to go back up to the police car."

Bob and Tracy have blocked out much of that night, notably the circumstances around the discovery of their daughter's death. Others, however, have vivid memories of Bob moments after the discovery. For Kaiden Barraclough, who was 100 yards away from the boathouse at the time, it was the culmination of a long night riddled with fear and anxiety.

"I remember hearing a shout and activity to my left, which I think was Bob running down there," she said. "I just froze. I saw two guys helping Bob come back up, kind of on a hill. I was struck that it seemed to me how normal he looked. His face looked completely normal to me. He wasn't crying, hysterical, or anything."

What his face didn't show, his legs did. Bob could hardly stand on his own. It took two men on either side to help him walk up the incline from the pond to the top of the steep hill that cut through the Blakes' property. As stunned as Bob was, he knew his next task would be a daunting one: Telling his wife that their daughter was gone.

CONFIRMING THE WORST

A few hours before Clinton Lambotte spotted Brenda's body, the Osburn family graciously offered to have their home serve as a safe place for many of the community's children to stay. When several of Brenda's friends, including Wilson and Amy Best, convened, there was still a concern that the seventh grader had been kidnapped, and the person or persons responsible was on the loose. Many of the parents who dropped their kids off that night were on the Blakes' property.

Because of the location of the Osburn home, everyone at the house was in a spot with a great view of the activity. The Osburns lived across the street from Gene and Tammy, and the house was at the top of a hill almost parallel to the location of the boathouse. In addition, the incline provided a transparent look into the valley that wasn't available from Douglas Road.

"We were just hanging out and talking, having fun," Kristi Osburn said. "We were probably just thinking nothing bad will happen; she'll probably show up. Everybody went outside, and everybody is crying, freaking out, thinking, 'What the hell is happening?' Everybody could hear them say, 'We found her body.' Then, we see all the cops."

Brooklynd Thomas was among those staying at the Osburn house that night. While others thought and hoped Brenda would show up, she knew something had gone terribly wrong.

"Some thought maybe she went with a boyfriend, but I knew differently," she said. "They decided that if it got later that it wasn't looking very good, and us girls probably did not need to be out anymore because it was getting more and more grim."

The girls at the house had to endure the shock of losing Brenda by themselves for a while without their parents. Within minutes, Shawnee County Sheriff's officers shut down the section of Douglas Road stretching from the north end of the Blakes' property to the Sievers'. For more than an hour, nobody could get to the Osburn house.

Some, like Mary Sievers, walked from the woods across the road and up the hill to the Osburns to be with her daughters. Though Crystal Sievers and the others girls could hear shouting, she was in disbelief until her mother arrived.

"I remember my mom telling us that they found her. I asked, 'Is she alive?' and she said she didn't know," Crystal Sievers said. "And I said, 'Is she dead, or is she alive?' and when she answered I remember just screaming. It really hit hard at that point."

Eventually, officers opened up the road for parents to pick up their daughters at the Osburn house. Best was so terrified that she asked her mother not to drive by the Blake house on the way home. Cathy Best ended up driving several miles out of the way, traveling along the desolate gravel of Carlson Road and around Dover to the family's house.

Misty Lange was standing in the yard when she heard the news from a parent. By the time she returned home later that morning, her grandparents already knew.

"That was weird because they were never awake that late," she said. "I remember crying. I remember being really upset. I remember not wanting to be alone."

THE INVESTIGATION BEGINS

Dave Reser took an interesting path into law enforcement. A Topeka native and football star, he graduated from Shawnee Heights in 1974 before playing center at Butler County Community College for a year.

Reser returned to Topeka in the mid-1970s, working at the Highland State Bank for several years before he decided he wanted to work outdoors. He became a police officer in the 1980s, beginning his career with the Shawnee County Sheriff's Department in 1986. By October 1991, he was a corporal.

Reser arrived in Dover at 11:30 p.m. that night to assist rookie detective William Vaughn. After he, Vaughn, and Alvin Moran interviewed the Mareskas, he spent most of the next two hours helping coordinate a search that consisted almost entirely of volunteers and members of the Dover Fire Department. A little after 2:30 a.m., Reser followed up on a tip that someone spotted a muddy footprint similar to the tennis shoes Brenda was wearing on K-4 Highway two miles north of town.

After Reser arrived to check on the footprint, which he determined was not Brenda's, Bill Kilian radioed the corporal to tell him that she was found dead. Reser and Kilian immediately went to the scene, entering the Blake property from Douglas Road, noticing fresh bicycle and vehicle tracks at a gate entering the pasture north of the house.

As the officers worked their way through the woods, Reser also spotted fresh, muddy vehicle tracks at a cement creek crossing, along with the aforementioned shovel guarded by Leon Sievers. Kilian and Reser arrived at the boathouse at 3 a.m.

"The vision of her laying there in that cold weather on that cold floor has just stayed with me all these years," Reser said. "My daughter was 2 years old at the time this took place. Being a parent myself, I just couldn't believe how somebody would do that to a child. I thought about that the whole time—that could have been my daughter."

Upon his arrival at the boathouse, Harry Carpenter was securing the crime scene. The longtime deputy stayed with the body for a while that morning as others looked for evidence.

"It's something I don't like to remember," he said. "It was bad; a bad thing to happen to such a nice little girl. I said I'd stay with her because I'd been around dead bodies and could handle it. I kept hearing noises, and it was possums and raccoons and things out at night. I didn't want them to get in (the boathouse)."

As Reser and Kilian made their way down to the crime scene, several volunteers walked back to Douglas Road, including a handful who worked with Sgt. James Honn on written reports. Among those was Larry Lister, who noted that he found tracks in areas that were not there during the initial search.

On his way back to Douglas Road, another volunteer, Dennis Riley, spotted impressions in the dirt that were "very distinct, not from a rolling tire, but from someone lifting and setting the bike directly down." The statement also said he saw a set of narrow tread vehicle tracks in front of the bike tracks.

Meek, who was in a group of three on the opposite side of the pond when Lambotte discovered Brenda's body, also wrote a statement. Meek played a critical role because he had a camcorder that night. Without a search warrant at the time, officers were several hours away from processing the crime scene. However, Meek recorded the scene less than 20 minutes after the discovery, providing law enforcement with an important piece of evidence.

"They asked me if I would go back and video tape the crime scene," Meek said. "It was very hard to go in, but I knew how important it was if they were going to catch the individual and hopefully prevent this from happening to another individual. It wasn't pleasant."

BRENDA IS WITH JESUS

Although Tracy drove with her husband during the earliest round of searches and visited the Blake home to speak to Jon Sr. and Jr., she spent much of the rest of the evening at the family's home, where her in-laws and several friends tried to comfort her. Before Barraclough joined the group of volunteers on the Blake property, she stopped by to see Tracy.

"I remember we were at her house for a little while, and she was just sitting there calm and complacently," Barraclough said. "I was shocked she wasn't more upset and agitated. It was almost like she already knew. She was saying things that didn't make sense. 'Oh, she'll be here in a moment.' Then, later, 'I know she's gone; it's OK,' and smile. She was just not connecting."

While the Kellers hoped their daughter was only hurt in a biking accident and needed help, they also feared the worst once they put the pieces of the puzzle together. Those fears became a reality when Bob heard Mary Sievers shouting "Code blue!" as he walked through the woods on the east side of pond. Moments later, he drove home to pick up Tracy and his parents, taking them to the grade school parking lot and stopping far enough away to be removed from the bustle of the command center.

"He took Tracy in his arms, and he said, 'Our Brenda is safe with Jesus,'" Jean said with tears rolling down her cheeks.

Roy's reaction is a memory that sticks with Bob.

"I remember my dad's voice as he totally bawled, kind of sobbed. I just remember that," he said.

The Kellers had the unenviable task of calling family once they returned home after 3 a.m. The series of calls began with Janice, who left the Wichita area with her husband in the middle of the night for Dover. Beverly, pregnant with her third daughter at the time, left Wichita shortly after sunrise that morning with her husband.

"We were trying to call people and let them know she was missing, and whoever called us called us again and told us they found her and she was gone," Beverly said. "I think they talked to my husband, and he said, 'Let's go cry.' I think I cried the whole time. I didn't know what else to do."

Aunt B, up most of the night praying for Brenda and her family, left at the same time as Janice, despite pleas from Jean to wait until the sun came up. Ever the motherly figure, Jean was worried about people driving at night. Her sister ignored those words, packing her bag and heading north within minutes. She arrived early enough to be with her nephew, who didn't sleep much that night.

"I spent time that night with Robert," Aunt B said. "He'd come in and sit on the couch, and then he'd get up and do something else. Nothing was normal about it. I don't think anything was normal, not for a long time."

While Aunt B comforted Bob, Jean and Roy tried to sleep in Pat's room, as he was spending the night with friends. After putting on her robe and getting ready for bed, Jean heard a knock at the front door and hurried downstairs to answer it, trying not to disturb her grieving son and daughter-in-law. She opened the door to a neighbor looking for her daughter, who spent several hours with Tracy earlier that night.

"I hated to, but I went back upstairs and knocked on the door and asked Tracy where she was, and she said they'd have to call so and so, I don't know where she's at," Jean said. "I went back down to tell her who to call, went back up, and there was another knock at the door. It was a police officer trying to find out where people were."

Jean was so shaken by Brenda's death that she fell on her way down to answer the door the second time, her knees giving on the stairway. She decided not to go back upstairs, spending a long night in the living room. As she sat there, John, who was out searching most of the night with friends, walked into the house and directly to his room in the back of the first floor of the home.

"I heard John come in, and I should have gone to him," a tearful Jean said, "but I didn't. I just sat there."

Tracy spent the night in her bedroom, leaving after sunrise to walk across the street to the church for the Sunday service.

"I thought weird things like, 'She has to be so cold,'" Tracy said. "Just weird, unsensible things. I kept thinking, 'God raised people from the dead, why won't he raise her from the dead?'"

MAKING THEIR WAY BACK

Gene and Tammy Blake rarely took extended vacations. As co-owners of the Las Vegas Hair Design salon on the south side of Topeka, they worked long hours. A few years before, they closed the last of four hair design schools, all named the Gene Blake School of Hair Styling. At one time, the couple had schools in Topeka, Emporia, Kansas City, and Olathe.

"We closed the schools because of the government," Tammy said. "We had one instructor embezzling money. She was taking the money and telling students when they needed the money, she would give it out. Come to find out, we got a little further into it, and one of the students said, 'Well, I didn't get my money.' We investigated and found out, and that kind of ruined things, just kind of set things off on the schools."

The Blakes had an admirable work ethic and flourished as stylists. It didn't take long for Las Vegas Hair Design to be a successful business with a steady clientele in the capital city. Running a business meant their vacations usually entailed a weekend here or there at their cabin in Burlington, where they spent most of their time at the Neosho River and John Redmond Reservoir.

But, earlier in 1991, the Blakes committed to a true vacation in Florida, planning to drive from Dover to the Sunshine State. By the fall, they were beginning to question whether or not they should cancel the trip, largely because Jon Sr. suffered a serious brain injury and couldn't take care of himself.

The Blakes thought they addressed that concern when they offered a room to Gene's cousin, Ivan. All they asked in exchange was Ivan's help around the house and in looking after Jon Sr., especially while they were in Florida.

"(Ivan) said, 'I think I can take care of things,' if we were going to take this vacation, and we had somebody take over the salon," Tammy Blake said. "We thought that would be a good deal."

That deal got a little more complicated a few weeks after Ivan moved in, when the Blake home grew to five people. Just a few months into his one-year sentence, Jon Jr. was out of the Osage County Jail. According to Osage County court records, his sentence was modified on Sept. 24, a change that called for Jon Jr. to spend 90 days in a pre-re-vocation program at the Osawatomie Correctional Facility, an 80-bed, minimum-security building on the grounds of the Osawatomie State Hospital.

However, the correctional facility was not able to accept him, and Jon Jr. was released to his parole officer, who in turn placed him with the Blakes in Dover. He began living there on Oct. 1, less than three weeks before Brenda's disappearance and death. In the span of a few months, the Blake home went from two people to five, including two with extensive criminal records and another on probation for domestic violence.

"It seems like everybody we've helped, something's gone wrong," Tammy Blake said. "My daughter said, 'Would you guys quit doing this?'"

In the weeks leading up to the Blakes' trip to Florida, there weren't any issues. Jon Jr. stayed to himself and helped around the house, feeding the horses and dog, as well as pitching in to take care of his father, who, though only 47, could barely walk up the stairs without falling over the railing, Tammy Blake said. What appeared to be a house of misfits was a quiet home most of the fall.

Jon Jr. was scheduled to be booked into the facility in Osawatomie on Oct. 17, a day before the Blakes headed for the East Coast. A few days before they planned to leave, though, Tammy Blake said she received a call from the Osage County Jail in Lyndon. The law enforcement officer who called that day asked if Jon Jr. could stay there another day, to which the Blakes agreed. However, an officer called again the next day.

"They said, well, I'd have to keep him over the weekend, and I told them we planned to go on vacation," Tammy Blake said. "They said, 'Oh, well, he should be fine.'"

Gene and Tammy discussed cancelling their vacation, but decided that they could trust Ivan to take care of Jon Sr. and the house while monitoring Jon Jr. Less than 24 hours after that decision, they pulled into a motel in Tampa, checked into their room for the night, and called their daughter to tell her where they were staying.

"She said, 'You gotta come home,'" Tammy Blake said. "We came straight back."

The Blakes had few details at the time, as Brenda's body hadn't been discovered. But their property was the focus of an extensive search for a 12-year-old girl. They stopped only for gas and arrived back in Dover the following evening to a stunned and angry community.

A LONG NIGHT WITH BRENDA

When Lambotte spotted Brenda's body in the boathouse, the search became a probable homicide investigation, kicking off a series of calls to multiple law enforcement officers. At 2:54 a.m., Sgt. R.J. Warrington took a call from dispatch, got dressed, and drove to the Sheriff's Department, arriving at 3:15 a.m. to load the unit's crime scene vehicle, a cream-colored box van decked out with cabinets on both sides, counters, lights, a generator, and dozens of instruments and pieces of equipment.

Before leaving for the department, Warrington called Ken Smith, one of his partners on the crime scene crew. Smith arrived to assist Warrington at 3:25 a.m. The duo filled the van with equipment and supplies, leaving at 3:45 and fueling up the vehicle and generator before heading to Dover, where they arrived at 4:23 a.m.

Smith died at 77 in 2020, but his wife, Rosemary Smith, said the case was one he talked about more often than the hundreds of other cases he worked.

"I remember that scene and what Ken went through," said Smith, who was a client of Gene Blake's at Las Vegas Hair Design. "It really bothered him. It was a young girl, and he had a granddaughter."

A third forensics officer, J.D. Sparkman, met Warrington and Smith in Dover at 4:45 a.m. Before Sparkman arrived, Warrington and Smith met with Detective Jack Metz, the lead investigator on the case. The officers discussed the investigation in preparation for processing the crime scene and searching the area for evidence once they obtained a search warrant.

Not long after Warrington and Smith got to Dover, Shawnee County coroner Wyke Scamman, who held that position into his 80s before leaving in 2012, arrived and approached Warrington.

"The coroner shows up," said Warrington while laughing, "and I go, 'What are you doing out here? We've got to get a search warrant. Why don't you go back to sleep and we'll call you.'"

As the forensics team waited for clearance to process the crime scene, Reser relieved Carpenter at the boathouse, spending nearly two hours with Brenda in the cold and dark.

"Once I got the building, that's where I stayed," Reser said. "At the time, I was concerned about somebody coming down there to remove the body because I had no idea if somebody had been arrested. If there was more than one of them, well, I was there by myself. The radios weren't working that well down there. If I needed help, I was S-O-L, basically."

ON THE SCENE

Metz grew up in Topeka, attending Highland Park High School, but he was familiar with Dover. His father took him to the rural southwest corner of Shawnee County to hunt, fish, and camp with friends. Metz also was familiar with Jon Sr.

"I knew (Jon Sr.) in high school with a few people he'd run around with," Metz said. "We weren't personal friends, but we'd run across each other every once and a while. He was just kind of wild, loved to fight, was in and out of trouble. I lost contact with him, but he was a rough customer."

By 1991, Metz was a veteran detective in the Sheriff's Department with a sterling reputation. Numerous fellow officers, attorneys, and news reporters vouch for his work, including one who said, "If Jack Metz tells you something, you can take it to the bank."

On Oct. 20, Metz was on call. One of five detectives in the unit, it was his two-week period to take the call on any major crime. Contacted by dispatch at 2:53 a.m., Metz got out of bed, dressed, and was on his way to Dover, where he arrived at 3:42 a.m.

Honn briefed Metz on the case, including details about Brenda's disappearance, officers speaking to the Mareskas and searching the Blakes' house and barns, and various witness accounts from the evening.

As Metz met with Honn, David Debenham was on the way to Dover. Born in Germany as the son of an Army man, Debenham grew up in Abilene, Kansas, attending Bethany College and Washburn University School of Law before working for the Shawnee County District Attorney's Office. As an assistant district attorney, he also was on call that night.

"If law enforcement needed a search warrant, you helped with search warrants," Debenham, now a retired district court judge in Topeka, said. "We didn't have as many homicides back then, so I called Bill Ossmann (a fellow assistant district attorney), because he'd been here longer and had more experience. I'd handled some homicides, but two hands are always better than one."

Debenham, who began working in the District Attorney's Office in 1980, also was familiar with Dover. The owner of a Harley-Davidson, he rode his motorcycle through the town dozens of times over the years. On the night of Brenda's death, he arrived shortly after Metz. The attorney, detective, and several officers gathered to discuss the case.

As the group waited for consent to search the Blake house and obtain a search warrant, Debenham and Metz watched the video Meek recorded, and the footage gave them a better picture of what happened to Brenda that night.

"We didn't go right to the boathouse because we didn't want to mess up the crime scene," Metz said. "They'd taken video, so David and I went to a house that I knew of and had been friends with the woman who lived there. We just viewed it, went back, and knew more what we had."

With a limited number of law enforcement at the crime scene, several volunteers stayed in the woods for a few hours that morning to monitor evidence they discovered, including bicycle tracks, vehicle tracks, and the shovel.

Lister found bicycle tracks running from the roadway of the barn closest to the pasture, and another set that went over the hill east of the pond. Leon Sievers came across tracks near the creek and Meek a set at the edge of the pasture, along with vehicle tire tracks in the mud where a narrow road passed over the small creek running through the property. Barraclough also discovered fresh, soft tracks on one of the paths in the woods.

Sparkman, who arrived in Dover at 4:45 a.m., relieved Reser at the boathouse 30 minutes later, and the latter met with Debenham.

"I remember it was cold, and I remember going out in the crime scene van to work on the consent to search," Debenham said. "I remember that Bob was very concerned about her being out there and getting cold. There wasn't any light in the (boathouse), and they wanted to make sure they didn't miss any evidence, so law enforcement didn't execute on the search warrant until the next morning."

Before the officers and Debenham wrote a search warrant, they worked on a consent to search to take to the Mareskas before sunrise. Crafted quickly with a pencil on yellow notebook paper, the document said:

"I, John Mareska Jr. and John Mareska Sr., do hereby consent to Shawnee County Sheriff's officers and the Shawnee County coroner to search the premises, surrounding buildings and property belonging to either Gene Blake, John Mareska Jr. or John Mareska Sr. in Shawnee

County, Kansas and seize any evidence and take any photographs which they may desire."

After the completion of the form, Honn and Alvin Moran drove to the Blake house, arriving at the front door at 5:34 a.m. Honn knocked on the door loudly several times with no answer. He then had the Sheriff's Department dispatch call the house. The phone rang for two minutes without an answer. All told, the officers waited for 12 minutes for a response from the Mareskas before leaving.

PREPARING THE AFFIDAVIT

Like Reser, Sgt. Mark Wanamaker took an unconventional path into law enforcement. He attended trade school in Kansas City out of high school and worked as a broadcast engineer for a Topeka radio station before moving to television in the same position at KTSB, now KSNT Channel 27 and one of two main stations currently in the city. As he began that career, however, Wanamaker became more and more interested in police work while serving in the Shawnee County Sheriff Department Reserve for four years.

"One of my friends was in the Reserve, and he got me interested in that," Wanamaker said. "I decided to make a career change, and I never regretted it. I never looked back."

By 1991 and with 15 years under his belt, Wanamaker had seen his share of homicides, including a few teen and child murders. He worked one of Topeka's most infamous crimes, the 1976 murder of Tirell Ocobock, an 18-year-old beaten to death with tree limbs on the morning of April 26.

"I was just a rookie, and I was the first officer on the scene for that," said Wanamaker, who worked for the Sheriff's Department for nearly 30 years. "That one was never solved. Child deaths affect cops more. It doesn't mean the adult is diminished in any way, but child homicide has a dramatic effect."

Wanamaker and his family – wife Shelley, son Scott and foster daughter Jamie – lived fairly close to Dover at the time of Brenda's death, moving from Topeka to a home between Dover and Auburn, a small town in Shawnee County eight miles to the southeast. Scott Wanamaker attended schools in Topeka's Washburn Rural school district, transferring to Dover Junior High before his eighth-grade year and just a few months before Brenda died.

"I had to tell Scott," Shelley Wanamaker said. "He was a mess that something like that could happen. With Mark, it was, 'How would I feel if it was my child?' No cop does well with children who die. We're Christians. We know the Lord has a reason for everything that happens, but it still doesn't help your emotion or mind."

As difficult as it was for Sgt. Wanamaker, he had the mindset every cop does: He had a job to do. Arriving in Dover a little after 4 a.m., he helped secure the crime scene. The Sheriff's Department's plan was to wait for daylight before walking in from Douglas Road to the crime scene to detect any evidence.

While Honn and Moran waited for the Mareskas to answer the door or phone that morning, Wanamaker, Reser, Pierce, Metz, Warrington, Smith, Debenham, and Ossmann met to work on an affidavit for a search warrant. Completed as the sun was rising, the four-page document described Brenda's disappearance, various witness accounts of seeing her the previous evening, the search of Blakes' house approved by the Mareskas, details surrounding the Mareskas' stay at the home, and the search for Brenda and discovery of her body.

The final paragraph stated: "Wherefore, affiant believes probable cause exists that a crime has been committed and prays that the court issues a search warrant to search the garage-like building located in Shawnee Co., Kansas and the open fields surrounding the garage-like building and to seize there from the following."

Included in the affidavit were collecting Brenda's body, clothing items, photographs and videotape of the scene, measurements of the scene, trace evidence (blood, hair, fibers, fingerprints, saliva, and semen), a shovel or other weapon, photographs and impressions of tire tracks and bicycle tracks, and Brenda's bicycle.

As officials finalized the affidavit, Pierce contacted the Topeka Police Department to request a flyover of the crime scene and Blakes' property to take photographs and video. Meanwhile, Metz and Wanamaker coordinated the search the department planned to conduct once they had a search warrant.

As law enforcement's involvement in the case ramped up that morning, many people in the community and friends of the Kellers were about to learn the devastating news.

SHOCK SETTLES IN

Donald Grubb and his wife knew for hours that Brenda died the previous night, so they woke their daughter up earlier than usual on a Sunday and asked her and her brother to come downstairs.

"I was like, 'Why are you getting me up this early?'" Aimee Grubb said. "I know I cried, then we got ready for church."

The service is one the Grubbs and others who attended that day won't forget. There was no schedule or message that morning, but the church was at capacity.

Bob didn't speak, so Glenn Lange led the gathering, which included singing several hymns, notably some of Brenda's favorite songs, and sharing memories of her.

"There was a couple hundred people stuffed in there," Misty Lange said. "I remember Tracy telling us that she wouldn't want us to be sad. We needed to remember the happy times, and that kind of stuff."

While Bob and Tracy attended church, Roy left for Topeka early that morning to ensure that the Free Methodist Church service went as planned, and Jean stayed at her son and daughter-in-law's house to welcome guests. As one might expect in a small town like Dover, dozens of people stopped by that day to deliver food and offer to help the family in any way needed.

Though John and Pat don't remember much about that morning, John does recall taking a long walk with his uncle to get away from the frenetic activity around the house and church. Pat remembers his parents' emotions that day.

"A lot of sadness and despair in both of them," he said. "I remember intense sadness."

As residents in Dover tried to make sense of Brenda's death, others with ties to the community were just getting the news that morning. Among them was Amber McGhee, who left town immediately after the volleyball tournament to spend the weekend with her father in Scranton, another community 30 minutes away in Osage County.

"I didn't know anything was going on until the next morning when my dad sat us down when we woke up," she said. "I didn't believe him until I called my mom. I remember just crying. I asked questions. I don't remember what the questions were or what the answers were."

On Sunday morning, school officials notified the teachers at the junior high and grade school. While many knew Brenda was missing the previous night, a few had no idea something was amiss.

"I drove back to Topeka (where he lived) on that Sunday afternoon, and (the school secretary) had left me a message on the phone. She was out of control with tears and sobbing; it was horrible," Ted Lassen said. "I was just kind of dumbfounded. It was just a shock."

At least one teacher, Allen Zordell, felt guilty, thinking he was the last person to see her that day as he waited for all the members of the team to walk home or catch a ride with their parents.

"When (the school secretary) first told me they found her, I was relieved, then she told me she was dead," he said. "I couldn't breathe; it was total shock. My wife was crying. I still get teary-eyed."

For decades, teachers in Dover were among the most important and revered people in the community. That proved to be no different after Brenda's death, as the staff at the junior high and grade school spent much of the rest of the school year trying to lift the spirits of their students.

"I felt the loss of Brenda in different ways," Terri Anderson said. "I felt it as her principal. I felt it as a mother. I felt it in that she was just a sweet person who I really cared about. I was broken-hearted. I didn't have the opportunity to grieve at that point because I had to start rallying."

CHAPTER NINE:

THE INVESTIGATION, PART II

Sunrise was at 7:36 a.m. on Oct. 20, less than five hours after Clinton Lambotte discovered Brenda's body and two hours after Shawnee County Sheriff's Department Sgt. James Honn and Wabaunsee County Undersheriff Alvin Moran attempted to rouse the Mareskas. As the sun came up, Cpl. David Reser, Sgt. Mark Wanamaker, and Shawnee County Assistant District Attorney David Debenham traveled back to Topeka to present the affidavit for a search warrant and deposition to Judge Charles Andrew, who issued the warrant at 8:30 a.m.

Meanwhile, the Sheriff's Department began its search in Dover. First, law enforcement scoured the ditches on both sides of Douglas Road several yards north and south of the grade school without finding any evidence.

At 8 a.m., Moran and Jack Metz drove to the Blakes' house to speak with Jon Sr. and Jon Jr. and obtain permission to search the home and buildings surrounding it. The officers needed permission because the search warrant only applied to the land and not those structures. As Metz walked up the sidewalk leading to the front door, Jon Sr. opened the door, giving Metz a view of the stairs leading to the second floor. Jon Jr. walked down the stairs as the officers entered the living room.

"Oh, come on in," a surprised Jon Jr. said loudly and nervously.

Without revealing that the department knew Brenda was dead, Metz explained to the father and son that there was a possibility Brenda was hiding or ran away, and they could help law enforcement by consenting to a search of the house and surrounding buildings.

As Metz spoke with the Mareskas, Mary Sievers walked from her home just 100 yards south of the Blakes' and entered their house through a side door. Sievers wanted to explain to officers that Jon Sr. had brain damage and might not understand what they were asking. As she walked toward the house, the Sievers' mastiff repeatedly bumped into her, trying to move her in the opposite direction.

"Dogs are funny," Sievers said. "He did not want me to go into that house, and he'd never acted that way before."

What Max the Mastiff knew, Moran knew. As Sievers entered the house and walked into the kitchen located just off that door, the undersheriff shielded her from getting any closer.

"(Jon Jr.) was really nervous, and his eyes were dilated, and Alvin was kind of pushing me back. I knew then that something was up," she said. "I told him I just wanted to tell him where the Blakes were, and I said, 'Is there anything else you need?' and he said no, and I got out of there."

Metz and Moran weren't in the house for long, but they did ask the Mareskas to sign the consent to search. Metz noticed that Jon Jr.'s hand was shaking when he handed him the paper, enough so that he struggled holding the pen. The younger Mareska had to place his palm on the paper to sign and date it, giving Metz a good view at both hands, which contained several fresh scratches. The elder Mareska showed no signs of nervousness when he signed the sheet.

As Metz and Moran continued speaking to the Mareskas, something else caught Metz's eye. As the sun shined through the window of the laundry room toward the back of the house, it reflected off a long red hair.

"It just glistened. It was like a neon light on that sweatshirt, and that was one of the first things we noticed," Metz said. "This girl's red-headed, there wasn't anybody around here with red hair, so that was a good indication that we needed to look a lot closer."

Metz and Moran thanked the Mareskas for the consent to search and informed them that they would be back to look through the house. Several officers were stationed along Douglas Road and on the property, including a police car in front of the house. If the Mareskas tried to run, they weren't going far.

WAKING UP TO A NIGHTMARE

By the time Metz returned to the crime scene van, which was being used as a command post, Wanamaker, Reser, and Debenham were back in Dover with a search warrant. Several other officers and personnel gathered with that group outside the van, and Metz led a briefing to coordinate the Sheriff Department's search of the Blakes' property.

As the officers met, reserve deputy Myron Stucky's post was in his squad car on Douglas Road, directly in front of the house to keep an eye on the residence, as well as Jon Sr. and Jon Jr. Throughout the morning, as law enforcement officers meticulously combed the area for evidence, the father and son went outside several times to get a better look at the activity.

"They were just loitering around," Stucky said. "I kind of looked at it like I'd be if anybody was parked out front of my house. It's like, 'What's going on?' They looked antsy. They weren't panicking like a cat in a cave, but they were up and down and in and out looking around. One time, I think they went out and fed the dog. Maybe (Jon Jr.) was trying to do normal stuff so it looked normal."

Dover was far from normal that morning. As the community woke up from and to a nightmare, a helicopter from the Topeka Police Department landed just off of Douglas Road, where forensics officer Ken Smith climbed aboard. The helicopter was in the air for half an hour, hovering over the Blakes' land as Smith took photos and filmed several minutes of video.

After Smith finished his work in the helicopter, the field search began from the road, with several officers and other personnel, including Debenham, crime scene officers R.J. Warrington and J.D. Sparkman, Major Ken Pierce, and Wabaunsee County Deputy Harry Carpenter, entering the pasture north of the house. While searching the field, the group found bicycle or motorcycle tracks and tracks from an automobile, marking the area with survey flags. Meanwhile, Smith walked from Douglas Road, through the pasture, down the woods, and all the way to the boatshed, taking additional photos and capturing video up to Brenda's body.

As Metz and Wanamaker entered from Douglas Road together, they walked to the northwest through the field to a small pathway in the corner of the pasture leading to the back of the property, before going to the west and southwest past a red barn and the pond behind the Blakes' house. They worked their way around the pond to the boatshed, arriving at Brenda's body at 10:32 a.m.

"The thing that I remember the most out of that whole deal is her naked body in the barn," Wanamaker said of arriving at the boatshed. "You could tell it was not a good ending. That's what sticks in my mind."

Several officers arrived at the shed within minutes of Metz and Wanamaker, including Warrington, Smith, and Sparkman, who began processing evidence in the shed and around Brenda, including taking photographs. The forensics team, with the assistance of Shawnee County Coroner Wyke Scamman, bagged her clothes and collected hair and blood samples, including blood from the back of the shed. Warrington also found a small stick, just a half inch in length and diameter with blood on it, inside the building. Warrington and Scamman examined Brenda's body before the forensics team began picking up evidence outside the garage.

Just northeast of the shed was a large pool of blood in the dirt and grass. It appeared part of the attack happened in that spot, which was a few feet away from a window in the shed that did not contain glass. It looked like someone dropped Brenda through the window into the boathouse.

"We looked at the window sill; there was blood outside, too," Warrington said. "We found stuff outside, and it looked like she'd been pushed inside. I took a chainsaw and cut the whole window out."

As the crime scene officers collected evidence in and around the boatshed, Metz contacted the Sheriff's Department to enact the dive team to travel to Dover and search the pond, where they anticipated finding more evidence.

THE LONG ROAD HOME

As Gene and Tammy Blake drove from Tampa through several states, they couldn't help but wonder if they were destined for a life dotted with tragedy. Several years before they met, Gene's first wife left him with their two sons, Marty and Darrin, who were only 5 and 2. Tammy came along nine years later in 1969.

"I went in to get my hair done, and he was my hairdresser," Tammy Blake said. "When I went to pay, I paid by check, and he said, 'Well, we need phone numbers.' And I said I don't give out my phone number because it's unlisted. He said, 'Well, it's company policy we have phone numbers.' I said, OK, and gave him my number."

Together, they raised Marty and Darrin, along with a daughter adopted in the early 1970s. They moved to Dover before Marty graduated from Mission Valley, where he was one of the most popular students, in 1980. Many in the community viewed the Blakes as odd because they had a vastly different lifestyle than most of the people in Dover.

"They would have parties when people would sit around and drink in the yard and barbecue," Mary Sievers said. "They'd have blue hair and pink hair because the Blakes did hair and worked with all these creative people. Dover really wasn't approving of them. They were kind of against the Blakes to begin with."

The Blakes may have seemed different, but a number of people said they went out of their way to help a person in need. Gene Blake hired people for odd jobs so they could have a little money and took people who were struggling out to dinner. Sievers said the couple was more welcoming than anybody when her family moved to town in the 1980s from the Catholic community of St. Marys, Kansas.

"When we moved from St. Marys, it wasn't readily accepted," Sievers said while relaying a story about a pastor in Dover who preceded Bob. "The minister came by to welcome us to the community. When we told him we were Catholic, he didn't stick around too long. We were always friends (with the Blakes). They're wonderful people, very generous and kind."

As the Blakes' hair business blossomed in the mid-1980s, they also owned a small convenience store in north Topeka and hired Marty Blake to manage it. They hired him a few years later to recruit students into their schools, a gig that was a perfect fit for his charismatic personality.

"He was a fun guy. Everybody liked him," Tammy Blake said. "The girls would come here at like midnight knocking on the door and say, 'We need to talk to Marty.' He did a great job recruiting for the beauty school. He could sell a refrigerator to an Eskimo."

Marty Blake's life was about to take off when he was diagnosed with HIV in 1986. He died at age 24 on Nov. 21, 1986.

"They didn't have anything that would help him," Tammy Blake said. "That was hard to believe. It was just hard. We had to go get counseling."

Just when it seemed like things were getting better, the Blakes lost the beauty schools. Then Jon Sr. suffered brain damage and moved into their home. Now, less than a year later, they were driving into a hornet's nest as they traveled back to Kansas.

"(Gene and Tammy's daughter) called us before the Blakes got back from Florida and said, 'They're going to kill my parents when they come back from Florida,'" Sievers said. "And I said, 'No, they're not.' We're going to go over there and wait for your parents. So, Leon and I went over there with our guns and waited for the Blakes to come home."

The Blakes were still hours away from home by noon on Oct. 20, right about the time the Shawnee County Sheriff's Department was beginning to focus on a prime suspect.

ON THE AIRWAVES

As the wife of a pastor, Tracy wore a number of hats in Dover. She was a mother of three, a cook at the schools, and heavily involved in church. What little time she had left went to working at the Christian radio station in Topeka, Joy 88 FM.

Warren and Susan Wilson, who ran the station, matriculated from the East Coast to the Midwest during careers in which they opened several Christian radio stations in cities such as Springfield, Missouri, Sioux City, Iowa, and Topeka. They started the latter from a trailer home at the base of a radio tower in 1985, the same year they hired Tracy part time.

"She took over the Saturday morning children's program and did a great job without having any radio background," Warren Wilson said. "She had a gift of gab. In some cases, that's all it takes on the radio; other stuff can be taught."

As the station's profile grew in Topeka, including moving to a building in the city, so did Tracy's. She became a popular personality and had a following from 1985 through 1991. Tracy was scheduled to work on the morning of Oct. 20, but called in late the night before to notify the Wilsons that she wouldn't be there.

The Wilsons woke up Sunday morning and received a call that Brenda was dead. They dedicated the entire day's program to Brenda, playing several of her and Tracy's favorite songs. They also fielded dozens of phone calls from devastated listeners.

"People called very saddened and very angry, very confused. They had all sorts of questions," Susan Wilson said. "What did the Kellers do wrong? People were grasping for answers because nothing like that happened. It was hard for them to accept."

Not as hard as it was for the Keller family that day, though. Once the church service finished that morning, they returned home to Roy, Jean, and several family members. Throughout the day, a stream of visitors stopped by their house to console the family, offer help, and provide them with food so they wouldn't have to cook.

Among those visitors was Kaiden Barraclough, who spent much of the night searching for Brenda and most of the morning with her daughter, Brooklynd Thomas, who was crushed.

"The implications of this reverberate on forever for Brenda and her family, and it reverberated in my family," Barraclough said. "My daughter didn't sleep for the longest time. She'd wake up in the middle of the night screaming night after night after night."

For members of the Keller family, various moments from that day stand out. Bob's sister Beverly remembers Tracy doing laundry.

"She was standing there folding, almost acting normal. I think it hit her later," she said.

"That day was awful," Bob's sister Janice added. "It was just awful for them. You're in shock. They were in La La Land. They just didn't know what to do, where to go. And we didn't know what to do."

IN DEEP WATER

Activated at 10:40 a.m., the Underwater Search and Rescue team of W.D. Beasley, Frank Good, and Tim Oblander arrived at their assembly site in Topeka 30 minutes later, packed their gear, and headed for Dover by 11:30 a.m.

In addition to asking for support from the dive team, Metz asked for two more detectives to assist in the investigation. A little after noon, Larry Baer and Mike Ramirez arrived at the scene. Baer and Ramirez began working at the Sheriff's Department in the mid-1970s and were a duo for two decades by 1991. A native of Lawrence, Ramirez went to Lawrence High School and then to Vietnam as a Marine. Baer, who went to Topeka High, also served in Vietnam. Though their paths didn't cross as they grew up in Kansas, they ended up in the same squadron during the war.

"Mike said, 'You from Topeka?' I said, 'Yeah,'" Baer said. "It was luck."

Ramirez and Baer became best friends, arriving in and leaving the country within two weeks of one another. Within a few years of leaving the Marines, both were working as patrol officers for the Sheriff's Office. By 1980, they were detectives for the department. On Oct. 20, 1991, they pulled into Dover within minutes of each other.

"There were a lot of people, pickups and stuff," Baer said. "I came down 57th Street, and I could see cars, lots of farmers. They had rifles on gunracks in all of those trucks."

Ramirez and Baer met with Metz about the case before walking through the pasture and woods to the boathouse. By the time they arrived at the shed, Brenda was in a body bag in preparation to be transported to the morgue. Metz showed his fellow officers the inside of the shed, including the large splotch of blood on the floor, along with the outside of the boathouse where officers found a significant amount of blood on the ground. The detectives discussed what happened the night before.

"I just kept thinking to myself, 'That poor little girl,'" Baer said. "I kept thinking she walked along this pass and was just scared to death."

The search and rescue team spoke to Metz before returning to their vehicle to bring diving gear to the pond. As they unloaded,

Brenda's body had to be moved by unusual means from the boatshed to Douglas Road because the ambulance could not handle the terrain on the Blakes' property.

"Getting to the boathouse was pretty rugged," said Allen Moran, Alvin's brother and a reserve officer for the Sheriff's Department. "I had a Bronco, and we went down through the terrain and got over to the building to her body and took it up to the road."

Moments later, the ambulance was on its way to Topeka, passing by the grade school and junior high, before turning east onto 57th Street, where it drove by the church and the Keller home.

"When the ambulance came by, I said, 'There she goes. I bet Brenda's body is in there,' or something, and my mom got really upset because she wanted to go so bad to where Brenda was and nobody would let her," Beverly said. "Of course, she didn't really want to see her. She wanted to be with her."

As Brenda's body was leaving town, Oblander and Good entered the pond while Beasley, the team leader, directed the search from the shore. With Beasley guiding them with a rope, Good and Oblander performed a search pattern near the end of the diving board. Within 15 minutes of hitting the water, the divers found Brenda's bicycle, marking the location with two buoys before bringing the bike out of the pond. It was about 26 feet from the shore and in water that was 10 feet deep.

The bicycle had a flat tire, the rear rim was bent, and the chain was off the track. It appeared that somebody pushed it for a distance with the bent rim because of the scarring on the metal sides where it rubbed along the frame. Warrington took the bicycle, which had scuff marks along the frame, to the crime scene van.

Oblander and Good continued to search, finding a Remington 1010 shotgun, but it appeared to have been stuck in the mud at the bottom of the pond for a long time. At 1:45 p.m., the dive team finished the search and left the scene to pack up their equipment and head back to Topeka.

MEDIA FRENZY BUILDING

Tim Hrenchir scrambled the night before to get a story in the paper before the Topeka Capital-Journal went to print. Even though newspapers had much later deadlines in 1991 than the vast majority of modern day publications, the story, which he finished around midnight, did not have information about Brenda's death. Still, Hrenchir had a hunch that the story was going to be a big one.

"The main thing, the main responsibility, is a sense of a lot of people are going to read this, and I want them to get an accurate picture," Hrenchir said. "You feel a responsibility to this girl to let people know about her and understand what's going on. At the time, we didn't know the horrible, gory details."

Warren Wilson was one of Hrenchir's first interviews that day. Tracy's boss at Joy 88 gave him a few contacts in Dover to reach out to for quotes, including Ruth Lange.

"She was very calm on the phone," Hrenchir said of Lange. "I was very surprised. She was very talkative."

As he tried to track down other leads, Hrenchir listened to Joy 88, where Warren Wilson spoke on the radio several times. That he was on the air that day magnified the importance of Brenda's death. He almost always worked behind the scenes and rarely was on the radio. Hrenchir did not travel to Dover that day, but he did send his younger brother, Pat, to the community to get a photo of Brenda to run with the story. It was a black and white image of a pretty young girl, one that exuded the innocence of a 12-year-old.

The reporter gathered enough information by the end of the day to write two stories. Hrenchir was the first journalist on the story, but he wasn't the only one. As officers continued their investigation that day, a media frenzy was building. But, on Sunday afternoon, Dover was still relatively quiet, with the exception of a heavy law enforcement presence on Douglas Road.

'NOTHING TO HIDE'

By 1:15 p.m., Jon Sr. and Jon Jr. had been in the Blake house for more than four hours as officers picked through the pasture, woods, and boathouse. Several times during that span, the Mareskas walked outside to try and see what was going on, without much luck.

Minutes later, Metz, Ramirez, Baer, and Allen Moran arrived at the front door, ready to begin a search of the house, while Wanamaker stayed with the dive team until they cleared the scene. As they approached the house, Moran noticed a small splatter of blood near the door on the porch. Jon Sr. greeted the officers at the door and allowed them to enter the living room, where Jon Jr. was sitting. Metz asked the Mareskas if they still consented to the search, and they said yes. Metz asked the father and son if they would wait outside during the search. Jon Sr. replied that they would, while Jon Jr. did not comment and walked to the front porch. An officer escorted the Mareskas to Stucky's squad car.

"They stepped out, and we put them out in the car. It was just very casual," Allen Moran said. "They didn't ask any questions, didn't even ask what was going on. It was pretty much lackadaisical."

The search began in the dining room and small basement, which did not contain any evidence. Metz moved to the laundry room located next to the kitchen. He walked over to a basket holding dirty clothes and began to sort through the items. About halfway down the makeshift hamper, he found a gray sweatshirt turned inside out. As Metz grabbed the shirt, he noticed it was damp and turned it partially right side up, revealing blood. He immediately put the shirt down and radioed Warrington to take photos and bag it. When Warrington began taking photos, he noted that the shirt also contained bright red hair. For veteran detectives who worked hundreds of cases in long careers, that type of evidence didn't come so easily at every crime scene.

"It was like he didn't have nothing to hide," Baer said.

"I would say he probably knew he was caught," Ramirez added.

The "he" was Jon Jr., who emerged as the prime suspect the previous night after he spoke to Carpenter, Reser, Alvin Moran, and William Vaughn. Fifteen hours later, as several detectives looked through his aunt and uncle's house, the younger Mareska sat in a car with his father and Stucky.

"We were there shooting the breeze; I was trying to keep it light," Stucky said. "One thing Jonny did say to me when they executed the search warrant was, 'Have they found that girl yet?' I said, 'I don't know. I don't know what's going on. I'm just up here to sit.'"

That wasn't the case, of course. Stucky was there because volunteers found Brenda dead. He'd known for hours and was stationed in front of the house to keep an eye on the Mareskas. When they were in his car, he tried to shift the conversation away from the investigation.

"I remember him saying, 'I hope she's OK,'" Stucky said. "I just dummied up. I said, 'I'm not part of that.' Most of the conversation we had was about dogs because I figured I could keep them occupied, and they wouldn't get agitated."

As Stucky spoke with the Mareskas, Jon Sr. and Jon. Jr. continuously looked back at the house, where the officers found and collected additional evidence, including gray sweatpants and another gray sweatshirt upstairs and a black nylon jacket in the southwest corner of the dining room. The sweatpants and sweatshirt contained blood and red hair fiber, and the jacket had blood stains on the right front pocket and a white stain on the left sleeve. After Metz found the gray sweatshirt in the laundry room, he left the house to speak to Debenham to notify him about the discovery and discuss interviewing Jon Jr.

As the officers carried bags of evidence out of the house, Jon Sr. and Jon Jr. continued to watch from Stucky's car. Though Jon Jr. asked numerous questions, his father sat quietly.

"Jon Sr. didn't say a whole lot, he really didn't," Stucky said. "They just acted dull, but he (Jon Jr.) was nervous in the fact that he asked about the girl. You could tell they were squirrely. They weren't nervous like you and I would be."

The Mareskas were with Stucky for more than an hour when Metz and Ramirez left the Blake property and walked to Ramirez's car on Douglas Road. As he walked away from the house, Metz asked an officer to bring Jon Jr. to his vehicle. Minutes later, the younger Mareska got in the car. Ramirez told Jon Jr. that they needed to ask him about the investigation and if he would be willing to go with him to Topeka for an interview at the Sheriff's Department. Jon Jr. agreed to an interview and left in Ramirez's car, with Metz following.

BAD THINGS HAPPEN EVERYWHERE

As Jon Jr. was about to head out of town with Ramirez, several community members watching the investigation from the road hoped the Sheriff's Department would let Jon Jr. run free so that they could take justice into their own hands.

"Some of the farmers asked us if we could just let him loose when we had him in the car," Baer said. "I said, 'No, we can't do that.' They said, 'Just tell them we hit you and took him away from you.'"

Many in Dover also believed Jon Sr. was involved, but none of the physical evidence at the time pointed to his involvement. Further, the detectives determined that the elder Mareska had no idea what was going on around him.

"He was a person of interest when we found out who was staying at the house, but he was really off," Metz said. "I can remember a statement he made before we took his son downtown. He was telling people, 'Well, they're taking my son up to the school to talk to him.' You could tell when we were talking to him that he wasn't all there. I don't think he comprehended what we were asking a lot of the time. He would wander off on another subject."

While the anger in the community was beginning to boil over as the investigation focused on the Blake house, the Kellers were in shock. Just 24 hours earlier, Brenda was home from the volleyball tournament, eating lunch, and preparing for her ride before the big

Ladies Aid event. Now, they were welcoming a steady stream of visitors trying to comfort them on Sunday afternoon.

Lavella Buchmeier, who was working as a hairdresser in Topeka that weekend, didn't know what happened until Sunday after she finished her shift. She and her kids, Autumn and Tyrel, drove to the Kellers' house immediately.

"I found out in the afternoon when I got home," she said. "Everybody was in town, and I was like, 'What's going on?' Tracy told me, 'He killed her.' You're positive you misunderstood and there has to be something else. It's like watching somebody talk, but your brain won't register what's being said. There were lots of people there. Tracy was completely blank and numb."

The Buchmeiers stayed at the Keller home for half an hour before coming home, where Lavella tried to console her son and daughter, who spent about as much time with Brenda as Brenda did with her own brothers.

"They were horrified. They didn't believe me," she said. "They wanted details, and I didn't have details. We kind of lived in Mayberry. Then, you realize that bad things happen everywhere."

At some point that afternoon, a cousin of the Kellers who worked as a school counselor asked about going to the junior high to get Brenda's belongings. Though she was only trying to help, just saying that got to Tracy, Aunt B said. Years later, Aunt B realized Tracy wanted to do that to see how Brenda left things, another way to remember her daughter.

The junior high wasn't empty that afternoon. Principal Terri Anderson asked the teachers to gather there for a meeting about handling the classroom when the schools reopened. Brenda's funeral was scheduled for Wednesday, Oct. 23, and the grade school and junior high were closed until the following day.

"My first duty is always to my students; I'm last," Anderson said. "It was just so very sad. I was flabbergasted, just broken-hearted. I had to really think about what I needed to do to protect those students. There were a lot of very sad kids."

STACKING THE EVIDENCE

By the time the officers in the house finished their search and others wrapped up a search of the property surrounding it, the Shawnee County Sheriff's Department had a treasure trove of potential evidence. In addition to the sweatshirts, sweatpants, and jacket found in the home, they found numerous other items.

One deputy discovered a blue bandana in the barn closest to the gate leading into the pasture north of the Blake house, and another a wooden dowel rod that appeared to have blood stains on it. Officers also collected a Dr. Pepper can and Coors Light can on the east side of the pond.

The department's physical evidence custody receipts on items bagged Sunday afternoon included the sweatshirts, sweatpants, two jackets (Brenda and Jon Jr.'s), red and black hair fibers, several blood samples, the clothes Brenda wore Saturday, the window frame from the boatshed, a Coke bottle, the blue bandana, the shovel, her bicycle, the shotgun, several rolls of negatives, and video tapes of the crime scene and property.

As Ramirez drove Jon Jr. to Topeka, Jon Sr. stayed in Stucky's police car for nearly two more hours. While his son was polite and talkative, the elder Mareska had little to say and was curt when he did speak.

"He didn't seem to be the brightest bulb on the porch; didn't seem real spiffy," Stucky said. "The dad acted like he was put out or irritated about what was going on. To tell you the truth, when I had them in the car, I thought it was the old man, that was my feeling. I'm not saying my feelings were right."

But by mid-Sunday afternoon, detectives honed in on Jon Jr. In Dover, officers remained around the Blake household until the early evening. Before Baer joined Metz and Ramirez at the Sheriff's Department, he interviewed Roger Lambotte, who saw Brenda riding her bike on Davis Road not long before she went missing the previous day. The report helped the investigators piece together a timeline and the route she took that evening.

At 3:05 p.m., Warrington, Smith, and Sparkman moved all of the evidence the department collected to the crime scene van, loading up the vehicle and leaving at 4:06 p.m. As law enforcement wrapped up the investigation on the Blakes' property, Ramirez and Metz were sitting down with Jon Jr. in an interview room at the department.

CHAPTER TEN:

THE CONFESSION

The drive from Dover to the Shawnee County Sheriff's Department is like many from a rural setting into a city. The roads leading out of the community weave through hills and farmland from the southwest corner of Shawnee County before merging into well-to-do residential areas on the outskirts of the west side of the state's capital city.

On the route Detective Mike Ramirez took that day, he and Jon Jr. traveled north on Auburn Road, which connects many of the small towns in Shawnee County and Osage County to Interstate 70. From Auburn Road, Ramirez and Jon Jr. drove on the interstate for a few miles before heading into downtown Topeka, where most of the state's government offices and the Sheriff's Office were and still are located. The 25-minute drive gave the veteran officer enough time to gain his suspect's trust.

"We just started talking," Ramirez said. "I learned from talking to him that he was from Lawrence, and he went to Lawrence High School. I went to Lawrence High School. We talked about the big Chesty Lion (the school's mascot) in the middle of the floor. It's just like good old friends all the way back to the station."

Something else about their interactions with Jon Jr. struck Ramirez and lead detective Jack Metz: his calmness.

"He was very quiet," said Metz, "and that's one thing that piques your interest is when they don't say, 'Why are you taking me?' or, 'What am I supposed to do?' There was none of this."

After arriving at the Sheriff's Department at 2:45 p.m., the detectives placed Jon Jr. in an interview room. As Ramirez and Metz discussed how to approach their suspect, he sat silently. His shoulder-length black hair was in a pony tail, and he was clean-shaven, with the exception of a mustache.

In Ramirez's office, the detectives believed that they didn't need to be aggressive or try to push Jon Jr.

"We basically decided since he was being cooperative, we weren't going to try to piss him off to try to get the truth out of him," Ramirez said. "I honestly believe if him and I didn't have the rapport, I don't think he would have spoken. He thought I was his best friend, and I made him believe that."

At 2:55 p.m., Ramirez and Metz went to the interview room and brought Jon Jr. back to Ramirez's office. At 3 p.m., they read him his rights, which he signed, and the interview began at 3:05 p.m.

ANOTHER SECOND CHANCE

On Aug. 27, 1991, less than two months before Jon Jr. sat in Ramirez's office to be interviewed about Brenda's disappearance and death, Devon Knoll, of the Lawrence Parole Office, spoke with Susan DeVoe, one of Mareska's court-appointed attorneys in the Osage County case, on the telephone, according to a Kansas Department of Corrections document. At the time, Jon Jr. was less than three months into a one-year sentence for stealing a truck in Lyndon and driving 30 miles to Burlington.

Three weeks before the phone call, he received a six-month concurrent sentence in Coffey County for attacking Teri Morin. Even though he was on parole for two burglaries in Douglas County and finished a sentence in Wabaunsee County for choking and beating up Cheryl Reeb in Harveyville less than a year earlier, the court convicted Jon Jr. of battery and not assault on Aug. 6 in Burlington. It was the second time in less than a year that he was convicted of the lesser of the two crimes, as assault carried a stiffer penalty.

"I looked upon it as a domestic violence incident," then-Wabaunsee County attorney Rob Matthews said of the Reeb case. "I think this is one of the most troubling things about being in law enforcement. You don't know how hard to come down on people."

A native of Nashville, Matthews moved with his parents to Kansas, where he attended Lawrence High and the University of Kansas. He practiced law as an assistant county attorney in Emporia, about an hour south of Dover, before moving to Alma, the seat of Wabaunsee County, in 1985. By the time he prosecuted Jon Jr., he'd been the county attorney for more than five years.

Matthews stopped practicing law in the mid-1990s to raise his children, but the case in which he prosecuted Jon Jr. and that resulted in a six-month sentence in Wabaunsee County Jail still gnaws at him 30 years later.

Matthews, however, wasn't the first, nor the last, who didn't bring the hammer down on Jon Jr. From October 1990 to September 1991, Jon Jr. served only nine months despite two battery charges, felony theft, and several other convictions, all in violation of his probation in Douglas County.

In a memo, Knoll wrote to DeVoe that the Department of Corrections had a 90-day pre-revocation program at the Osawatomie Correctional Facility, if the court allowed it on a diversionary basis. Four weeks before that conversation, on July 30, Judge James Smith sentenced Jon Jr. to a year in the Osage County Jail for felony theft, to run consecutive with any pending parole violations.

Less than two months after the verdict, however, Jon Jr., being represented by longtime partners DeVoe and Kathleen Neff, was back in the Osage County courtroom, where his sentence was modified, setting the wheels in motion for his release from jail. DeVoe and Neff, who had a practice together in Osage County for years, declined to be interviewed, citing attorney-client privilege.

On Sept. 24, 1991, Jon Jr. and Neff appeared before Judge Smith in the Osage County District Court, with county attorney Cheryl Stewart representing the state. That hearing was regarding Jon Jr.'s motion for a sentence modification to spend the final 90 days on his sentence in the pre-revocation program at the Osawatomie Correctional Facility. As the hearing began, Stewart, Neff, and Judge Smith had the following exchange:

"Your honor, may it please the court, the state's position is that if this defendant can be released into a drug and alcohol treatment program, we would have no objection," Stewart said.

"Is that what the 90-day pre-revocation at Osawatomie is?" Smith asked.

"If I may be permitted to answer, your honor, yes it is. I have spoken ..." Neff said before being interrupted by the judge.

"I want to know if the state concurs with that," Smith said.

"Yes, your honor, we would concur with that," Stewart said.

"Generally, I have no objection to allowing him to enter such a program under the terms contained in the letter from Mr. Knoll," Smith said. "And we will grant probation from the remainder of that sentence, giving him credit for the time he does serve in such institutional diversionary program. If, in fact, he violates that institutional diversionary program, it will be a violation of probation here granted, and subsequent to re-entry into the jail to serve the remainder of the sentence imposed. Other than that, I do not believe any other terms or conditions of the program are necessary."

With that, Jon Jr. had another chance, assuming he didn't violate his probation during the program.

"I don't remember his underlying sentence, but the judge put him on probation," Stewart said. "He pled guilty, got his sentence, and I figured the parole people take care of that kind of business. Once the county let go of him, and he's released from county custody, he's in the state's custody."

As it was, Jon Jr. was to be released from the Osage County Jail and transferred to the facility in Osawatomie within a few days. He never got there.

THE INTERVIEW BEGINS

Surrounded by law enforcement for hours, Jon Jr. held up remarkably well for a man who likely knew he was the prime suspect in Brenda's murder. That was about to change.

As the interview began a few minutes after 3 p.m., Ramirez told him about the investigation, including finding Brenda dead in the boatshed. When asked if he knew anything about her death, Jon Jr. said he didn't. He also denied knowing if his father was involved.

"I said, 'What can you tell me about this little girl?' and he said, 'I don't know what you're talking about,'" Ramirez said. "He lied to us through the whole interview."

Metz quickly switched tactics, asking Jon Jr. to walk the detectives through his day. He said he woke up at 8 a.m. on Oct. 19, making breakfast for himself and his father, before leaving with his cousin-in-law. Ivan then took Jon Jr. to his house in Tecumseh, where Ivan showed him the work he was doing to remodel the home.

After spending a short time at that property, Ivan drove both of them to St. Francis Hospital, where Ivan received an insulin treatment for his diabetes. Jon Jr. said while his cousin-in-law was in the hospital, he walked a few blocks north to the Full Moon Saloon and drank beer until Ivan came to get him. They left the bar at about 5 p.m. and arrived back in Dover at about 5:30 p.m.

Jon Jr. continued to deny knowing anything about Brenda's death, so Metz asked him how he got several fresh scratches on his hand. His answer was that he worked on a car in the garage after he arrived home on Saturday evening, stating he fixed the body of the vehicle. Believing this was another lie, the detective countered that he looked at the car, which was covered in dust, and that it wasn't touched.

Jon replied that he worked on the battery, but Metz said there wasn't a spot on the front of the car that wasn't covered in dust. Jon Jr. continued to say he worked on the car, even when Metz said that the only dust disturbed on the car was around the trunk and trunk lock. After going back and forth, Metz noticed that the veins in Jon Jr.'s neck were bulging, a tell-tell sign that his suspect was nervous and possibly lying.

Ramirez pointed out to Jon Jr. that he looked extremely nervous, without a response. To try to get him to relax, the detective started talking again about both attending Lawrence High School. Once he calmed down, Ramirez asked Jon Jr. if he didn't commit the murder, did his father? The younger Mareska adamantly denied that his father was involved, saying his father would never kill anyone. He also said he didn't even see Brenda walk by the house on Saturday.

"As you're questioning him about something you know, but he doesn't know you know, well, we just kind of throw it at him," Ramirez said. "The more we know, the better the interview. When him and I were together, the only thing I was interested in was him telling me that he killed her and how he killed her."

Metz and Ramirez began to press their suspect, with Metz telling him that he saw Brenda's body in the boathouse and that she had bright red hair, the same color of hair the officers found on the bloody sweatshirt they collected from his aunt and uncle's house. Metz also pointed out that crime scene officers found dark hair, like Jon Jr.'s, on her body, to which he did not respond.

As the officers continued speaking to him, Metz asked Jon Jr. when he last had sex. He said he was with a woman named Anita at the Full Moon Saloon while he was waiting for Ivan to pick him up. Jon Jr. couldn't remember her last name, but said he had sex with the woman, a prostitute who worked in the saloon, in an apartment above the bar.

Metz replied that he didn't believe him, but he would attempt to verify the story.

After this exchange, the detectives left the room, leaving their suspect to sit alone in Ramirez's office. Metz noted in his report that Jon Jr. was twisting his fingers and moving his hands and arms up and under his shirt as the blood vessels bulged in his neck.

During the time Metz and Ramirez left Jon Jr. to sit alone with his thoughts, the officers radioed Sgt. Mark Wanamaker, still on the scene in Dover, and asked him to bring Jon Sr. to the Sheriff's Department for an interview. By that point, Jon Sr. had been in Reserve Deputy Myron Stucky's squad car for several hours. Detective Larry Baer, also finishing up the investigation in Dover, drove back to the Blakes' home, picked up Jon Sr., and took him to the station, with Wanamaker following. During the ride to Topeka, Jon Sr. told Baer that he was in a fight and in the hospital for three months, and that his memory wasn't sound.

When Metz and Ramirez returned to the office, Metz asked Jon Jr. how long it'd been since he spoke with a minister. He visited with one three weeks before while he was in jail. Metz asked him if he would like to speak to one now. Jon Jr., clearly upset, dropped his head, looking down without answering.

"(Metz) started talking about religion, and I asked (Jon Jr.), 'What religion are you?' and I told him I was Catholic," Ramirez said. "And he was saying he thought God would never forgive him. So, I told him, 'If you want to tell us the truth, God will forgive you.' He hushed up a little bit, and I said, 'What would make you feel better? If you want to tell me what happened …'"

Jon Jr. replied: "Well, I'd just like to pray that God will take care of me for what I've done."

With that, Ramirez said, "So, let's do this." In his office, he and Jon Jr. dropped to their knees and prayed together.

"Do you feel better?" Ramirez said he asked. "He said, 'I do,' and I said, 'Maybe now you can tell me, and God will forgive you for it.'"

After numerous attempts to get a confession from Jon Jr., Ramirez felt like his suspect was more vulnerable than ever and asked him to tell them what happened that fateful night.

FROM JAIL TO DOVER

A few days after Judge Smith signed off on the modification to Jon Jr.'s sentence, he was still in the Osage County Jail. Though he was scheduled to be transferred to the correctional facility on the grounds of the Osawatomie State Hospital, Jon Jr. never arrived.

"My understanding was they contacted the parole department, the place that he was supposed to go. There was a nurse there that was supposed to do the intake, he wasn't available," Stewart said. "So, they weren't going to be able to intake him into the system that weekend."

Jon Jr. spent several days in the Osage County Jail after the sentence modification before one of his attorneys contacted Stewart, the county attorney said.

"He had a parole hold, so I drug my feet a little bit on the journal entry because I was waiting on the parole people to contact the sheriff, so I could get a go-ahead on what they're doing. I was letting the parole people communicate because typically the parole (people) would come get their people and get them out of jail," Stewart said. "One of the attorneys came in and said, 'Hey, Cheryl, he's been here on probation, nothing is going to move until you get the journal entry done.' So, while they were there, either I or the secretary typed the journal entry; they signed it, I signed it. I walked it upstairs, got it to the judge, it got signed, it got filed, which released him from probation on our case."

Judge Smith said he had no recollection of signing the journal entry, which allowed Jon Jr. to be released. In an article written by reporters Steve Fry and Steve Schwartz and published in the Topeka Capital-Journal on Oct. 22, 1991, Stewart explained that Jon Jr.'s "attorney questioned the county's authority to detain because the judge had said nothing in court about returning Mareska to jail."

"Once we figured out that we weren't supposed to have him, the jail contacted the parole officer," Stewart said in the article.

According to the Topeka Capital-Journal, the Kansas Department of Corrections apparently declined to keep Jon Jr., and the state allowed him to be placed with his uncle and aunt, the Blakes, in Dover. According to the Osage County Jail ledger for that day, he left the facility on Oct. 1. He was scheduled to report to the Osawatomie State Hospital on Thursday, Oct. 17.

The Blakes took Jon Jr. in because he didn't have anyone else. Less than a year from a severe brain injury and coma, Jon Sr. wasn't capable of taking care of himself, let alone his son, and was living with his sister and brother-in-law. Tammy Blake said she and her husband weren't aware of the extensive record their nephew accumulated in a short period of time.

"He was pretty pleasant. When he was here, he was really nice," Tammy said. "We didn't have any problems with him. I didn't know what he did. I figured he couldn't get into too much trouble with no vehicle."

Others, however, saw a different person, one who made them nervous. Mary Sievers was at the Blakes' house one day that October when Jon Jr. asked if her daughters could ride with him down to the corner store in town for a soda.

"Fortunately, we said no," she said. "I just didn't want them going anywhere with him, a young guy and two young girls, and we didn't know him that well. I think they were just as happy that we said no."

On another day that October, Marilee and Crystal Sievers were visiting the Blakes and playing pool while their parents sat in another room. As the sisters moved around the pool table to find the right angle for their shots, Jon Jr. watched them closely.

"At the time, you didn't pay any attention to that," Crystal Sievers said. "That's creepy now. He was always just creeping. He looked strong, what you picture as your typical muscular, tattoo guy. But it didn't occur to us that he was abnormal."

That did occur to Kristi Osburn, who often was hanging out with the Sievers. She remembers playing cards with the Sievers, Blakes, and Jon Jr.

"He always made me uncomfortable," she said. "He just didn't feel right to me. I couldn't identify it at the time because nobody had ever looked at me like that before."

Jon Jr. also caught the eye of Osburn's dad, especially when Jon Jr. was sitting on the porch in the morning. The Osburn parents often left early for work, and their three daughters were home alone awhile before they went to school. Osburn said her father had a bad feeling about the younger Mareska and would turn off his lights as he drove down the family's driveway.

"Jon used to sit outside and watch the road," Kristi Osburn said. "He was worried he would see him leaving and would be leaving his three daughters there."

Any concerns those in the area had, however, were supposed to be gone on Oct. 17, when Jon Jr. went to the Osawatomie Correctional Facility. But the hospital rescheduled his check-in for Oct. 21, two days after Brenda's murder.

JON JR. FINALLY TALKS

Sensing Jon Jr. was about to crack, Ramirez looked at him and asked softly, "Do you want to get this off your mind?" Ramirez added that it was time for Jon Jr. to help himself and start a new life by owning up to what he did that night.

"He knew he'd been caught, and I think he had remorse for doing it," Ramirez said. "He didn't really cry. He had tears in his eyes, but he didn't cry."

Even though he was emotional, Jon Jr. didn't answer the question about getting the crime off his mind the first time Ramirez asked.

When the detective asked again if he wanted to tell them what happened, Jon Jr. looked up and nodded his head.

He began by saying he went to the barn by himself after returning to Dover at about 5:30 p.m. Saturday. While in the barn, he saw Brenda pushing her bike down the road, walked behind her as she was pushing her bike, and grabbed her by the hair. He told her to come with him, walking her to the fence on the Blakes' property just west of Douglas Road, and forcing her to throw her bike over it before both of them crawled through the barbed wire.

Jon Jr. picked up the bike, grabbed Brenda by the hair again, and forced her to push the Schwinn down to the pond. At the pond, he made her push the bike to the edge of the diving board and throw her prized possession into the dark, murky water.

After she dropped her bike into the pond, Jon Jr. walked her up to the boathouse, took her inside, and made her take her clothes off. After she disrobed, he made her walk outside and back behind the boathouse, hiding them from anybody driving by on Douglas Road. He then had her lie down, and raped her, before rolling her over and sodomizing her.

Metz and Ramirez asked Jon Jr. what happened after he raped Brenda, and he said he made her turn over again on her back before choking her with his bare hands as she looked into his eyes. Once she lost consciousness, he picked Brenda up and dropped her through the empty window and onto the hard, cold floor of the boathouse. He walked around to the front, picked up her clothes, and threw them on her body.

While Ramirez sensed regret from Jon Jr., Metz did not.

"No, no, none at all," Metz said. "He had a tendency to go after girls, and we probably prevented it from happening again, because if he did it once, he'd do it again if the opportunity arose."

The officers asked Jon Jr. if Brenda attempted to resist and scream at any point, and he said that she did not. That statement is one fellow detective Larry Baer doesn't believe.

"He started doing his thing," Baer said of a possible scenario from that night, "and she begged him and begged him. She said, 'If you let me go, I won't tell anybody.' And he just laughed."

Another point of contention with the detectives is what actually happened to Brenda that night. Jon Jr. vehemently denied that he hit Brenda, even though she had dozens of bruises and cuts.

"We told him the victim had severe bruises on the upper body and a cut on her head, like she'd been struck with an object," Ramirez wrote in his report. "Mareska said he did not know anything about those bruises. He said he did not strike the victim in any way. He did say at times he told the victim to shut up, but he did not hit her."

It seemed odd to the detectives that Jon Jr. confessed to raping and sodomizing a 12-year-old, but he wouldn't admit beating her when the evidence pointed to a brutal attack.

"There's some criminals that will beat, sodomize, and rape a person, and they may tell you, 'Yes, I beat her; yes, I raped her, but I didn't sodomize her. Or, 'No, I didn't rape her, I did sodomize and beat her," Metz said. "I have never understood why there are just certain things they don't admit, but sometimes, from what I've learned, it's 'OK you raped her and sodomized her, but you didn't have to beat her because she was so small.' He beat her. It was obvious she'd been beaten."

Metz also asked Jon Jr. why he killed Brenda instead of raping her and letting her go. He did not answer.

"I think he knew (what he was going to do) when he was taking her back there and had her throw that bicycle in the pond," Baer said.

When he finished attacking Brenda, Jon Jr. said he walked through the woods to the back of the Blakes' house, went upstairs, and took off his clothes before taking a shower. For the rest of the night, he watched TV before going to bed. He woke up early the following morning and washed the jeans and boxer shorts he wore when he killed Brenda.

When asked why he didn't wash the bloody sweatshirt, Jon Jr. said he forgot. He also told Ramirez and Metz that he was wearing the same pants and boxer shorts that he wore during the rape and murder, and that the black tennis shoes he wore were under a blanket in a storage room next to his bedroom on the second floor of the Blakes' house.

Once he finished the confession, the detectives asked Jon Jr. if his father knew or if he told anyone what he did, to which he replied, "No." He then consented to repeating his confession on video tape and allowing a crime scene officer to take head and pubic hair samples, along with scrapings from his fingernails.

Before the officers began recording, Metz asked Jon Jr. if he felt better after confessing. He hung his head and didn't respond.

INTERVIEWING JON SR.

Baer and Wanamaker arrived with Jon Sr. in the final stages of his son's confession, sitting him in an interview room away from Jon Jr. As Metz recorded the video, Wanamaker met with Ramirez and Baer, learning that Jon Jr. said his father was not involved in Brenda's murder. Wanamaker asked the detectives to interview Jon Sr. to ensure that he didn't participate. After entering the room, Ramirez told the elder Mareska that his son confessed to killing Brenda.

"Mr. Mareska looked startled and shocked, asking if we were sure his son had confessed to the crime," Baer wrote in his report. "Again, Detective Ramirez advised, yes, his son had confessed to it, and we had a statement. Mr. Mareska just held his head down, shaking it."

The detectives asked Jon Sr. if he knew anything about the crime, and he responded that he didn't know about the murder or his son's involvement. At 4:45 p.m., Ramirez left the room, and Baer finished the interview. Baer asked Jon Sr. what he did the previous day. He said he worked on the house, but was in the Blakes' house with his son and a friend whose name he couldn't remember. That friend was Ivan.

Jon Sr. said his son left the house shortly after 5:30 p.m., believing he was going fishing in the pond on the property. He said Jon Jr. returned when it was dark at about 7 p.m., cleaned up, washed some clothes, and watched TV. He could not remember what Jon Jr. was wearing. Baer asked Jon Sr. again if he knew anything about Brenda's death, and he replied again that he didn't, telling the detective that he "would probably never understand how it was eating him inside."

Baer concluded the interview asking if Jon Jr. said anything to him once he returned from fishing. Jon Sr. said that he didn't. At 4:55 p.m., Baer left the room.

"A lot of people were real upset that we didn't arrest the father," Wanamaker said. "There's nothing to demonstrate he was involved. The evidence wasn't there to make an arrest. I guarantee you he would have been arrested if we'd had the evidence. There was no evidence whatsoever that he was directly involved."

After the detectives wrapped up their interviews with the Mareskas, Wanamaker drove Jon Sr. back to Dover. Although Jon Sr. asked to speak with his son, the department's reports do not contain information of that happening. As Wanamaker and Jon Sr. headed back to the Blakes' house, crime scene officer Richard Warrington arrived at the station to take samples of Jon Jr.'s head and pubic hair, along with scrapings from his fingernails, at 6:10 p.m. Because he was wearing the pants and boxer shorts he wore during the crime, Warrington also took those items, which Jon Jr. swapped out for a pair of coveralls.

Back in Dover, Wanamaker dropped off Jon Sr. and entered the Blakes' house, where he found Jon Jr.'s tennis shoes, which appeared to be covered in blood, and bagged them as evidence. On his way back to Topeka, the sergeant stopped by the Kellers and told Bob and Tracy that the department had a suspect in custody for the murder for their daughter.

"That was hard. It was pretty solemn," Wanamaker said. "I think they were somewhat relieved that we had accomplished that, but it sure didn't make the pain go away."

At the Sheriff's Department, Ramirez asked Jon Jr. if he was willing to have his blood drawn, and he agreed. Along with Baer, they left for Stormont-Vail Hospital, where a lab technician drew his blood at 6:55 p.m. By 7:10 p.m., they were back at the Sheriff's Department to pick up an arrest report on Jon Jr. from Metz. Baer and Ramirez then drove Jon Jr. to the Department of Corrections facility in Topeka, where they booked Jon Jr. on charges of kidnapping, rape, sodomy, and first-degree murder.

Pam Leptich, one of Brenda Keller's favorite teachers and who delivered the eulogy at her funeral, took this photo of Brenda not long before her death.

Bob Keller shared this photo of his daughter with the Kansas Legislature during one of his speeches at the Statehouse.

Brenda Keller's marker is one of the most prominent headstones in the Dover Cemetery.

Built in 1931, the Dover Federated Church remains the only church in the small community. Bob Keller has been the pastor for more than 40 years.

*The interior of the church looks much the same
as it did when Brenda was alive.*

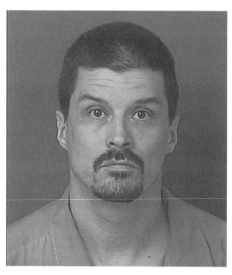

*A Kansas Department of Corrections photo of Jon Mareska Jr. in
2012. He is eligible for parole in 2031, when he will be 62 years old.*

CHAPTER ELEVEN:

THE AFTERMATH

By the time the detectives booked Jon Mareska Jr. into the Topeka Correctional Facility for the kidnapping, rape, and murder of Brenda, they had been working for hours. Jack Metz, the lead detective on the case, had been grinding away for 17 hours when he sat down with fellow detectives Mike Ramirez, Larry Baer, and Sgt. Mark Wanamaker.

Though the officers had plenty of work left to ensure that Jon Jr. stayed in jail, they were content with the investigation and the arrest of their prime suspect by Sunday evening, less than 24 hours after searchers discovered Brenda's body. From 8 to 8:30 p.m. in Ramirez's office, the officers discussed the case, concluding that they had done all they could at that point and would resume the next morning.

"It (a quick arrest) is not uncommon," Wanamaker said. "This one was pretty pointed as to who did it. Basically, he confessed to it, and that's about all you need."

Going into the second day of their investigation, the Shawnee County Sheriff's Department had a bevy of potential evidence. Crime scene officer R.J. Warrington checked in receipts for hair samples, fingernail scrapings, Brenda and Jon Jr.'s clothes, blood, photo negatives,

Brenda's rape kit, and more. Fellow officers submitted Jon Jr.'s bloody tennis shoes and videotapes from the confession and crime scene.

At the end of the long day, Metz couldn't help but think about Brenda and how her life ended.

"Because she was a child, because of her age, it's one of the more brutal ones," Metz said. "I've worked several homicides with adults, and none of them are good, but this guy had a mean streak in him."

The detectives also got an answer to a question many had as they searched the house and investigated the crime scene: Why didn't Jon Jr. try to make a run for it in the middle of the night?

"I think it was Wanamaker who told me, 'I asked him why he didn't run, and he said that cop could have killed me,'" said Wabaunsee County deputy Harry Carpenter, referencing his experience with Jon Jr. less than a year earlier in the county jail. "He was afraid of me because he knew damn good and well I'd do something, if I needed to."

The Kellers, meanwhile, were numb. Bob was already busy planning his daughter's funeral with a family friend, and Tracy was trying to stay busy with visitors stopping by throughout the day. One minute, she was folding laundry. The next, she was cleaning.

"I remember that it was a very nice fall day, and she and I were out on the porch," Janet Baldwin said. "She was sweeping. She just kept sweeping and sweeping. And she said, 'I lost my girl, Janet.' It gives me chills and tears to this day."

That evening, Jean, Roy, Janice, and Aunt B left for Topeka, staying the night at Roy and Jean's house. When they arrived, Jean went upstairs to her room, knelt down beside her bed, and looked to God for answers.

"I remember feeling like I wanted to pray, but I couldn't get through it," Jean said. "I remembered how Jesus will get through to God for us, and I just had to leave it with Him."

When Jean tried to give her grief to God, Roy went to her. As he started to drop to his knees, his wife let go of her emotions.

"Jeannie was in the position like she was kneeling, and Roy went over and she exploded," Aunt B said. "She almost screamed. It was just terrible."

That was the beginning of a long struggle for Brenda's grandmother. Over the next several months, Jean, already a slight woman, lost a significant amount of weight and merely survived the holidays.

"It just killed my mother," Janice said. "For a while, she couldn't talk about Brenda without crying."

"Mom hurt when her grandkids hurt. She poured everything into her grandkids," Beverly added. "If anything, she probably loved them harder (after Brenda's death)."

Janice, a young mother who was expecting another child at the time, didn't wear makeup for several months because she cried so often. John and Pat began to compartmentalize immediately, rarely talking about their sister's murder. To this day, they have little memory of the days, weeks, and months following Brenda's death.

Tracy changed forever the day she lost her daughter. Overnight, her personality shifted from bubbly and outgoing to reserved and quiet.

"Brenda was just a part of me. I loved sharing with her," she said. "I was pretty much out of it for a very long time. I think I really experienced what it means to have a broken heart."

WHERE'S IVAN?

When Ramirez and Baer booked Jon Jr. into jail, Ivan hadn't been heard from in more than 24 hours. At 11 p.m. on the night Brenda went missing, Jon Jr. told officers Alvin Moran, William Vaughn, and David Reser that Ivan left the Blakes' house sometime after 5:30 p.m.

Several witnesses, including Eva Riley, supported Jon Jr.'s statement. Riley and her husband told Metz they saw Tammy's car backing out of the driveway of the Blakes' home between 6:05 and 6:10 p.m. that night.

A few minutes later, according to Metz's report, Bob Marling saw Tammy's car heading eastbound toward Topeka at about 6:10 p.m. Though Ivan often worked on his place during the day, he usually stayed at the Blake home overnight. On this Saturday, however, he didn't return to Dover, and the Sheriff's Department's attempts to locate him that night were unsuccessful. Ivan did not return on Sunday, and officers didn't track him down until the day before Brenda's funeral.

While Ivan's whereabouts were unknown, Gene and Tammy Blake arrived home Sunday night to a devastated and angry community. As details from the case emerged, notably that someone staying at their home was arrested for the murder, some people in Dover blamed them.

"It was a hell of a drive back from Tampa," Tammy Blake said. "No one would really speak to us. It was a very cold shoulder, and it lasted quite a while, a long time. Of course, you feel guilty being gone. I don't think I'll ever get past that guilt. Turning around to come back to such a disaster ... that was just so overwhelming."

Rumors that Jon Jr. didn't act alone started almost immediately, especially when people learned that Jon Sr. – many residents didn't realize Ivan was staying there – was living with the Blakes. The day after Gene and Tammy got home, they started receiving anonymous phone calls. Some people told them to leave. A few threatened to take justice into their own hands.

"I was very angry about what they'd done to the Blakes," Crystal Sievers said. "(The Blakes) are so kind. They would never have allowed him (Jon Jr.) in their house if they had any idea. I don't know how people blame the Blakes. I feel so much loyalty to them after everybody has been so horrible to them after all they've done for everybody and us."

Many of the menacing phone calls were directed at Jon Sr. Though investigators cleared him of being involved in the murder, a contingent of people were convinced he participated. The threats were frightening enough that Gene and Tammy, fearing for his life, moved Jon Sr. to Topeka, where he stayed with his mother in her apartment across from the Topeka Zoo.

GOING UNDERCOVER

In the early 1990s, the Topeka Capital-Journal was one of the most respected newspapers in the Midwest. The paper formed in the 1870s following a series of mergers, culminating with the Topeka Daily Capital and Topeka State Journal. The paper prided itself on being the state's most reliable source of news and provided coverage from Liberal in the southwest corner of the state to Hiawatha in the northeast corner.

In October 1991, the Capital-Journal boasted a circulation of more than 100,000 across the state. If a story appeared in the paper, thousands of people were going to read it. In a time long before Twitter and iPads, the paper often broke news to readers.

That was the case on the morning of Monday, Oct. 21, 1991, as people sat down for breakfast and coffee. Written by Tim Hrenchir, the lead story spanning five columns at the top of the front page featured the headline "Girl's murder shocks small town," with a pull quote from Dover principal Terri Anderson: "I just can't say enough positive things about Brenda. She was a beautiful girl inside and out."

Hrenchir's leg work on the story showed. He had quotes from Anderson, Ruth Lange, and Joy 88 manager Warren Wilson. The piece was a feature introducing readers to a little girl beloved in a small town similar to hundreds of communities in the state.

A second story written by Hrenchir, "Suspect arrested in slaying," rested next to the first article and stretched from the top to the bottom of the front page in the sixth and final column. It summarized the arrest of Jon Jr. and provided details surrounding Brenda's disappearance and the search for her. Though the story didn't contain quotes, it referenced Wanamaker's statement in a press release that Jon Jr. was arrested on charges of first-degree murder, aggravated kidnapping, rape, and aggravated sodomy. The piece also noted that a Sheriff's Department dispatcher said an "unrecognizable" body was found early Sunday morning.

"We knew Brenda was dead, and that the term brutally murdered had been used," Hrenchir said. "It was the biggest (story) I'd covered at that point."

Hrenchir pointed out in his second story that Brenda's murder was the first homicide in Shawnee County outside of Topeka since February 1984, the murder of Clarence Lavin Jr., a case that remains unsolved. It also referred to Brenda's obituary on Page 5B. Nestled at the bottom of the page, the obit was surrounded by the death notices of people much older, including a 95-year-old woman immediately before and an 87-year-old man immediately after. The notice listed her mom, dad, brothers, and all four grandparents as survivors, as well as Brenda's involvement in church, the church youth group, Topeka Youth Band, and Friends of the Topeka Zoo.

At the time many were reading Hrenchir's stories, fellow reporter Roberta Peterson arrived for work at the Capital-Journal's building a few blocks east of downtown Topeka. A veteran journalist, Peterson had worked at the paper for more than seven years after serving as a professor of journalism at Kansas State University. A talented wordsmith who had a way with people, Peterson often wrote the heart-wrenching stories many reporters couldn't capture.

"Whenever it was something sensitive, they would make me go," said Peterson, "even though it was never my job, and I don't consider myself really good at that."

While Peterson had covered a wide range of stories all over the world during her career, she had never been a general assignment reporter. At least until there was a shift in the newsroom with the arrival of a new managing editor.

"They had all this drama going on in the newsroom," she said. "This guy came in and decided he was going to turn the whole newsroom upside down. So, if you were near the top, you went to the bottom. The thing was I could be a general assignment reporter, and he knew that'd make me quit. So, that's what he offered me. I said I was willing to do any story, and he didn't believe me."

On Peterson's first day in the new role, the managing editor assigned her to cover Brenda's funeral.

"I'd been there several years, and that was the first assignment," she said. "He figured I'd refuse to do it because the family had requested no media. It was a very heavy thing."

Brenda's story also hit Peterson close to home. The day before the murder, Peterson's son went missing. A year younger than Brenda, he left the family's house in the Potwin neighborhood of Topeka with a friend without telling his parents. For an hour, the Petersons felt the crushing anxiety Bob and Tracy Keller felt just 24 hours later.

"The really short version is he was fine, but for an hour, we didn't think so. I never had anything like that happen before," she said.

The combination of stress at home and being assigned to cover a funeral the media wasn't supposed to attend gave the seasoned reporter pause.

"I was afraid I should just go on and say forget it; this guy's going to put me in the worst possible position," she said. "I didn't want to crash the funeral. I didn't want to be there, and not being honest about the fact that I was with the newspaper … it was just bizarre."

Peterson eventually accepted the assignment to cover the funeral, a decision that had a significant impact on Brenda's story and people following the case.

LIKE LOCUSTS

While the Kellers asked the media not to cover the funeral, that didn't stop reporters from flocking to Dover in the days leading up to the service. It went from a sleepy bedroom community to a media hub overnight, complete with TV trucks, cameras, and daily stories and news segments.

Julie Gomez, who was a year behind Brenda, moved from the east side of Topeka to Dover with her family in 1990. Though Gomez grew up in a bigger city, she was shocked by the sudden explosion of activity.

"I remember them (media) being there, the presence they had," she said. "I just had never dealt with something like that and had never seen so much media. I won't forget that. In this small town, all the media that was there for my friend that was murdered. When this happened, I think it shook everybody."

TV stations competing for a juicy interview weren't afraid to cross boundaries. Amy Best, who spent nearly as much time at the Dover Federated Church as Brenda, said news reporters set up shop in front of the church, where many of the children in the community were hanging out with friends.

The schools also were a popular spot for journalists, even though the junior high and grade school were closed until Thursday, Oct. 24. While the students weren't there, most of the teachers were working. Anderson and her staff worked diligently to build a return plan that helped their students experience some semblance of normalcy after a traumatic event.

"The thing that made me so angry was the media coverage came swarming into Dover like locusts," Pam Leptich said. "I was just very angry the way it was handled. I stayed angry because I just wanted everybody to go away."

School officials and other adults shielded Brenda's schoolmates the best they could. The Mission Valley Unified School District sent 11 counselors to Dover to meet with children who needed help coping. Mark Erickson, a school psychologist in Kansas for 25 years, became a spokesperson for the district.

"The media was there bugging the teachers and principal, and one of the things the principal wanted me to do was talk to the media and try to keep them from bothering the teachers," Erickson said. "And, she didn't want them talking to the kids. We were trying to help them deal with having one of their classmates have a tragic ending."

Reporters did manage to interview a few kids, including some who were in grade school. Though they didn't end up with much material to use on the news or in articles, the boldness of the media further vexed people.

"To be honest, they were kind of like vultures, standing around waiting for somebody to talk to," Allen Zordel said.

Leptich didn't understand what the perspective of a grade-schooler added to the story.

"They would ask a third grader or a fifth grader, 'Are you sad?'" she said. "I thought, 'Get the hell out of here.' You ask a third grader, you can't even be sure if they know Brenda is gone. A third grader might say, 'I just want to get something to eat.'"

Before Peterson went undercover for the funeral, she wrote a sidebar for the Capital-Journal's Oct. 22 edition that focused on what Brenda meant to Dover, as well as ways a community can handle tragic news accounts. Peterson did not interview any students, quoting Erickson and Anderson, who said in the article: "Everyone loved Brenda. She was artistically talented with very deep religious convictions. She didn't preach at us, but lived her faith, and that brought so much to our lives. They (her classmates) are really more like siblings than classmates. They are grieving deeply."

It was the lead story that day, however, that took the town's fury to another level. Paired with Peterson's sidebar as the centerpiece on the front page, reporters Steve Swartz and Steve Fry wrote a story titled "Suspect was supposed to be in jail."

The piece detailed Jon Jr.'s first court appearance, via video link between the jail and courthouse, on Monday, noting that his bond was set at $100,000, but the lead paragraph said that he was supposed to be in the Osawatomie Correctional Facility on the day Brenda died.

Containing a mugshot of a rough-and-tumble looking Jon Jr. with long, flat hair and a dark moustache, the story listed his prior convictions and said that the person who was scheduled to check him into the pre-revocation program wasn't at work that day, so he was scheduled to be admitted the week of Oct. 21.

"Despite the fact Osawatomie wasn't ready for Mareska, he was allowed to leave the Osage County Jail on Oct. 1. He was released to the custody of his uncle," Swartz and Fry wrote.

The article also summarized the Sept. 24 sentence modification hearing and Jon Jr.'s defense attorneys questioning the county's authority to keep him in the jail, and quoted County Attorney Cheryl Stewart: "Once we figured out that we weren't supposed to have him, the jail contacted the parole officer."

Swartz and Fry contacted the Department of Corrections for an explanation as to why the parole officer placed Jon Jr. with Gene and Tammy, but the department spokesman said that parole supervision records weren't open to the public, and he couldn't comment on the case.

"Stewart said she could have made a recommendation to the court about where Mareska should or shouldn't stay. But, she said, it was a 'whirlwind hearing,' the articled stated. "And, Stewart said, even though Mareska had a criminal record from several counties, his background was no worse than many defendants with which she deals."

Learning about some of the details of Jon Jr.'s release infuriated many in Dover.

"I would hold the legal system responsible for making poor decisions with an individual that you know likely had some severe mental illnesses, as well as violent tendencies, and not properly monitoring him," Autumn Buchmeier said.

Stewart was vilified by many for years after Brenda's death. During a visit to the church her family attended in Scranton after the murder, a man walked up the aisle, stopped in front of her and said, "You're Cheryl Stewart?" When she answered that she was, he hatefully responded, "You're the one that got my friend's daughter killed. You're disgusting; you shouldn't even be in this church."

"I just looked at him; it's all I could do. I might have said, 'Sir, I didn't kill anybody,'" Stewart said. "I understand being upset, but you know that certainly didn't feel good, and my kids were just looking at me like 'What are you upset about, mom?' They weren't very old. Guess what: I never went back. I definitely feel for the family because that's a very tragic thing. Nothing can take that back.

"I was the only one that caught flak, from the newspapers, from all the people around. I was the only one that caught it. Nobody blamed the defense counsel. Nobody blamed the judge. Nobody blamed the jail. Nobody blamed the sheriff. Nobody blamed the Department of Corrections that didn't come get their guy. When they blamed me for it, I thought that was rather slanted."

THE AUTOPSY

Willard "Wike" Scamman came to Topeka in 1963 as an anatomic and clinical pathologist who graduated from Vanderbilt's prestigious School of Medicine. Nearly 30 years later, at the age of 59, Scamman's resume included Lattimore-Fink labs, small hospitals in western Kansas, and three hospitals in the capital city. By 1991, he'd opened the first blood bank in the area, ran his own practice for a decade, and worked in the county coroner's office.

Scamman, who retired at age 85 in 2017 after working in Topeka for more than 50 years, conducted Brenda's autopsy on the Monday morning before Brenda's funeral. Also attended by Assistant District Attorneys David Debenham and Maggie Lutes, Public Defender's Office investigator Jim Kinney, and officers Metz, Warrington, J.D. Sparkman, and Ken Smith, it revealed the brutality of her murder and that there was no doubt that the murderer beat her severely, possibly with an object.

Though Jon Jr. told detectives he didn't hit Brenda, she had dozens of injuries that showed otherwise, including lacerations and abrasions from her head to the top of her foot. She had deep cuts on her shoulders and chest, including one four inches long and an inch wide, along with deep vertical abrasions on her lower back, upper right arm, and legs.

Brenda's body was bruised virtually everywhere, including the lower body, left forearm, and legs. She had tears in her vagina and anus severe enough for Scamman to list them as traumatic injuries.

"This is the case I probably think about more than any of them," Debenham, a father of three daughters, said. "I think it's because of the nature of this case. This is just one of those sad cases with good people that had awful things happen. She was so young, totally innocent."

Brenda was beaten so severely that she had internal bleeding in several areas, including outside of the brain and between the brain and surrounding membrane from a head injury. Scamman noted that she had a subdural hemorrhage of the spinal cord in the middle of her back, along with bleeding around the larynx and pharynx, due to strangulation.

Those injuries were among eight listed as traumatic, along with the tearing in her vagina and anus, a rupture of the left lobe of the liver, bleeding in the mesentery (the organ that attaches the intestines to the abdominal wall) and upper abdomen, multiple abrasions, and deep bruising of the skin.

Many of the injuries on their own would have been enough to kill Brenda, notably the brain injury, ruptured liver, and bleeding on the spinal cord, larynx, and pharynx.

"It was terrible, just terrible ... how long was she alive when he was doing that?" Metz said.

HER FIRST MURDER CASE

Lutes began working in the District Attorney's Office in the fall of 1988, not long after she graduated from the Washburn University School of Law. Also an alumna of Kansas State, she was a young attorney working her way up in October 1991. In her own words, Lutes was working "very low-level entry cases" in the years leading up to Brenda's murder. Lutes grew up in a place similar to Dover, a small western Kansas town, Pratt, where she lived in a rural setting.

"I rode bikes up and down a dirt road, and I grew up on a dairy farm," she said. "It was about a six-mile by three-mile community, and there was at least one house every mile. There was about five of us kids, and I was one of the oldest ones. We used to ride our bikes all the time.

"I've prosecuted a lot of cases where you go, 'It was just a matter of time.' It was just sad. This was not that. This was every parent's nightmare."

Lutes was visiting her parents in Pratt, a city with a population of 6,700 located less than an hour from the Oklahoma border on U.S. Highway 54, on the weekend Brenda died.

"I heard about the case as I was driving home Sunday evening, and I just remember being overwhelmed," said Lutes, now an assistant district attorney in Wichita. "I remember thinking, 'I have got to work on this case.' I was drawn, led, whatever you want to call it, that I needed to be a part of this case."

Lutes went to work early Monday, immediately talking to Debenham.

"I went in, and David was working on it, and Dave and I got along really well," she said. "I said, 'I've never done a case like this, could I help you with this?' He was like, 'Absolutely.'"

With that, Lutes worked on one of the most notorious cases in Shawnee County history. One of her contributions was an idea she pitched to Debenham right away.

"I remember telling Dave that if this case is going to trial, we really need to understand more about this community and who she was within the community, even as a child," she said. "I think we should go to the funeral, but not tell the family. We should just kind of be in the background."

INTERVIEWING IVAN

In addition to Jon Jr.'s first appearance in court via video link on Monday, Assistant Public Defender Cindy Sewell submitted a request to seal the affidavit and complaint in the case. Shawnee County District Judge Matthew J. Dowd granted the request, issuing a gag order for all the attorneys and law enforcement officers.

As it was, the Sheriff's Department was far too busy continuing their investigation to worry about discussing the case with media. Baer and Ramirez resumed their search for Ivan on Tuesday, driving to his house in Tecumseh several times in an attempt to set up an interview. Finally, at 1:30 p.m. that day, the detectives connected with their person of interest, asking him to set up an appointment for Wednesday. Two hours later, Ivan surprised the officers by dropping by the department.

When Ivan sat down with Baer and Ramirez at 3:48 p.m., Baer explained the investigation and told Ivan he wasn't under arrest and could leave whenever he wanted. The officers began by asking him when he moved in with the Blakes, to which he responded at the beginning of September. He also said Jon Jr. moved into the house "two to three weeks ago" and that Jon Sr. was living at the house when he moved in.

Ivan told the detectives that his son went to stay with his ex-wife for the weekend on the Friday before Brenda's disappearance. On the day of Brenda's death, Ivan's plan was to get up early and drive to Topeka to work on his house before receiving an insulin treatment. That morning, Jon Jr. asked if he could go with him.

Ivan said that he and Jon Jr. stopped at Banjo Belly's, a café in south Topeka not far from Forbes Field, a civil-military airport, for breakfast before going to his house in Tecumseh, where they stayed for a while before driving to St. Francis Hospital at about noon.

When Ivan told Jon Jr. that his treatment would take a couple of hours, Jon Jr. said he was going to meet friends at a tavern, the Full

Moon Saloon, a few blocks from the hospital on 6th Street. After leaving the hospital later that afternoon, Ivan went into the bar, had a beer, and played darts with Jon Jr. and a woman he didn't know.

Ivan said they left the saloon and arrived back in Dover at 4 p.m., but wasn't sure of the exact time. However, that time didn't line up with what Jon Jr. said during his confession or witness accounts.

After pulling into the Blakes' driveway, Ivan said he and Jon Jr. went inside, where the former stayed for 10 to 15 minutes before leaving to drive back to Topeka. He stopped at Wendy's, ate dinner, and returned to Tecumseh, where he stayed until Sunday morning.

Baer and Ramirez asked if Jon Jr. was drunk, and Ivan responded that he did not appear to be when they got to the Blakes'. The officers also asked if he appeared to be high or was selling drugs in the bar, and Ivan said no again.

Ivan told the detectives he'd never seen Brenda riding her bike and that he typically left Dover between 6:30 a.m. to 7 a.m. in the morning to drop his son off at Shawnee Heights High School in Topeka before working on his house. He said he usually didn't return to Dover until 7 p.m. or later.

When Ivan finished the interview, he told Baer and Ramirez that they could call him if they had any more questions.

'HE WAS TRIPPING'

On the same day Baer and Ramirez interviewed Ivan, fellow detectives Richard Mergen and J.D. Mauck stopped by the Full Moon Saloon to track down information on Jon Jr. They interviewed Jeff Ford, who was tending bar on Saturday afternoon.

Mergen and Mauck began by checking on Jon Jr.'s story about a woman named Anita, and Ford told them that she was not in the bar on Saturday and was working at another bar after leaving the Full Moon Saloon several months earlier.

The detectives also asked Ford about the room upstairs where Jon Jr. said he had sex with Anita. Ford responded that the rooms were privately rented to another man and not part of the business.

When Mergen and Mauck showed Ford a photo lineup, Ford recognized two people who were in the bar, including Jon Jr. on Saturday. The other man was not in the bar that day.

Ford stated that Jon Jr. "was in and out" of the tavern that day and drank several large drafts of beer. He said that he remembered Ivan, who did not talk much while he was there and "watched other people."

Ford added that Jon Jr. offered to sell him 100 pounds of marijuana and acid that day, showing him a bud of the former that was wrapped in a Kleenex. When the officers asked him if he was drunk or high, Ford said "he was tripping" and may have been under the influence of drugs. Ford also noted that Jon Jr. drank about six large beers in the three-and-a-half hours he was at the bar.

Ford, who saw news reports showing Jon Jr. on TV the day after the murder, said that Ivan and Jon Jr. left the bar in a red car with "TAMSTOY" on the license plate at 4:30 p.m.

As Mergen and Mauck interviewed Ford, Wanamaker responded to a call from Sandy Mitchell, who wanted to tell officers about the voices she heard on the Blakes' property during the search for Brenda. Mitchell told Wanamaker that the voices were close as she waited outside the barn east of the pond.

Mitchell told Wanamaker she never saw the person or persons speaking, including the individual who said, "Oh, God," and was not 100 percent certain that that was what the person said. Mitchell said she did not see anybody when she shined her flashlight in the direction of the voices.

Many law enforcement officers working that night speculate that Jon Jr. was attempting to conceal the crime when he realized there were several people on the land.

"The other thing that sticks out in my mind about this case, is I heard they actually found where this clown had dropped the shovel and his intent was to bury her, but he got interrupted by the search party," Wanamaker said. "Absolutely, he was going to hide her. He was going to bury her so nobody could find her. Chances are, he may have been well aware there were search parties out. I think he waited until dark, was going to bury her, and got interrupted."

'NO WAY, NO WAY, NO WAY'

As Terri Morin drove to work on the Monday after Brenda's murder, she was in a good mood. Five months removed from her ordeal with Jon Jr., she was beginning to move on and focused on her job at Wolf Creek. Her mood shifted when she turned on the radio.

"I heard he was arrested for raping and killing a little girl, and I thought, 'Oh my God!'" Frederick said. "I actually turned around and went back home and went to bed. I'm happy nothing happened to my kids, but that poor girl. That devastated me more than anything to hear that and think that could have been me. It was crazy."

Many others who knew Jon Jr. were stunned when they saw on the news or read in the paper that he was arrested for murder. Some didn't believe it was true or that he was guilty.

"A friend of mine called and said, 'You need to turn on the news,'" Becky Taylor said. "I remember turning on the TV and seeing him on the screen, and I thought, 'What the hell?' Jon's been in jail a lot, but never been on TV. I remember sitting down and seeing 'murder' underneath his name, and I was like, 'Wow. No way, no way, no way.'"

Taylor and Jon Jr. were close, even after their breakup in high school, but he didn't reach out to her after he was arrested. He did call Kim Hardesty.

"When that happened, I had just seen him on TV," she said. "It scared the hell out of me. At that time, my daughter was only 4 years old. I just freaked out. There was a bunch of us who were in the program together, and, boy, my phone started ringing off the wall. We were all just shocked. It scared me so bad that when he called I told him, 'Jon, I can't believe this.'"

Jon Jr. told Kim during that call that he didn't kill Brenda. She asked him not to call again. He did anyway, and she didn't answer the phone.

"I didn't even follow the story," she said. "I told him I didn't have nothing to say and didn't want to have anything else to do with him."

Jon Jr. made one other phone call in his first few days at the Topeka Correctional Facility, a brazen one to Tammy Blake to ask her and Gene for help.

"I just blew up," she said. "We had people, company here at the time to help. I told him, 'You've ruined our lives. Don't ever, ever call me again.'"

That was the last time Tammy Blake spoke to her nephew.

CHAPTER TWELVE:

'MY STRAWBERRY IS GONE'

While murders in the rural sections of Shawnee County and the surrounding counties such as Wabaunsee and Osage were rare, the area wasn't immune to infamous homicides. Twelve years before Brenda died, one of the most notorious crimes in northeast Kansas had ties to Harveyville.

On May 20, 1979, just two months after Brenda's birth, 12-year-old John "Jack" Hanrahan left his family's home in Topeka to ride his bike across a field to Gage Bowl, where the boy played pinball. Wearing a blue or gray shirt, beige pants, and brown shoes, Jack made it to the bowling alley but disappeared after playing several games.

Ten days later, after a massive search and public outcry, a 16-year-old fishing on Dragoon Creek discovered the 4-foot-11, 85-pound child's body nine feet inside the Osage County line and just outside of Harveyville in Wabaunsee County. Many of the law enforcement officers involved in Brenda's case worked the Hanrahan investigation as members of the Major Case Squad, a consortium of police and sheriff's departments in northeast Kansas assigned to significant cases.

"I have a lot of memories on that one," Bill Kilian said. "I was at the scene out in Harveyville after the boy was found. We developed at least two persons of interest, and one of the suspects was a priest."

The M-Squad found Hanrahan's bike the day after he vanished about a mile south of the bowling alley, but officers never discovered the clothes he wore that day. By the time the teen found his body in the creek, Hanrahan had to be identified through dental records and skeletal X-rays.

Because the area of discovery was so difficult to access, the squad theorized that whoever kidnapped him dumped his body from a bridge up the creek. The autopsy revealed that Hanrahan was sexually mutilated and strangled. With little to go on, the Topeka Police Department struggled to solve the case. A few months after the murder, William "Freight Train" Gautney, a serial killer who traveled across the country on trains, was charged. However, the charges were dropped when officers obtained information placing Gautney out of the state on May 20.

"You've got to have the evidence," crime scene officer R.J. Warrington, who worked the Hanrahan and Keller cases, said. "You hate to see stuff like that happen. That's the stuff that sticks with you."

The lack of physical evidence in the Hanrahan murder has amplified the notoriety of the case for more than 40 years now. Despite thousands of leads and the identification of a prime suspect in the late 1990s, plus a subsequent trial and acquittal, the 12-year-old's murder remains unsolved to this day. The failure to give the Hanrahan family justice fueled officers for decades, including while working on Brenda's case.

"I think about this case from time to time; I think about all of them," said Jack Metz, who began working at the Sheriff's Department two years before Hanrahan's murder. "A lot of police officers will say it doesn't bother me, but, yes, it bothers us when you get a child like that."

REALITY SETS IN

She had a connection with all of her students, but Brenda was special to Pam Leptich. At a time in their lives where the hormones of 12- and 13-year-olds were raging, Brenda was a calming influence, she said. Leptich remembers the last time she saw Brenda, who gave a speech during class the Friday before she died.

"I can still see her there," Leptich said. "I remember she was a little shy about speaking in front of the others. There was nothing hidden about that child."

Like all of the teachers at the Dover schools, Leptich struggled mightily in the days after Brenda's death, especially how to handle the return to classes the day after the funeral. But, Bob and Tracy gave her an opportunity to help Brenda's classmates and teachers, as well as the rest of the community, cope when they asked Leptich to deliver the eulogy.

"I didn't know how I was going to approach it, so I went out into the country, drove around for two hours, and took a recorder with me," she said. "I just started saying things and giving my memories of Brenda. Once I decided the track I wanted to take, that I wanted to go with, it wrote itself."

While that request provided a bit of a distraction for Leptich, others in Dover desperately looked for something similar. For the kids, that meant hanging out at the church, where numerous parents took turns hosting get-togethers to try to keep the children's minds on anything but what happened and to keep them away from the news media. Aside from TV trucks, reporters, and cameras, Dover resembled a ghost town on the Monday and Tuesday before Brenda's funeral.

"You think the world is going to stop," Kristi Osburn said. "Life goes on, but you don't know what to do. I remember it being a blurry, weird time."

It also was a time of guilt. Many of the members of the volleyball team on the bus with Brenda on Oct. 19 remembered that she asked them to go for a ride with her that day. They asked themselves if she would still be alive had they said yes. Her closest friends had to regroup.

Overnight, a town where people left their doors unlocked while they slept went on lockdown. Doors and windows were double-checked every day, and parents slept with their kids at their feet and guns on their nightstands.

"My kids' biggest nightmare from this whole event is they can remember their dad standing in the backyard with a gun," said Penny Lister, "and they were like, 'Dad's going to shoot somebody.' This was a game-changer for everybody because all of a sudden we were not protected here. We were not safe anywhere because if it can happen in Dover, it can happen anywhere."

THE WAKE

To say the weather in Kansas is unpredictable is putting it mildly, especially in the fall. One year to the day before Brenda's visitation and funeral, the temperature ranged from a low of 31 degrees to a high of 66. Eight days after the service, on Halloween night, a winter storm blasted the region. But on Oct. 23, 1991, the weather couldn't have been better with a low of 62 degrees and an unseasonably warm high of 88, combined with a bright sun and a 15-mile-per-hour breeze.

Though many have blocked out the wake taking place before the funeral, several of her friends have vivid memories of seeing their classmate in a casket, including one who said it looked like she was "obliterated." Others said Brenda did not resemble the striking young girl they knew.

"I remember walking in and walking up to the casket and standing there and looking into the casket, seeing her face … and her face was just huge," Autumn Buchmeier said. "You could see dark blue streaks under her skin, and I remember asking my mom what those were and why it looked like that."

Others couldn't bring themselves to look at their friend in that state.

"I felt down or started getting sick, and I didn't look at her," Crystal Sievers said. "To this day, I have not forgiven myself for not looking. I beat myself up for that moment my entire life, not being strong enough to look, and I think that has caused a lack of closure."

The Kellers did their best to hold it together. Still, Brenda's brothers would have rather been in a cave than surrounded by people watching them grieve.

"I didn't want people to feel sorry for me," Pat said.

Roy, the stoic member of the family, scanned the church from a distance, watching his granddaughter's friends hang their heads and weep as they walked between the pews, until he saw one of Brenda's best friends overwhelmed with sadness.

"I stayed clear to the back, except when Misty (Lange) was walking through," he said. "She was broken."

Tyrel Buchmeier did his best to console Pat, but, even at age 9, he came to the realization that life was never going to be the same in Dover.

"Hypothetically, the Friday before this, you'd ride your bike all over," he said. "You'd ride up to the school, you'd play basketball, you'd ride your skateboard. You did whatever you wanted as a kid. All your parents knew is you were in Dover,.and that was good enough. Before, it was you hop on your bike and, 'Hey, Mom, I'm going to do X,' and you just went and did it. I remember shortly after this telling my mom I'm going to do X and she said, 'No, you're not.' I just remember that Dover was changed. And in 12 hours."

QUITE THE SPECTACLE

As they prepared to walk across the street to Brenda's wake and funeral on Wednesday, her family endured a range of emotions. Bob's sister Beverly felt like she was in a dream, still struggling to believe such a horrific tragedy could happen to them. John and Pat put all their energy into not crying. Roy and Jean tried to be strong for their family but also planned to be in the background as much as they possibly could. Bob, in the role of pastor, stayed busy trying to comfort visitors.

Before the Keller family left for the church, they received a phone call that morning from Gene Blake. He offered his condolences to Bob and Tracy, apologizing for any perceived role he and his wife played in Brenda's death.

"I didn't blame them," Bob said. "How many times do any of us do something, and we don't know what's going to happen? I don't hold them responsible."

Shortly after the call, Bob brought his family together for a prayer. From Grandpa Roy to 9-year-old Pat, they held hands as Bob spoke about mercy and how they should forgive Jon Jr.

"We have to be able to forgive," Jean said of her son's words that day. "If we didn't forgive, we would be hurting worse than we are. I feel like I've forgiven, but I'll never forget."

When the wake ended and the Kellers were walking to the junior high for Brenda's service, they realized how much she meant to the community. By the early afternoon, shortly before the funeral began at the school, there were hundreds of people in Dover. Cars lined both sides of Douglas Road for more than a mile, and there was a throng of people outside the building who couldn't get inside.

"Everybody was there," Tyrel Buchmeier said. "I don't think there was anybody within 10 miles of Dover who wasn't there that day. The family was too well-known."

There also were hundreds of people at the service who didn't know Brenda or her family. With the media coverage came well-wishers from across the country. Bob and Tracy received letters from people in several states, and dozens of the cars on Douglas Road had license plates from places other than Kansas. For some in the community, the idea of becoming a spectacle wasn't welcome.

"I was amazed by the people there, but also mad because they didn't know her," Amy Best said. "I think the biggest struggle was very few people understood, and so many people being sad. What right did people have? I remember being mad about that."

FROZEN IN TIME

There were two groups of people some Dover residents didn't want to see as they mourned for Brenda: the media and the Blakes. Though the Kellers asked that the former not attend, there were reporters with cameras and microphones. One tried to interview Lange as she left the church for the junior high.

"Misty cussed her out and said, 'How do you think I feel?'" Brooklynd Thomas said.

Reporters bore the brunt of anger from many in Dover, even if they were just doing their jobs. Being there didn't sit well with Roberta Peterson, the Topeka Capital-Journal writer working undercover. That changed moments after she arrived when she realized several of her friends were attending the service.

"I get there, and I don't know these people at all, but the main sanctuary is full of people I know," she said. "They think it's natural that I'm there and pull me toward the front. I still felt bad about it. What it came down to was all I really did was tell his (Bob's) story, and that was what the public wanted to hear at that point."

Getting a spot near the front was fortuitous. By 1:45 p.m., the junior high was completely full. The small gym contained so many people that the other rooms in the school and the basement served as additional seating. Room by room, folding chairs filled quickly, and stereo speakers in each provided the sound. In her story in the next day's paper, Peterson wrote, "When Brenda Keller's funeral began at 2 p.m., later arrivals lined the school halls, sat on the stairs and eventually gathered in groups outside the building, where extra speakers were placed." Estimates of the number of people who attended ranged from 600 to 1,000.

"Because she (Tracy) was in radio at the time, there was a lot of the outpouring of support," Bob said. "You just felt like the church, the body of Christ, was lifting you up in prayer."

Keller family friend Byron Waldy, who later served as a counselor for John and Pat, officiated the service, talking about wonderful memories and respect those he spoke to in the days leading up to the funeral had for Brenda. Peterson's article said he spoke of Brenda's love for animals, riding her bike, and whistling.

"As if in response," Peterson wrote, "the gusty Indian summer winds whistled loudly through the windows and rattled the shades in the rooms throughout the junior high."

Several schoolmates, almost all of whom sat at the front of the service in the gym, shared their memories and love of Brenda. They led the large group in singing some of Brenda's favorite songs, including "Awesome God." Another tune, Amy Grant's "I Will Remember You," which includes the line "See that I don't want to say goodbye, our love is frozen in time," touched Sievers deeply.

"I still can't hear that song without crying," she said.

One of the most poignant moments came when Leptich delivered the eulogy. She struggled with the decision to speak at the service, then spent hours thinking about what to say. As she walked to the podium in the gym, with the sun streaming through the windows and the school's painted Tiger mascot shining on the wall off to the side, she looked at Brenda's classmates and her students before speaking directly to them:

"Memories happen because something is too good to let go. Each of us will tomorrow, the next day and the next have our memories of Brenda. The special way she touched lives, and life is more than a memory and more than something too good to let go. The poet Barrie wrote, 'God gave us memories so that we might have roses in

December." Brenda gives us memories so that we never have to say goodbye.

"Brenda's whistle, her special way with special words, her quiet, consistent kindness, her love of all living things, the way she turned plain canvas into visions, will be with us each time a kind word is spoken, each time a joy is shared, each time a living thing is protected, each time we smile.

"We miss her presence among us because we want more from her. We miss her presence among us because we want to give more to her. But we have not lost the chance for either. We can forever give to and receive from Brenda.

"Kids, whistle again. Laugh again. Pet your dogs and cats, tease Mr. Z, and again and again know that your friendship, one for the other, makes Brenda happy. Throughout our lives, any day we say a good word, laugh a long laugh, feel good enough to whistle, treat a living thing with kindness, we can say, 'Thank you, Brenda.'"

'FORGIVENESS IS AVAILABLE TO ALL'

While Beverly and her husband Steve were at the service, a small bug crawled toward them and several others, and somebody close by attempted to squash it. Steve waved the person off, saying, "Don't do that. Brenda wouldn't want you to do that."

That was a fitting tribute among many that day for the little girl, but the greatest one came as the funeral came to a close. Bob, who originally planned not to speak, changed his mind. He gathered his strength, walked to the podium, and looked at the hundreds of people crammed in the gym. His first words, "My Strawberry is gone," brought more tears, but his message was one of forgiveness, and his goal was to lift a community buckling to hate.

"I was hearing a little bit about anger," he said. "I was hearing about people burning the Blakes' house down, and I just thought I needed to defuse things."

Peterson realized immediately that she was in Dover to share Bob's message of compassion. In her story, she quoted much of his speech:

"Brenda would have understood that I could not pass up the opportunity to talk to a crowd of this size. It (a picture in his office that Brenda liked) is called 'The Homecoming,' and it depicts a person in the arms of Jesus Christ being welcomed to heaven. That is what keeps us going. We know that, last Saturday, Brenda experienced that greeting, and in His healing, caring arms, all grief and pain was swept away.

"But she's not there because she loved animals, or drew pretty pictures, or wore T-shirts that said she was going to heaven. She's there because she asked God to forgive her of her sins, accepted that forgiveness and received Christ as her Savior and Lord.

"And that forgiveness is available to all, even to the man who took her life.

"I saw my daughter in her casket for the first time yesterday. She was holding her Bible in her arms. I opened it to the place where she had been reading, where her bookmark was. And there, in bold type, were the words, 'Love your enemies.' I have to believe that God was speaking to me, and perhaps Brenda, too. Through this tragic time, we have to remember to love, and not to hate."

The message, particularly Bob asking for forgiveness for the man who murdered his daughter, had a resounding effect on those attending the service. Dottie Wendland said to herself, "Bob, how can you do this?" Janet Baldwin was overwhelmed that he could forgive at all, let alone so quickly. Her husband, Greg, noticed that someone who just couldn't forgive so soon got up and left the service. Best wondered if Tracy, John, and Pat shared the sentiment or were angered by it. Others, like Lister, said it was one of the most courageous things they've ever seen.

"It was like he wasn't there, like he was super-human. I just don't know how he did it," Lister said. "There were probably people there who had never set foot in a church, maybe had never heard a true salvation message. He did a fantastic job."

Several people, including Lavella Buchmeier, said it strengthened their trust in God.

"To listen to Bob speak, to talk about forgiveness so soon … was the most amazing moment in my Christian faith, my walk with God," she said.

Ultimately, Bob wanted his last tribute to his daughter to be one she would have believed in, a message from God.

"Robert felt like that was the last thing he could do for Brenda," Jean said. "And he delivered a terrific message."

Bob didn't consider his speech that day super-human. He felt like he had to help others as much as possible.

"I don't know how other pastors do it, but when I'm pastoring a funeral, whether it's an older person, or someone who is a good friend, or it's a child, you have a professional reverence to do your job," he said. "You don't want to be out there crying. You're there to provide comfort. I remember wondering why I wasn't falling part … I was doing a job. I wanted to see if there was a way to help. I think in my mind that's what I was doing. I don't think I was strong. I had all those people, and there's that sense that you had to make it so this counted for Brenda, so I shared what I did about God's grace."

Years later, Bob expanded on his message.

"I didn't say at the funeral that I'd forgiven Jon Mareska," he said. "We started expressing forgiveness from God's willingness to forgive. When I see stories about other people who go through this, or other girls that are treated like this, I become extremely angry. That's why I like to watch movies and things (about crime). It helps me ventilate. I'm not any special anything, but I think it helped us to forgive, to say we forgive, so that those feelings wouldn't just destroy us."

NOT WELCOME

Many in the community didn't care to see Gene and Tammy Blake at the service. Though the couple received anonymous threatening phone calls and pressure from others to move, they stayed strong and attended the funeral after calling Bob. The reception the Blakes received that day was chilly.

"They were there and we sat together, and that may have had something to do with people being cooler to us," Leon Sievers said. "People didn't talk to them at the funeral."

The Blakes managed to stay busy in the days leading up to the funeral by scrambling to protect Jon Sr., the target of many of the phone calls. They temporarily placed him with his mother in Topeka, and Mary Sievers helped the Blakes find a permanent home for Jon Sr. away from Dover.

"People were threatening to kill Big Jon," Mary Sievers said. "Tammy called and said, 'Is there anything you can do to help me?' and I said yes. I pulled some strings at the VA and got him admitted there, so they got him in for an evaluation."

That evaluation was finished and submitted on the day of the funeral. According to Shawnee County Sheriff's Office files on Brenda's case, Abigail Moore, a doctor at the Colmery-O'Neil Veterans Administration Medical Center in Topeka, wrote District Court Judge Charles Andrew, requesting a court order for the treatment of Jon Sr.

In the letter, Moore wrote, "Mr. Mareska is a mentally ill person who is considered a danger to himself due to his inability to comprehend the dangerous situation awaiting him at home. He exercises poor judgment and lacks insight into his illness and what has transpired in the past few days. ... He has been unable to live alone since the accident of 12/7/90, which caused brain damage. ... The community (Dover) met and requested of the family, in the form of threats, that Mr. Mareska not be allowed to live in the area. ... He has threatened to 'get even with, to kill the person who hurt him.' He is referring to the man who caused the injuries which caused his brain damage."

Moore's statement was accompanied by a document from Nancy Hildreth, a social worker at the VA Medical Center. She submitted an application for determination of mental illness to the court, noting that Jon Sr. "has been unable to care for his own personal hygiene, is not able to prepare meals," according to the department's case files.

Moore and Hildreth declined to comment on the letter and application, citing physician-patient and social worker-client privilege.

"I did that for Tammy, not him," Mary Sievers said. "And he subsequently ended up in a nursing home."

The Blakes, who endured the loss of their oldest son just seven years earlier, had plenty to handle. Though most weren't sympathetic, others felt for the family.

"I'd been neighbors with them for several years, and I liked Gene and Tammy," Allen Moran said. "I know Gene and Tammy were just devastated when they found out what happened, and they were kind of shunned by the community. I know they didn't have anything to do with it, but they were blamed for allowing it to happen. They suffered a lot themselves."

More than 30 years later, there are several people in Dover who have not said a word to Gene and Tammy Blake since Brenda's death.

WHEN DOVES STAY

Once Bob finished his message, the service moved to the cemetery to the south and just off Douglas Road, less than a quarter mile from the school and the same distance from where Brenda died. Because there were so many people at the event and so many cars along the road, everybody walked down the highway to the spot where her headstone would rest.

"It was a huge, huge funeral," Ted Lassen said. "I've never seen anything like it in Dover. There was a huge entourage of police, there were motorcycles. It's probably the biggest event they've ever had in Dover."

The Kellers did their best to keep it together. Jean got through her son's message of forgiveness, but she didn't make it through the final portion of the service at the cemetery, leaving with her sister.

"We had to go out and sit in the car," Aunt B said. "Jeannie said, 'I can't talk to anybody.' I said, 'You don't have to talk to anybody.'"

Tracy appeared to be handling the event well, though she says years later that she was "out of it." Janice noticed at one point that Tracy even laughed when some people talked to her that day, but said, "I thought, 'How could she laugh?' and I judged that. I realized you're not there really. You're going through the process. Later, that hurt really comes."

Among the convoy of people at the cemetery were law enforcement officers from the Sheriff's Department and attorneys from the DA Office. All were there to pay their respects, but they were also working. David Debenham and Maggie Lutes took in the environment, getting a sense of the psychology of the community and the impact Brenda's murder had on it. Meanwhile, members of the Sheriff's Department videotaped the service to see who attended and find more potential evidence.

"We were back where we could hear it," Lutes said. "It was very moving, very moving. The community was so overwhelmingly grieving. There was overwhelming sadness at such a loss of this beautiful child who had so much going for her."

Overwhelming sadness was an apt description for the mindset of Brenda's schoolmates. Two days before the funeral, Bob asked Waldy if they could find a way to include Brenda's friends and other children at the school in the service. Waldy, who previously worked for Warren and Susan Wilson at Joy 88, called Susan to see if she had any ideas.

"It was that Monday that this woman called and said they have a service or business where they will bring white doves and release them," said Susan Wilson, who took a van of employees to the service. "They asked me if I wanted to hire them to do this, and I said, 'Well, I don't know.' Byron called me and said the students are just so distraught and want to do something to help. What can they do that's tangible that might help them in their healing?"

Moments after Brenda was laid to rest with several hundred people surrounding her burial plot, her classmates lined up, took a dove, and released it. One by one, the doves took off for the sky, but instead of flying out of the area immediately, as they typically did, they fluttered into the trees surrounding the cemetery and watched over the crowd for several minutes.

"The husband and wife told me, 'This is unbelievable. As soon as they're released, they go straight home. They're flying around in the trees,' Susan Wilson said. "They knew there was something going on, something more than us.'"

When the doves did leave the trees, they flew to the southwest. A few minutes later, as Larry Lister and his son, who did not attend the funeral, worked in their yard, several doves coasted into the yard, flew around a tractor on the property, and turned to the north before leaving Dover.

"They went out and came back over to the south, and my thought was surely they're not going to go back over the Blakes' house," Penny Lister said. "But they probably did. There was a reason."

THE HARD PART

Once the service ended, and after dozens of people spoke with the Kellers, the crowd slowly dissipated as attendees walked to their cars and headed home. While the Buchmeiers drove to their house just west of Dover, Autumn Buchmeier leaned forward from the backseat, sticking her head between the two front seats to talk to her mother.

"I was propping myself between the seats and asked 8 million why questions and was not getting any good answers," she said. "I understand as an adult why I didn't get any answers."

The service was a transition for many that day. From the shock of Brenda's murder, to the enormous grief that was just beginning, to questions lasting a lifetime … many of which will never be answered.

Once the Kellers were home, they realized that Jean was gone. As it turned out, she was alone with her granddaughter, as she had been thousands of times before.

"Mom was missing, nobody knew where she was," said Beverly, "and they found her. She had gone over to the cemetery and was just there by herself."

After several days of planning his daughter's funeral and trying to comfort his family, Bob finally had a chance to breathe that night. He knew reality was about to set in.

"That's when the hard part came in ... the hearings and court," he said.

CHAPTER THIRTEEN:

THE NEW NORMAL

Normalcy. Dover craved it after Brenda's murder. Her friends and other children yearned for the freedom to ride their bikes up and down the roadways leading out of town. The adults yearned for the security of knowing that they didn't have to worry about their kids.

The day after the funeral, the community took a step toward something resembling normal when the grade school and junior high reopened. For days, students and teachers did their best to keep busy.

"I don't think that there was any getting over it. It lives on in everybody's mind," Terri Anderson said. "There were lots of tears from classmates, and a lot of mention of her faith. There was some fear, too, but the counselors were there."

The district deployed a small army of counselors to the schools, including Mark Erickson, who doubled as the liaison to the media, which was still in town looking for stories. The counselors spoke to a number of kids in the week after Brenda died.

"I thought there would be a lot more anger, as angry as I was," Erickson said. "The media had fourth and fifth graders talking and asked them what they thought of it, and I told them that's a difficult question for a 10-year-old child."

All the support from the community wasn't enough for some. Pat went back to school almost immediately, but felt embarrassed and thought everybody was looking at him. Amy Best struggled so much that she only stayed in school for a few days before her mother took her on a trip to Chicago.

"I was just not comfortable being there," she said. "I needed to get away."

Dottie Wendland had one student, a little boy, who wouldn't stop crying.

"Most of the kids were pretty somber about the whole thing for several days," she said. "I just felt like the best thing to do after that was kind of go on and do things as ritualistically as we normally did and keep the kids going."

Some of the teachers found reconnecting with John and Pat to be a challenge. Pat never spoke about his sister, and John skipped school often. Allen Zordel, who taught and coached all three Keller children, had a difficult time even talking to the brothers after Brenda died.

"It was quiet," he said. "Everybody was on eggshells. John was pretty much the same, as much as could be expected, but Patrick lost a lot of his orneriness. He had been like Dennis the Menace."

While life got closer to ordinary the further the community got from Oct. 19, there was a Dover before Brenda and a Dover after Brenda. Her schoolmates were sad for months, and some struggled for years.

"It was prevalent. I remember her being talked about frequently," Pam Leptich said. "There was an emptiness and sadness that lasted the whole year. But everybody locked eyes, understanding we were suffering, and I said maybe the best thing was to have class like Brenda was there."

But she wasn't there, and that void deeply impacted her younger brother. During nearly every recess, as his classmates played, Pat was far off in the distance, away from the action. After a few days, Wendland realized he was at the edge of the grade school grounds, sitting against the fence separating the field from the cemetery. Day after day and recess after recess, he settled into the grass, looking forlornly to the south at his sister's headstone.

"He'd be gone, and there was another boy that would go down and be with him," said Wendland, "and I thought that was such a good thing. He was such a good friend. He just would go down and be with Pat. And it was like, 'I'm here and you can talk to me.'"

The boy was Pat's best friend, Tyrel Buchmeier. Day after day and recess after recess, he was by his side.

SHORT, BUT POWERFUL

On the day classes resumed at the junior high and grade school, Roberta Peterson's story on the funeral ran in the Topeka Capital-Journal. Printed on the front page with the headline "Brenda's father: Put hate aside," the article was the centerpiece and included a large, five-column photo of the pall bearers carrying Brenda's casket out of the junior high gym and placing it in a hearse. The left side of the photo, shot by longtime photographer John Bock, showed the Kellers walking out of the school, with a solemn Roy, Bob, Tracy, John, and Pat looking at the ground.

"John used a lens like you've never seen to make it look like he was that close, because he was not," Peterson said.

Earlier in the week, Peterson nearly quit when the newspaper's managing editor assigned her to cover the funeral after the family asked that the media not attend. She also was limited to writing a short 12-inch story, another guideline from the new editor and a practice almost unheard of at the time.

However, writing a succinct piece about Bob's harrowing message and one with rich descriptions of the setting proved to be perfect. Not being able to quote anyone but Bob from his speech made the story that much more meaningful.

"There were people I could have quoted, but not the main people," she said. "The constraint in the end actually made it a little more powerful because of the way people reacted to it. I have a very strong faith, and it was one of those things where I really felt like I was being put there."

Though she was pleased with what she wrote and the praise the Capital-Journal received for its coverage, Peterson still felt awful. The day after the funeral, she wrote Bob and Tracy a note, apologizing for not adhering to the family's request.

"I just said I was very uncomfortable knowing they'd requested not having anyone there, and he (Bob) said God put me there," Peterson said.

Though a few reporters didn't abide by the guidelines set by Anderson and Erickson regarding interviews, most of them were professional. Within a week of the murder, the coverage eased considerably as the community attempted to move on and begin healing.

One week after Brenda died, the junior high held a dance to celebrate Halloween. That was another difficult reminder for Tracy, who said Brenda was going to dress as a Tootsie Roll for the dance and to go trick-or-treating. The school originally planned to cancel the event, but several of Brenda's schoolmates protested.

"Nobody danced, but we were all together," Crystal Sievers said. "I think that's what we needed, to be together."

TIME FOR A BREAK

Bob always loved football. He played it growing up, starting on the offensive line at Minneapolis High School in the early 1970s for Dick Tatro, who served as a football coach for more than 30 years across Kansas. Roy said his son might have been even better at the sport if he didn't hate to hurt people. Nonetheless, Bob was part of a Lions team that posted the first winning season at Minneapolis in nine years with a 5-4 record in 1971.

Twenty years later, just a little more than a week after his daughter died, Bob hoped football would provide a little break from the hysteria. A longtime fan of the Kansas City Chiefs, he looked forward to watching the Monday Night Football game on TV between the Chiefs and their rival, the Los Angeles Raiders. Unfortunately, it was a short break.

"There was a knock at the door, and somebody I didn't know came over and was crying," Bob said. "I think they were thinking that they were comforting me, but they were crying. All of a sudden, I said, 'Tracy, I've got to get out of here. I can't do this anymore.' And we went."

After the funeral, a family friend offered to let Bob and Tracy stay in a cabin at a campground in Council Grove, a small town an hour southwest of Dover. Reality hit Bob during the couple's short stay.

"That's when it really hit me that the pastoral profession thing, it's not a fake thing, and you can't turn it off. I was in that role," he said.

Bob and Tracy weren't the only ones who needed to get away. While they were tucked away in a cabin in east central Kansas, Gene and Tammy Blake were staying in their small cabin off the river in Burlington. After days of anonymous phone calls, cold stares, and even one couple knocking on their door and asking them to leave town, the Blakes had enough.

"People were turning against us," Tammy Blake said. "We stayed in our cabin because we couldn't live here. The community was making it uncomfortable."

While the Blakes and Kellers were out of town, a local monument company went to work building a headstone to place at Brenda's grave site. The marker, funded partially by donations from members of the community, might be the most prominent one in Dover's small cemetery. Located at the east end of the yard, the headstone is made of white marble with a rectangular foundation. A heart-shaped top piece rests in a curved base, which features engraved pictures of a rat, in honor of Charlemagne, a turtle, and a smiling snake head.

The top stone has an etched Bible at the top and an image of a dog at the bottom, with Brenda's full name, date of birth, and date of death between them. A stone vase for flowers sits to the left of the base. About three feet to the left of the marker is a cement bench for people to sit while visiting Brenda.

"Bob's a little embarrassed about the grave," said Bill Lucero, a long-time friend. "He thinks it's a little over the top and thinks it makes them too important within the community. At the same time, I think he appreciates how much everybody showed they cared."

The Kellers returned home in the middle of the week, narrowly beating the snowstorm on Halloween night, which came on a Thursday in 1991. The storm, which dumped several inches of snow in northeast Kansas, was so powerful that most of the state's high school football games were postponed, and nobody in Dover went trick-or-treating. Not that many of the kids were in the mood less than two weeks after Brenda's death.

ONGOING INVESTIGATION

With a preliminary hearing scheduled for Dec. 10, the Shawnee County Sheriff's Office had about six weeks to gather additional evidence and conduct more interviews in Brenda's case. On the day after the funeral, detectives Mike Ramirez and Larry Baer interviewed Darrin Blake, the youngest son of Gene and Tammy. During Ivan's interview earlier in the week, he told the detectives Jon Jr. called Darrin Blake on the morning after Brenda's murder.

When the detectives interviewed Darrin, he said that Jon Jr. called him at his house in Topeka shortly before noon to say that he signed papers allowing the Sheriff's Department to search the house.

"He said that Mareska made it sound like he didn't know what was going on," said Ramirez's report, "'cause he had been asleep on the couch that morning when they awoke him conducting the search."

As the investigation continued, lead detective Jack Metz called Bob and Tracy on Nov. 4, asking to speak with them to clarify the details surrounding Brenda's disappearance. On the following day, Bob, Tracy, Roy, and Jean traveled to the Sheriff's Department to meet with Metz.

The detective asked the Kellers if their daughter had issues with anybody along the route she rode her bike on Oct. 19, to which Tracy replied that she never had a problem. Metz also asked if Brenda had any mechanical issues with her bike. Tracy said that the chain would come off at times, but her daughter had not had any problems with her bike recently. Bob added that the chain was typically an easy fix.

The Kellers outlined Brenda's day again, and one new detail emerged when Tracy noted that Jon Sr. didn't refer to Jon Jr. as his son.

"She then asked if anyone else was home and was advised by Jon Mareska Sr. that his nephew was there," Metz wrote in his report. "She asked if she could speak to his nephew and was told no, he was asleep on the couch. Mrs. Keller then stated that she wanted to get into the house to speak with anyone else in there. She asked for a drink of water and was granted entry by Jon Mareska Sr. She stated she went in and observed who she later learned to be Jon Mareska Jr. asleep on the couch. She had Jon Mareska Sr. try to wake Jon Mareska Jr., but was unable to wake him."

The following week, on Friday, Nov. 15, Tammy Blake arrived at the Sheriff's Department's crime lab in her Camaro. The department requested that the Blakes bring the car in to be processed for evidence. Crime scene officer R.J. Warrington vacuumed the driver's and passenger seat, the back seat, and the floorboards before taking photos of the interior and exterior. Warrington and fellow officer J.D. Sparkman looked for blood and other stains but found no signs of either. Thirty-seven minutes after she arrived, Tammy Blake left the department in her car. Warrington sent the particles and other items vacuumed to the Kansas Bureau of Investigation (KBI) for analysis.

The lab didn't finish processing those items for several weeks, but the Sheriff's Department did receive results Nov. 21 on other evidence in the case. According to the report submitted by the Bureau's forensic examiner the week of Nov. 25, Brenda's left shoe and sock, soil taken from outside the boathouse, her sweatshirt, jeans, right sock, the stick, and both of Jon Jr.'s shoes contained blood consistent with her type. In addition, blood found on her sweatshirt, the window frame, and the black jacket was consistent with the blood types of Brenda and Jon Jr.

Tested before advances in the technology, the blood and other bodily fluids were not examined for DNA. Investigators analyzed blood and saliva samples, along with vaginal, oral, and rectal swabs, at the laboratory.

The small stick was the only place where the Sheriff's Department found seminal fluid. The results on the semen revealed that the donor was a non-secretor. As part of the small population of males who are non-secretors (about 20%), the KBI's report stated that Jon Jr. "would be included as a possible donor." A non-secretor is an individual whose fluids contain very little, if any, blood type antigens.

The KBI preserved a portion of Brenda's blood, as well as Jon Jr.'s blood and saliva, for future analysis, if needed. More than 30 years later, the Sheriff's Department still stores much of the evidence from the case.

That week was a busy one for detectives, who also conducted a follow-up interview with Ivan. Two days before Thanksgiving, on Nov. 26, Metz and detective Tim Byers drove to his house early in the afternoon and asked to speak to him about the case. Ivan said he could stop by the Sheriff's Department after he picked up his son from school. An hour later, before driving to the school, he traveled to downtown Topeka, telling Metz "he wanted to get this over with before he picked up his son."

The officers explained that there were discrepancies in his previous interview that they needed him to clarify, and that they wanted Ivan to walk them through his day on Oct. 19 again. He reiterated that he left the Blakes' house early that morning with Jon Jr., had breakfast with him at the café in Pauline, and visited Ivan's house on Ratner Road before driving to St. Francis Hospital for an insulin treatment.

Ivan said that he joined Jon Jr. at the Full Moon Saloon, where he had one beer and played darts. He told the detectives that he was in the bar for 15 to 30 minutes before he and Jon Jr. left for Dover. He added that he could not remember if he drove along K-4 Highway northeast of Dover or Auburn Road to the east of the community, but "believed he arrived at the Blake residence around 4 p.m. to 4:30 p.m." Ivan said he went into the house for no more than 30 minutes, grabbed some clothes, and left.

Byers and Metz asked what Jon Jr. did after arriving back in Dover, and Ivan said he didn't know if he stayed inside or went outside. He saw Jon Sr. playing pool in the house by himself. After picking up the clothes, he drove back to Topeka on Douglas Road and 57th Street.

Metz responded by saying that witnesses saw the car he was driving that night heading east on 57th after 6 p.m., which was later than the time he indicated leaving Dover. Ivan said it was possible and that he wasn't sure of the times. He added that he remembered lying down on his bed and "might have dozed off for a few minutes, but it was not very long, but he could have lost track of time."

When the detectives pressed Ivan on the inconsistencies in his story, he said he understood and wanted to cooperate. "He was sure he had made a mistake on the time or just misjudged the time that he was there," according to the report.

When the detectives finished questioning Ivan, Metz asked him if he would give the department permission to take samples of his head hair, pubic hair, blood, and saliva. He readily did so, but asked if he needed to contact an attorney. Metz responded that he was not under arrest and could leave any time he wanted.

Before providing the department with the hair and saliva samples, Ivan told Metz that he was diabetic and impotent. He said he spoke with his doctor about it, and that "he prefer we not put this in the report, but if it became necessary, we could speak to his doctor in reference to this."

Moments later, Ivan left for St. Francis Hospital, where a staff member drew his blood and submitted it to Warrington.

AN EXTRA CHAIR

The holidays were always a big deal to the Kellers, and they gathered at Thanksgiving and Christmas every year, usually at Roy and Jean's house. As Bob, Janice, and Beverly had more children, the meals became large and exhaustive. That didn't change in 1991, even though Thanksgiving, on Nov. 28, was just a little more than a month removed from Brenda's death.

"I just remember how hard that was," Jean said. "Brenda was always kind of the life of the party."

Jean tried desperately to help the family adjust without her granddaughter, going as far as counting the chairs multiple times at the long line of tables she and Roy connected in their living room. Somehow, she still miscounted.

"I swear somebody came in and put another chair down because there was just one chair too many," she said. "Our first times back together as a family were so very difficult."

Try as they might, it was still a somber day, even after the family went to the church, where the children rode their scooters on the ramp in the parking lot. Later, several members of the family went to a movie.

"They just needed something to forget," Jean said. "I remember how everybody tried so hard to make it a fun time."

Not long after she hosted Thanksgiving, Jean had an extremely difficult day thinking about Brenda. Tracy stopped by for a visit and spoke with Roy, who said, "Mom's having a hard time today." Tracy walked into the kitchen, where Jean was trying to work, wrapped her arms around her mother-in-law, and held on tight.

"I'd been crying, and I just couldn't stop," Jean said. "She put her arms around me, and we both cried for a little while."

'THE EASY WAY OUT'

Few cases impacted attorney David Debenham more than Brenda's. He grew up in Lindsborg, a small town in central Kansas known for its large Swedish, Nordic, Scandinavian, and German heritages. The city also is the location of one of the state's most gruesome crimes, the triple-murder of three children 7 and younger by their father, Christopher Jones. Those murders took place just a few days shy of the eight-year anniversary of Brenda's murder.

"A lot of small towns, you think nothing like this is going to happen," Debenham said. "I don't know if Lindsborg ever had a murder."

Brenda's case also hit close to home because Debenham's oldest daughter was only 3 years old in 1991.

"It's one of those father-daughter things," he said. "You think about your daughter, and you think, 'Oh, God, bad things happen to good people.' As a father, you think, 'How am I going to protect my kids as they go through the years?'"

Debenham worked closely with the Kellers throughout the various court proceedings, beginning with preparing them for the preliminary hearing held less than two weeks after Thanksgiving. Going into that hearing, Bob and Tracy knew the death penalty wasn't an option, as Kansas abolished capital punishment from 1972 through 1994. Despite what happened to their daughter, neither wanted the death penalty for Jon Jr.

"That's the easy way out," Tracy said. "I would not want him to be out because I would never want him to do that to someone else."

"Biblically, the Bible says if you take a life, your life is forfeited, so I cannot say like some people do that it's just wrong," Bob added. "With the system now, the cost of the death penalty is so high, with the appeals and all the years."

The Kellers showing empathy for the murderer of their daughter moved Debenham, who worked with dozens of families of victims who wanted vengeance and "people to swing for their crime."

"They were unbelievable to work with," he said. "(Brenda's) grandparents, father, and mother met with us on numerous occasions. We were always amazed that they wanted justice, but they weren't vindictive. They hurt deeply, but we were amazed at how they could reasonably talk about it."

Several times during the next six months, Bob and Tracy met with Debenham to discuss the possibilities: Is the case going to trial, is the District Attorney's Office going to offer a plea or accept a plea offer, and what approach would the attorneys take?

"You look at yourself and think, 'How would I react in this situation?'" Debenham said. "We were always amazed at how well they kept it together."

THE PRELIMINARY HEARING

Tensions were high on the morning of Tuesday, Dec. 10, for the preliminary hearing in the State of Kansas vs. Jon H. Mareska Jr. Held at the Shawnee County Courthouse in downtown Topeka, the hearing featured a small army of security due to threats against the defendant, along with a requirement that every person entering the courtroom that day pass through a metal detector manned by deputies.

Byron Cerrillo, widely regarded as a sharp and sly lawyer, represented Jon Jr. Cerrillo worked at the Sheriff's Department in the mid-1980s before becoming a public defender in Shawnee and Johnson counties. Cerrillo worked some of the highest profile cases in Kansas before he died in 2006, including representing serial killer John Edward Robinson in the early 2000s.

"I'm not going to lie to you ... he was a little slimy at times," former Shawnee County attorney Maggie Lutes said. "He was not above a little shade here and there, but he was a good attorney, and he was going to do a good job for his clients. He was very skilled, and he had done a lot of cases by then."

Cerrillo demonstrated his craftiness that morning. As several witnesses waited to enter the courtroom, he and Jon Jr. walked up to them, and Cerrillo tried to introduce his client to each one, Penny Lister said.

"He wanted us to shake his hand," she said. "(Jon Jr.) did not offer, he just walked. His attorney was a piece of work."

It took a while to fill the courtroom because officers searched purses for weapons, in addition to guiding people through the detector. Jean set it off several times while walking through, even after she emptied her pockets and purse.

"That lady would look at me, and I would put everything I had out," she said. "Finally, I went through and it went off, and I just said, 'I think it's the broken heart of a grandma.'"

Minutes before the proceeding began, the courtroom was at capacity, with 52 spectators and members of the media in the small space, according to the Topeka Capital-Journal. Reporter Steve Fry's story noted that three Department of Corrections officers sat within 15 feet of Jon Jr., while a fourth guarded the hallway door.

"They (Cerrillo and Jon Jr.) went into the courtroom through the back because they were worried about taking him past the windows in the courtroom, which normally is where they would have gone," Lister said. "They were so worried about somebody shooting him."

Accompanied by Cerrillo and fellow assistant district defender Al Bandy, Jon Jr. appeared before Judge James Macnish, a native Missourian and Marine who worked as a district court judge for four decades in Shawnee County.

ON THE STAND

The preliminary hearing was extensive, which Debenham planned. That strategy included putting seven witnesses on the stand and entering 30 pieces of evidence. The attorney knew testimony was critical to the state's case, and that they could lose witness accounts to numerous circumstances.

The witnesses that day were Bob, Lister, Ramirez, coroner Wike Scamman, dive team member W.D. Beasley, and search volunteers Clinton Lambotte and Thomas Horn. The evidence included 28 photos, many from the crime scene, the videotape of Jon Jr.'s confession, and the waiver of rights the defendant signed.

Scamman's testimony was the longest, consuming more than 30 pages of the 114 recorded for the hearing. Much of the time, the coroner answered questions about Brenda's injuries, including that many of them were fresh. During the cross examination, Cerrillo asked Scamman to explain what he meant by fresh, to which the doctor responded that the injuries were within an hour or two of her death.

Scamman added, "Even though she was strangled, she was still alive lying on the floor."

Many of the details of Brenda's gruesome murder weren't public until the hearing. During the preliminary, Scamman described in depth just how much she suffered the night she died. He spoke about the bleeding in her spinal column, the deep bruises all over her body, the tears in her vagina and anus, and the torn lobe in her liver.

"There would be blood loss from this, and you could die from this if you didn't have any other injuries," he said.

Scamman also outlined the critical injury in Brenda's upper body: the hemorrhaging in a vein running from the abdomen to the heart, caused by a blow to the abdomen.

"When you say it's due to trauma, what are you referring to?" Debenham asked Scamman.

"It's due to some blow or force to the upper abdomen that caused the tearing of vessels and caused the hemorrhage," Scamman answered.

Bob was the next witness, but he wasn't on the stand for long. Most of his testimony detailed Brenda's day until she went missing.

MUDDYING THE WATER?

By the time Lister took the stand, she had already had an odd morning. First, she waited to walk through the metal detector leading into the courtroom. Like most of the Dover residents at the courthouse that day, she hadn't seen many detectors. Then came the surreal moment when Cerrillo tried to introduce her and the other witnesses to Jon Jr. As she testified, she was struck by the defendant's demeanor.

"He sat there with his head down, didn't make a comment," she said. "He was very reserved and together, but his eyes said something different. He looked scared."

Lister's testimony was important because she was the last person to see Brenda alive, other than the killer. She explained that she drove past Brenda while she was walking her bike about "maybe 50 yards" north of the Blakes' house. Lister waited for a few minutes in the circle drive at the grade school while her daughter dropped off pies for the Ladies Aid dinner. At no time, she said, did she see Brenda pushing her bike past the school, which was only a half mile north of the Blakes', nor did she see Brenda on the way home.

During Cerrillo's cross examination, Lister said she realized the Kellers were looking for Brenda when her daughter's friend called to ask if she had seen her that night. Larry Lister called Bob immediately to tell him that his wife saw Brenda pushing her bike north of the Blakes' at 5:30 p.m.

According to the transcript of the hearing, neither attorney asked Penny Lister about her account of seeing three men in the front yard of the Blake house seconds before she drove past Brenda. Years later, she said she was told not to talk about seeing Jon Jr., Jon Sr., and Ivan on the picnic table.

"I was not allowed to tell what I saw because they didn't want it to come out because Jon's dad was there and some cousin (Ivan) was there," Penny Lister said. "They didn't want that told because they had a confession, and he was already going to jail anyway, so we just don't need to know. Don't bring that up because then that muddies the water for getting him convicted."

Lutes disputes that statement.

"I'm just here to tell you that Dave Debenham would never tell somebody that. He would say, 'Say what you saw,'" Lutes said. "It didn't come from me, and it didn't come from David Debenham. What law enforcement told her, I can't vouch for, but I'd vouch for David Debenham. There's not a chance on this planet that he said that to her."

'SHE WAS NOT THERE'

Lambotte lived in Dover his entire life, with the exception of two months in Eskridge, up to the day he found Brenda's body. Within weeks of that night, he moved out of Shawnee County to Morrill, in northeast Kansas and just a few miles from the Nebraska border.

Lambotte, who later returned to Dover and served on the Mission Valley school board, declined an interview, but those who know him said discovering Brenda had a profound impact.

"All of us took it to heart, but for him to find her," said Brooklynd Thomas, who rode the school bus Lambotte drove, "it was too much for him."

Lambotte returned to Shawnee County for the prelim, describing to the court how he found Brenda.

"I walked up on the front of the building and shined my light back in it," he said. "It just happened to shine right on her, and that's – that's what I saw. The only other thing in there was just some leaves."

Debenham asked Lambotte what he saw the first time he pointed his flashlight inside the boathouse.

"I first looked in there and I said that that was her, and then, just for a split second, I thought it was a mannequin because the Blakes doing hair and stuff," Lambotte said. "She was real white, and it just didn't look like her, so I thought it was a mannequin. Then I seen a little pool of blood, and I said, 'No, that's her.'"

Debenham entered into evidence a photograph of Brenda laying on the floor of the shed, asking a few questions about the scene that night. A sullen Lambotte answered "yes" quietly enough that Debenham asked him to speak more loudly.

During the cross examination, Cerrillo asked Lambotte if he knew searchers checked the boathouse before the final wave during which he found her body.

"I don't know for sure if it had. I had heard that it had been," Lambotte said. "I think somebody said that the first or one of them consisted of three or four guys. I had heard them say they was down there once."

On redirect, Debenham asked Lambotte specifically if he knew if previous searchers looked in the boathouse.

"I knew the shed was over there, and I said, well, has anybody checked over there, and nobody could really give a sure answer if anybody had looked in there," he said. "And I still to this day don't know if anybody ever did actually go over to it. Some of them said that they seen it from the pond but never went over there."

Years later, Larry Lister, who was among the group on the Blakes' property looking for Brenda before the final search, said that he did look in the shed on the evening of Oct. 19.

"I was at the building," he said. "There was nothing in it."

Debenham finished his redirect with Lambotte at 11 a.m., and the court took a 15-minute recess before Tom Horn, the EMT who checked Brenda's vital signs, took the stand.

'THOSE DEAD EYES'

Horn also lived near Dover most of his life going into the hearing. He told the court he became a certified EMT less than a year before Brenda's murder and described the scene early on the morning of Oct. 20.

"I went into the building, observing everybody as I went in so I did not disturb anything," he said. "I took her wrist … her wrist was not flopping around, so it was semi-stiff, her body was real cold. I checked her carotid pulse, it was absent. I checked breath sounds, and they were not present. I checked her pupils, and they were dilated. From my observation and my training, she was not alive."

Horn was on the stand for only a few minutes and followed by Beasley, who detailed the Underwater Recovery Team's work on the day after Brenda's death, including finding her bike about 25 feet from the shore. During the cross examination, Cerrillo asked Beasley if the team found any bicycle tracks outside of the pond, to which he responded "No."

Cerrillo also asked if the chain was off the bike when it was removed from the water, and Beasley said he believed it was. The attorney showed the witness a photo of the bike after it was recovered with the chain off of it.

"It's on it?" Cerrillo asked.

"Yes, I can see chain hanging down right along in here," Beasley answered.

"OK. When I mean on, I mean on the sprockets," Cerrillo said.

"Quite frankly, I didn't pay any attention to that," Beasley replied.

Despite battling Bell's palsy at the time, Ramirez was the next and last person to take the stand. A short, stocky man with a stoic demeanor, the detective wore sunglasses that day because the illness affected his eyes and speech. Most of Ramirez's testimony focused on Jon Jr., including identifying him for the record, describing how they met, and testifying about the defendant's confession.

The detective said that he and Metz spoke to Jon Jr. about the investigation at about 2:30 p.m. Oct. 20 and asked if they could interview him.

"I told him that we were investigating a homicide and that I was wanting to ask him some questions in regards to that particular investigation," Ramirez said. "I asked him if he was willing to go downtown to the Sheriff's Office for an interview, and he stated, 'Yes.'"

Ramirez noted that Jon Jr. was not under arrest and free to leave at any time, but voluntarily left Dover with him. The officer said that once they arrived at the Sheriff's Department, Ramirez and Metz placed their suspect in a small interview room, then moved him to Ramirez's office five to 10 minutes later. Before the detectives began interviewing Jon Jr., they read him his Miranda rights. At that point, Debenham entered into evidence the interview information form Jon Jr. signed that day.

"After we received consent to talk to Mr. Mareska, I went into detail regarding the investigation," Ramirez said. "I asked him if he had any knowledge of the homicide and he stated, 'No.' We continued interviewing Mr. Mareska for some time. Eventually, Mr. Mareska admitted to both Detective Metz and myself that he killed the young victim."

After Ramirez told the court how Jon Jr. described abducting, raping, and killing Brenda, Debenham asked the detective if he asked about the bruises and injuries on the victim.

"Yes, sir. I asked him if he had ever struck the victim, and he indicated he had not," he said. "He did indicate that he told her several times to shut up. … He said that all she kept insisting was not to hurt her."

Debenham asked Ramirez about videotaping the confession, then admitted the tape into evidence. For the next several minutes, those in the court watched as Jon Jr. detailed his crime on camera.

"This was 1991. At this moment, video confessions were extremely rare, and his was either the first or one of the first viewed in a district court," said Fry, who covered the courts for 30 years and worked at the

Capital-Journal for more than 40 years. "I was surprised that we were going to get to see that because this is the defendant actually talking, and it was viewed by the public."

Jon Jr. describing a heinous crime impacted those in the courtroom. For many, it was the first time hearing what he did to Brenda. As Tracy listened, she covered her mouth with one hand. Fry remembers Jon Jr.'s plain delivery in speaking about the rape and murder.

"He was sitting there in court with this blank look, and that is exactly the way he was throughout the entire thing," Fry said. "There was no emotion whatsoever. I was just looking at a picture of him, his most recent picture at the Kansas Department of Corrections, and those dead eyes are the same ones in court, just nothing there."

During Cerrillo's cross examination, he pressed Ramirez as to why he was the one who did most of the talking during the interview with Jon Jr. while Metz was the lead investigator. Cerrillo also pushed Ramirez on his tactics during the interview, pointing out that the detectives told the defendant that Brenda was found dead, where she was found, and where the divers found her bike.

"You go into specific details with Mr. Mareska Jr. as to what you know about the case?" Cerrillo asked.

"Yes, sir," Ramirez replied.

"At some point in time, though, he changes what he's telling you and tells you that he did it, though, right?" Cerrillo asked.

"Yes, sir," Ramirez said again.

"You resorted to, not a bag of tricks, that's not the proper way to characterize it, back to your experience to see if you could get Mr. Mareska to change his mind, didn't you?" Cerrillo said.

"Yes, sir, I interviewed him," Ramirez said.

"Per the interview techniques, in order to get someone to talk about, you have had training for it, haven't you?" Cerrillo said. "And part of that is to try to put a guilty conscience on the individual, right?"

"No, sir, I wouldn't say part of that is," Ramirez said.

Cerrillo asked several questions about what the detectives asked Jon Jr. regarding the last time he visited a minister, as well as telling him he would feel better if he told them what happened that night.

"Now, when he did tell you that he killed Brenda Keller, he was co-operative, wasn't he?" Cerrillo asked. "And part of your investigation as a detective is to find out very specific details, right? Because you know it's possible people can confess and not really know too much about the crime, right?"

"Yes, sir," Ramirez replied.

If that line of questioning was designed to place doubt on the strategy Ramirez and Metz used, it wasn't effective, largely because of the way Jon Jr. confessed on tape.

"That confession was just awful," Fry said. "I don't recall that there was very much expression in him whatsoever. If he had cried or paused because of the emotions, I would have noted it."

BOUND FOR TRIAL

The State rested after Ramirez completed his testimony, but Debenham closed with a statement about the court binding Jon Jr. over due to the charges against him and that he planned the attack on Brenda.

"As far as premeditation, maliciousness, your honor, the defendant told the detectives that he grabbed Brenda Keller by the back of the hair, forced her over the fence, took her to the pond, made her throw the bicycle into the pond," Debenham said. "There is one reason and one reason only to throw that bicycle into the pond, and that's because he knew at that point in time she was never going to walk alive on the face of this Earth again.

"It's true the defendant said, when he told the detectives, he didn't know anything about the bruising. It is conceivable that he's told us part of the truth in his confession, that he has left out some omissions of fact, the deep bruising, the rupture of the liver, the subdural hemorrhaging of the brain, the injuries of that nature.

"The State would believe that based on the act of having Brenda Keller toss that bicycle in the pond where it would not be recovered, taking her out a quarter mile off Douglas Road, raping and sodomizing her behind an abandoned garage-like structure, strangling her while she was looking at him, that there is more than ample evidence that this crime was malicious, without cause, without provocation, without any rhyme or reason, that the defendant had more than ample time to think over his intentions and what he planned to do in this case."

Judge Macnish ruled that the evidence submitted during the hearing indicated that it demonstrated probable cause on the counts of murder in the first degree, aggravated kidnapping, rape, and aggravated criminal sodomy. He entered a plea of not guilty on behalf of Jon Jr., who stood mute, and scheduled a trial for Feb. 17, 1992.

CHAPTER FOURTEEN:

A PLEA FOR LIFE

Clad in nativity clothes, the grandchildren put on a performance for Roy and Jean every Christmas before Brenda died. The kids joyfully planned a play before singing and dancing while Steven Rue, Beverly's husband, played the trumpet and Bob sang. The scenes were one of many traditions in the Keller family.

In addition to a massive family meal, Jean meticulously organized the holiday every year, including a color scheme for the tree, extensive decorations around the house, and carefully selected gifts for everybody. Christmas in 1991, however, was survival, especially for the family matriarch.

"I remember Jeannie saying if it hadn't been for Janice, I never would have made this Christmas," Aunt B said.

Janice, still struggling mightily herself with emotions ranging from the upcoming birth of her third child to crying daily due to the loss of her niece, pulled it together enough to buy all of the family presents for Jean.

Bob and Tracy were just beginning to grieve, balancing keeping their family together with the crushing weight of an ongoing investigation and upcoming trial. Bob equated each meeting with attorneys and every court appearance to tearing the Band-Aid off of an open wound.

On dozens of nights over the months after Brenda died, Bob awoke to the heart-wrenching sound of his wife crying. There was nothing he could do for Tracy.

"Tracy, if you know her, she sings all the time. She hums, sings, not for people, just singing. The kids at school said when she was a cook they could tell where Tracy was because they could hear her humming," Bob said. "It took her song. She quit singing for four years."

That holiday season was far from joyful for the Blakes, as well. The Mareska family wasn't close, but they did gather for a Christmas dinner every year. It was one of the few times Tammy and Jon Sr. got to see their brother, Chip, who lived an hour away in Emporia. Seeing his older brother, who was already suffering from brain damage, after his nephew committed such a heinous crime devastated Chip.

"It gave me a sadness, and more so for my brother's sake," he said. "My brother wouldn't know what end was up. I just felt bad for him. It would affect how people, even in his condition, would approach him. It was heartbreaking for me just knowing that a member of the family did that. They were trying to help that young man out, and he basically destroyed their lives."

Many in Dover were continuing to direct their anger at the Blakes, but the couple was steadfast in staying on their farm. Gene Blake was adamant that he wasn't going to let the group of people who believed he and his wife were at fault drive them out of town.

"My sister loved that farm," Chip Mareska said. "To them, that's home."

THE INVESTIGATION CONTINUES

In the weeks leading up to Christmas, the Shawnee County Sheriff's Office received the lab results from the items collected in Tammy

Blake's car. The Kansas Bureau of Investigation (KBI) compared the articles forensics officer R.J. Warrington vacuumed with the rape kit and the head and pubic hairs from Jon Jr. According to the Bureau's report, the examination of the vacuumings did not reveal any hair consistent with Brenda's head hair, and no pubic hair was in the material collected.

During the course of the investigation, a self-proclaimed psychic from Silver Lake, a small town about 10 miles west of Topeka, contacted the Sheriff's Department saying he had information about the case. The individual, Reginald Franzen, gave Detective Larry Baer a six-page, handwritten statement, including a diagram from his vision of a girl's body resting against a tree.

Before Baer spoke to Franzen, he read his statement, then asked fellow detectives Richard Mergen and J.D. Mauck to review it. Franzen wrote that his first knowledge of Brenda's murder was on Aug. 14, more than two months before she died, and that he submitted to a Shawnee County District Court judge information about several homicides in the area, including Brenda's.

"I am what is commonly referred to as a psychic. Ordinarily, this word conveys notions or premonitions, which people try to describe as best they can," Franzen wrote. "My connections, as usually connections are not visible, were visible to myself. I was informed during that testimony that a life would be lost, sometime later. They stated to me that it would be a horrible crime, that she would be 12 years old and be described within an article by the Capital-Journal as the girl with flaming red hair."

In his statement, Franzen also wrote that he was told through his psychic powers that the suspect was a man named Dr. Stuart Twemlow. A revered psychiatrist, Twemlow studied at the Menninger Clinic in Topeka and had a private practice for more than 30 years before he died at age 81 in 2022.

Franzen said that Twemlow was the prime suspect in not only Brenda's murder, but also the murder of Karen Estes, a 42-year-old mother and grandmother killed in 1989 in Topeka. But there was nothing to tie Twemlow to Brenda or Estes, and the psychiatrist was regarded as an innovator and caring man in his field. After the detectives read the report, Baer met with Franzen, telling him that he could not discuss the investigation due to the gag order on the case.

"After reading his report and his notes, I find there is no similarity to what actually happened and to what he was stating in his report," Baer wrote in a report he filed for the District Attorney's Office. "There would be nothing we could use for any help from him at this time."

While that interaction had no evidentiary value, the Sheriff's Department did receive an important report during the first week of January 1992 when the KBI completed its analysis of Ivan's blood sample. The Bureau compared his blood to the genetic material on the stick recovered from the crime scene. The report stated that he was a type B secretor, and because the seminal fluid on the stick was from a non-secretor, he was eliminated as a possible donor.

NEGOTIATING A PLEA

Kansas is a deep red state with a House and Senate dominated by conservatives, but it has elected numerous Democratic governors through the years. Among those was John Carlin, a dairy farmer from Salina, Kansas, who served in the House of Representatives for nine years before being elected as governor in 1979.

The state stopped practicing the death penalty in 1972, when the Supreme Court abolished capital punishment and reduced all death sentences to life in prison. Before then, Kansas had not executed anyone since June 1965 with the hangings of George York and James Latham, spree killers who murdered seven people in 1961.

Kansas also abolished the death penalty from 1907 to 1935, but was relatively active in enacting the sentence from its inception in 1853 to 1965, with 76 executions. Among those were the two individuals responsible for the most infamous crime in the state's history, the murder of the Clutter family on a farm in Holcomb that Truman Capote chronicled in his masterpiece, "In Cold Blood." Perry Smith and Dick Hickock, who killed the family of four in November 1959, were executed by hanging in 1965.

Executions resumed in the United States in 1976, but Kansas did not bring back capital punishment. Legislators attempted to reinstate the death penalty several times in the late 1970s and 1980s, but Carlin vetoed the bill. By 1991, the state not only didn't have the death penalty, but also didn't have a life without parole sentence.

Behind the scenes, Debenham and Maggie Lutes were negotiating with Byron Cerrillo on a plea agreement for Jon Jr. A plea sentence wasn't what many of the people in Dover wanted. A large contingent in the community believed Jon Sr. and Ivan should be punished, too. Cerrillo, known widely as an aggressive, voracious advocate for his clients, knew the District Attorney's Office had more than enough evidence to convict Jon Jr. and hoped to avoid the state's heaviest punishment at the time, a "Hard 40" sentence.

Though the state made the decision, they met with the Kellers several times to discuss possible sentences. One of the reasons the District Attorney's Office was willing to work on a plea was the unpredictable outcomes of a jury trial. Debenham knew that 12 people may decide on a lesser sentence, and jury trials often come with appeals.

"One of the things you've got to look at is the victims," Debenham said. "I don't think there's an easy answer. It was difficult, but it would have been more difficult if we'd had the death penalty. There's some closure in a plea and sentence."

"I don't remember that there was ever any strong indication of anybody else being involved in it," Steve Fry said. "If that came up anywhere during the questioning and so forth, Byron Cerrillo would have had access to that, and he would have brought it up. He would have wanted to deflect blame off his guy onto anybody else.

"Cerrillo was a pit bull. He really was. I saw him go after children that were raped by an adult. He was doing his job, but it was not fun to watch. If he would have had any notion, I think it would have surfaced somewhere."

Debenham and Cerrillo settled on a sentence essentially as harsh as a Hard 40. In a plea the Kellers supported, the attorneys agreed that Jon Jr. would serve life on the murder and kidnapping charges, plus 10 years to life on the rape and sodomy counts.

Because there was not a life without parole sentence in 1991, anybody convicted of a life sentence was eligible for parole after serving 40 years. Though many individuals were never paroled and served a life sentence, they still had a sliver of hope, which the plea deal gave Jon Jr.

THE FINAL PLEA

Debenham and Cerrillo finalized the plea agreement early in 1992, and it became public knowledge on the afternoon of Feb. 6 when the attorneys, along with Lutes, Assistant District Defender Albert Bandy, and Jon Jr., appeared in the Shawnee County District Court. The State heightened security, with three corrections officers guarding Jon Jr. and three Sheriff's Department deputies monitoring the courtroom. In the proceeding before Judge Fred Jackson, Debenham read a letter submitted as evidence outlining the plea negotiations:

"Pursuant to the plea negotiations, your client will enter a plea of guilty to Count One, premeditated first-degree murder; Count Two, aggravated kidnapping with the intent to hold Brenda Keller to facilitate the commission of the crime of rape or aggravated criminal sodomy; Count Three, rape; and Count Four, aggravated criminal sodomy.

"Although the Court is not bound by any agreement between the parties, the State and the defendant have agreed to be bound by the following sentence: Count One: life; Count Two, life; Count Three, not less than 10 years, not more than life; and Count Four, not less than 10 years, not more than life."

The Kellers asked in the plea that Jon Jr. be punished for each crime committed on their daughter. The sides also agreed that the sentences would run consecutively to each other and with any pre-existing sentences, which included his parole violations stemming from the burglaries in Douglas County. When Debenham finished detailing the plea, Judge Jackson asked Jon Jr. to come forward.

"You've heard the statements of the counsel concerning the plea negotiations and signed the letter agreement. Do you understand the plea negotiations?" Jackson asked.

"Yes, sir," Jon Jr. replied.

"You're charged in a complaint with one count of first-degree murder, one count of aggravated kidnapping, one count of rape, and one count of aggravated sodomy. Do you understand the charges?" Jackson said.

"Yes, sir," Jon Jr. replied.

"Were these offenses committed while you were on parole?" Jackson said.

"Yes, sir," Jon Jr. said again.

"Do you understand that the Court would be obliged by law to make any sentence imposed in this case consecutive to any sentence in the case which you were on parole at the time?"

"Yes, sir," Jon Jr. replied.

When Jackson finished questioning Jon Jr., Debenham again described the crime for the record, detailing Brenda's day until Jon Jr. kidnapped and attacked her before raping and murdering her. As he spoke about the events, Tracy, sitting in the front row according to Fry's article in the Feb. 7 edition of the Capital-Journal, dropped her head and stared at the ground.

"The hardest thing," said Detective Mike Ramirez, "is the parents didn't want to hear what happened. I hated seeing that."

At the end of the proceeding, Judge Jackson asked Jon Jr. how he pleaded to each of the four counts. Plainly, he said "guilty" to each charge. The judge set sentencing for March 9, one day after what would have been Brenda's 13th birthday, but the hearing later was postponed until April 13. As Jon Jr. left the courtroom, deputies blocked spectators from leaving until he was gone.

'THE QUIET LITTLE TOWN NOW LIVES IN FEAR'

A few weeks after the plea agreement proceeding, the Kellers learned that Judge Jackson would read notes from victims before the sentencing. Just 11 days before Brenda's birthday, Bob and Tracy circulated a letter in Dover asking for friends and community members to submit their words to Jackson. In part, the Kellers wrote:

"The Court has engaged in a presentence investigation. During this time, the judge will be reviewing all factors available to him prior to imposing a sentence. We have learned that he will read all letters addressed to him on this matter. The family has been asked to respond to the following question: Please describe what being the victim of a crime has meant to you and your family."

Bob and Tracy planned to speak at the sentencing and asked Jean and Clayton Comfort, Tracy's uncle, to make statements at the hearing. The request to their friends in Dover resulted in a plethora of letters mailed to the judge, ranging from Brenda's closest friends, to teachers, to patrons of the Dover Federated Church. Later given to Bob and Tracy, most of the letters asked the judge not to let Jon Jr. out of prison.

"Brenda would agree with me that neither of us would want this guy getting out because one death is too many," Amy Best wrote. "I know how much it hurts."

Amy's parents, Cathy and Gary, told Jackson about the devastation Brenda's murder caused, including a loss of innocence for the children and the change in the Kellers.

"There has been a personalization of every crime we hear about now – in movies, in news, in conversations – that causes us to grieve to some extent for all those that we now understand are so changed by the crime. Every day, we recognize other ways this event has changed our lives," the Bests wrote.

Comfort, a retired major general in the Marines who flew a fighter jet and served two tours in Vietnam, also sent a letter to Judge Jackson. Brenda's great uncle wrote that she was the "epitome of youthful promise and a joy to behold." He described the months after his niece's death as a feeling of helplessness "as we finally realize that no magic exists to restore Brenda and the promise she represented."

Many of Brenda's friends and schoolmates shared their memories of her with the judge. Jill Wilson wrote about mud fights with her. Julia Gomez remembered that Brenda didn't care "if you were a nerd or didn't have any cool clothes. She liked you the way you are."

Misty Lange told Jackson about a trip to Silver Dollar City in Springfield, Missouri, because "I wanted to ride the rides, and she wouldn't because she wanted to look at the crafts." In a rare moment of humor in the letters, Lange wrote that inmates shouldn't be given TVs or phones and that they shouldn't have more rights than children under 18.

Michelle Johnson, who was two grades ahead of Brenda, recalled her tattling on the kids in track who didn't run as far as they were supposed to during practice. In a poignant moment about her hometown, Johnson wrote, "Nothing has been or ever will be the same in Dover. The quiet little town where children would play through the streets now has a few children playing in their own backyards, guarded by a fence. Dover, the quiet little town where everyone now lives in fear. There is a missing place in our hearts, a hole."

The adults wrote about the devastation Brenda's murder caused their children. Darlene George, a longtime member of the church and whose kids attended school with Brenda, told the judge that the graphic media coverage cost the children in Dover their innocence. Ruth Lange said losing Brenda "left a gap in our lives that can't be filled." Principal Terri Anderson wrote, "The ache in our hearts and the nightmares will never completely go away." Sonny Van Cleave, the beloved custodian of the schools, shared a story about the time he stepped on a worm, bringing tears to Brenda's eyes.

Roy and Jean's letter to Jackson included sharing a conversation between Brenda and her grandmother after one of John's football games: "I said, 'Brenda, you girls were sure chattering away this evening.' She said, 'Oh, Grandma, we have so much to talk about, all the things we want to do and what we plan to be.'" Those dreams will never be fulfilled, the Kellers wrote. Roy and Jean also told the judge that their grandsons, son, and daughter-in-law were left with an emptiness that will never be filled.

'WE KNOW IT WILL GO ON AND ON'

Roberta Peterson has a way with words and a way with people. Her professional, yet caring nature allowed her to connect with people from every walk of life, including Bob and Tracy. Originally reluctant to speak with the media about their daughter and her murder, the Kellers discovered quickly that they could trust the longtime reporter.

One of the reasons for that connection was that Peterson understood the Kellers' struggle because it hit close to home. Less than seven years before Brenda died, the grandmother of Peterson's husband was murdered in one of the country's most notorious death penalty cases. Ruth Pelke, a 78-year-old Bible teacher from Gary, Indiana, died at the hands of four teenagers in 1985. Paula Cooper, 15, Denise Thomas, 14, Karen Corder, 16, and April Beverly, 15, attacked Pelke under the veil of asking for Bible lessons. Cooper stabbed Pelke 33 times in the chest and stomach with a foot-long butcher knife before the girls stole $10 and the keys to the grandmother's car.

Three of the girls received sentences ranging from 25 to 60 years, but Cooper got the death penalty at age 16. Pelke's family made news a few years later when they issued a public statement to forgive Cooper. Bill Pelke, Ruth's grandson, chronicled this in his book "Journey of Hope."

In 1988, Indiana's Supreme Court changed Cooper's sentence to 60 years when the state raised the minimum age limit for execution from 10 to 16. She eventually served 28 years before being released at age 43 in 2013.

"Their (Bob and Tracy's) forgiving him stood out," Peterson said. "I went through some of that with my husband. These were the only two places where that (forgiveness) felt genuine and real and really had an impact on other people."

That common bond made it easier for Peterson to approach the Kellers about writing a story leading up to the April sentencing. After meeting with Tracy at the Capital-Journal, Peterson obtained the family's permission to not only interview them and write a story, but also have a photographer in their home.

"I always got the feeling that they'd been comfortable with me since the funeral," Peterson said. "I think they knew I wasn't there to turn loose on their blessing."

Published as the lead story on Sunday, March 22, Peterson's feature piece dominated the front page, with two large vertical photos, taken by photographer Jeff Taylor, on either side of the copy. The one on the left was of Tracy sitting on Brenda's bed with the last dress she bought her daughter lying next to her. In the shot, Tracy looked forlornly out the window in Brenda's room, which the family left as Brenda had it. The photo on the right was of Bob sitting on the family home's porch swing while reading a book about coping with the loss of a loved one. The headline stretching across the top of the paper read "Pain still fresh for murder victim's family."

In writing the lead to the story, Peterson thought about the weather. Kansas winters can be harsh, brutally cold with below-zero temperatures on several days, biting, gusty winds that feel like they cut to the bone, and the occasional snowstorm. As she was preparing to write the feature on the Kellers, the state was just beginning to emerge from a frosty winter. Peterson thought about the weather beginning to turn and realized it served as a perfect, yet humbling metaphor for the family.

"I was just thinking how hard that was," she said, "things coming back to life, but not everything."

The article began, "Spring has returned to Dover. The grass is green and wildflowers are springing up along the winding roads. Bicyclers also are beginning to appear along those byways. Brenda Keller loved to ride her bicycle in Dover, and spring was her favorite season. But spring is here, and Brenda isn't."

As Peterson wrote, the Kellers were entering the most painful time after a murder. At five to seven months after the crime, the shock begins to wear off and the reality sets in, according to the National Organization of Parents of Murdered Children.

"The realization is hitting us now that Brenda hasn't gone someplace and will be coming back," Bob told Peterson. "All those special things she did ... there is no one to do. Before it was just a shock. You don't think about living the rest of your life without her."

Peterson wrote about Brenda's gifts, from writing and art, to her dedication to improving in sports. The story also detailed the struggles of her brothers. John wanted his parents to be less protective, and Pat was angry, an emotion on display when he got mad at his grandmother for trying to help him carve a pumpkin for Halloween. Brenda helped him with that project for years, triggering his temper.

"Pat and Brenda, being the youngest, had fought a lot and picked on each other," Tracy said. "But they really loved each other."

The Kellers also told Peterson about their trip to Colorado not long after Brenda died. They stopped to take a family photo, and when it printed, it hit all of them that Brenda wasn't in the picture.

"This is the hardest it's been for me. For so long, I was running on remote control," Bob said. "It was as if I had stepped into a boxing match and was taking severe blows, but for months I had plenty of reserve to withstand it. Now, we're in the 15th round, and I'm not responding well. I can't even handle the regular pressures of life."

Peterson's story also provided more information about Brenda's disappearance than had been reported in previous months, including details about Bob and Tracy searching for their daughter after the Ladies Aid event, as well as Bob assisting in the search of the Blakes' property. Bob said that the memories of that night return anytime he heard a helicopter. He also told Peterson about the hours after he had to tell his wife that their daughter died.

"I was numb," he said. "I remember walking through the house later and finding Tracy in Brenda's bedroom. I went in and saw her. She was holding Brenda's pillow."

The Kellers also spoke about the support they received from the community and beyond. Tracy said they got dozens of cards and money in the mail, including enough of the latter that they bought a new van for the church. Bob and Tracy liked one of the poems someone sent them so much that they placed it on the back of the headstone.

"Someone wrote it for us and mailed it, and now we don't even know the name of the person," Tracy said. "But it was as if Brenda had written it herself."

The exhaustive media coverage, especially in the weeks after the murder, hurt the Kellers. Tracy said the family felt ashamed because so many people learned, in vivid detail, what happened to their child.

"How much should be told?" Bob said. "We wanted her privacy protected."

Despite what Jon Jr. did to their daughter, the Kellers weren't bitter. Tracy said she felt deeply for the mother of the man who murdered Brenda.

"I know how I feel losing Brenda," she said. "His mother has to be having a very hard time."

Peterson finished the article with Bob telling a story about someone he grew up with who killed a woman. That crime happened just months after Brenda died, in January 1992. Steven Bailey, who played with Bob in Minneapolis when both were kids, shot his girlfriend in

Topeka, killing her. He was sentenced to 15 years to life and is still incarcerated in the Ellsworth Correctional Facility.

"It gives you a different perspective, to identify with someone on the other side," Bob said. "Who are the killers? They're people, like the victims. Who knows what makes them change?"

THE END OF PROMISE

For weeks, Becky Taylor was distraught. She couldn't believe her first love, the young man who held her hand in public and acted like a gentleman just a few years earlier, could murder a 12-year-old girl. Jon Jr. called Taylor shortly after he was arrested. Over the next few months, he called several more times.

Taylor was married at the time, and her husband wasn't pleased that his wife was receiving phone calls from a man charged with such a heinous crime. He told Taylor that she needed to stop talking to him, or he'd get out of jail and kill her, too.

"I was like, 'No, he's not,'" she said. "I feel 100% confident that if he got out, he would not harm me in any way."

Jon Jr. had little support and few friends at that point. He hadn't seen his mother in five years, and his father was in a nursing home, closing on dementia. The Blakes cut all ties with their nephew. Taylor did what she could to help him, including contacting Cerrillo.

"I went in and said, 'I dated this guy, and there's no way,'" she said. "He asked me if I would testify on his behalf, and I said, 'Of course.'"

Taylor drove to Topeka for the first two court proceedings, sitting in the hallway most of both hearings. At one point, as she nervously waited, she looked up and watched as Shawnee County Sheriff's deputies escorted Jon Jr. out of the courtroom. That was the last time Taylor saw him. She told Cerrillo that he would have to subpoena her to appear, because her husband insisted that she not testify.

"I never got subpoenaed. I waited and waited and nothing. The only thing I could figure is was Jon didn't want me there," she said.

"My reasoning is he didn't want me to hear and think that bad of him. The next thing I know, he's been sentenced."

The weather on the day of the sentencing was fitting for a dreary scene in a hearing featuring heart-wrenching victim statements from Bob, Tracy, Jean, and Comfort. As the proceeding began at 2:45 p.m., a steady rain pelted the courthouse, with winds gusting up to 30 mph. Moments after Judge Jackson opened the sentencing, Jean took the stand. Just a few weeks before, she wrestled with a decision on speaking.

"I remember Robert calling, and I said, 'Oh, Robert. I couldn't do that,'" Jean said. "He said, 'Well, you just think about it, Mom. If you want to, you can.'"

That night, Jean woke in the middle of the night and decided testifying was something she had to do for her granddaughter. She spent several hours writing her message. As she begin speaking in the courtroom, she said it was as if Brenda said to her, "Won't you speak for me, Grandma?"

As Jean talked, she looked directly at Jon Jr., who did not show emotion at any point during the hearing, but did appear to be listening, according to Fry's story in the next day's edition of the Capital-Journal. As she spoke to Jon Jr., Jean told him how special grandchildren are to grandparents. She shared a story about spending time with six granddaughters and one grandson two weeks before that day in court and how she made special treats to eat. She realized as she was cooking that she would "never again plan for my Brenda." It turned a joyous moment into a sad one.

"This precious little girl loved life and respected it so much," she said. "She did not want anyone to kill any living creature. She would say, 'Oh, don't kill it. It hasn't done anything to you. It deserves to live.' Brenda deserved to live."

Though Jean later forgave the man who killed her granddaughter, she wasn't ready on this day. She told the court she knew God would forgive him and prayed that she could do the same. She concluded by saying that Jon Jr. should not have the privilege of freedom.

Comfort took the stand next, telling the court he was speaking for Brenda's cousins, friends, and classmates. His statement focused on the "joyful promise" that his niece held and how a wide range of negative emotions, including anger and fear, replaced that promise.

"We know that the Court cannot bring Brenda back to us," he said, "but we do pray that the fullest measure of accountability be affixed to the brutal killer."

Tracy's statement was one of despair, loss, and emptiness. Her voice broke several times and she spoke quickly while leaning toward the judge, details described in depth by Fry in his article.

"I long to have Brenda come home, to see her around the corner and hear her whistling," she said. "I didn't need to see her. I could usually hear her coming, and I long to hear her come through my front door. And, instead of turning on the TV and play with her friends, she would come find me and hug me and say, 'I love you, Mom.'"

Tracy told the Court about all the things she missed about her daughter. She would no longer go on long bike rides or walks with her. She no longer had a "coach" to encourage her to push herself. She would never get to see her daughter play basketball or jump the hurdles in track. She would never look in the paper and see Brenda's name on the honor roll. She would not get to experience the things mothers cherish: the first date, graduation, a wedding, and Brenda's children. She would never have her daughter sitting next to her in church as they shared their love for Christ.

"She'd get as close to me as she could," Tracy said. "It's gone forever. I can't ever get that back."

In the most heartbreaking moment of the hearing, Tracy shared that during this time of year, she would be "frantically running around" to get Brenda an Easter dress that the family could afford.

"Instead, I planted flowers on her grave," she said before asking the Court to impose a sentence protecting other girls and women from Jon Jr.

Like his mother, Bob spoke directly to the man who killed his daughter. He began by telling Jon Jr. that he left a hole in the hearts of everyone who loved Brenda. Bob then reminded Jon Jr. that the week of the sentencing was an important one for Christians, who were celebrating Easter, telling him that Jesus prayed for the men who killed him.

"Jesus' words tell me that in spite of the worst that a person could do to him, he still loved them," he said. "And those words tell me that in spite of the worst you could do to Brenda, God loves you."

Bob told Jon Jr. that while he was disgusted with what he did, he would forgive him, as God would.

"I believe Brenda would forgive you, and I know that my wife and I are also willing to forgive you, as well, if you ask," he said.

"If only" were the two words Bob used the most often. If only he checked on Brenda earlier. If only he happened by her at the right time. If only he sensed she was in danger earlier.

"I sometimes find myself full of regret," Bob said.

He also spoke at length about Brenda's friends, naming Best, Wilson, Jana Blodgett, Robin Self, and Brooklynd Thomas. When he saw those girls and the young girls in his family, he thought about danger that they might not see.

"I don't ever want to pick up the paper and see what happened to Brenda has now happened to one of them," Bob said.

A LINE TO REMEMBER

"Death is death."

That quote, from Cerrillo, is one of the things Bob will always remember about the courtroom. To this day, it gnaws at him. Moments after Bob left the stand, Debenham entered several photographs of

Brenda's injuries into evidence. Cerrillo objected immediately, telling Judge Jackson that the district attorney was using them to "inflame the Court and public." Debenham countered that he wanted the judge to understand the brutality of the attack Brenda endured.

"Your honor, death is death," Cerrillo replied.

The judge overruled, but the defense attorney's cold response struck a nerve.

"I know court is court, but I'll never forget him saying, 'Come on, death is death.' That really bothered me," Bob said.

Debenham spoke next, outlining the charges Jon Jr. pleaded guilty to and saying that the sides agreed that the sentences were to run consecutively, which the Kellers asked for during the negotiations. The district attorney also reminded the judge that the defendant was on parole in Douglas County for the crimes he committed in 1988. Debenham mentioned two statutes in the state of Kansas that applied to Brenda's case, one stating that a dangerous offender be treated in custody for as long as needed and the other that the lowest minimum sentence should be consistent with public safety, the needs of the defendant, and the seriousness of the crime.

Debenham reminded the Court that Jon Jr. consistently committed crimes from 1988 through 1991, escalating from burglary to assault before killing Brenda. He also spoke about the impact the murder had on the people in her life.

"These are individuals who are unable to sleep, and they have nightmares; children who shouldn't have such nightmares, who shouldn't be aware of the things they've heard about this case," Debenham said.

One last time, Debenham detailed the kidnapping and murder of Brenda. The injuries were so numerous that outlining them consumes two pages of the court transcript.

"Dr. Scamman noted that even though Brenda Keller was strangled, she bled a considerable amount after she was on the floor of the shed," he said. "It was his opinion that she was not dead."

Cerrillo, who entered a Presentence Investigation (PSI) report into evidence earlier in the hearing, spoke for his defendant next. He said it was Jon Jr.'s decision not to fight a life sentence, partially because he didn't want the Kellers to experience any more hurt. The attorney talked at length about his client's childhood, telling the court that he was sexually abused when he was 3 to 4 years old.

"Anyone who knows when you're sexually abused when you're a young child like that you turn out to be addicted, you show bursts of outrage and anger," he said.

Though the Shawnee County District Attorney's Office file on the case contained psychological evaluations, those are not available to the public. Nonetheless, Cerrillo used several details in the PSI during his closing statement. He told the Court that Jon Jr. grew up watching his mother and father fight, and that he didn't see his father from the time of his parents' divorce as a boy until he was 17.

"His mother remarries, remarries another severely alcoholic individual who also brings the same type of relationship into the house," he said. "That is his mother is the one who continually gets beaten over and over and over again."

Cerrillo stated that Jon Jr. started using his mother's cocaine and drinking at a young age, feeding his addiction and anger. Like his father years before, his mother "disappears" from his life when he left Oklahoma to move in with his father.

"The anger toward women, that's what he's been around all his life," Cerrillo said.

Jon Jr.'s mother disputes the notion that she and her son were in homes that were constantly violent.

"He had issues with his stepdad because his stepdad was strict," said LaDonna Thomas. "He was good to him, too. He had issues as a child because his dad ignored him. (Jon Sr.) was abusive toward me one time."

As Cerrillo continued, he said the PSI performed at the Bert Nash Community Mental Health Center in Lawrence painted a picture of Jon Jr. as a man who had no self-worth and craved structure.

"Jon believes that there is something wrong with him," he said. "He feels lost, headed for disaster."

As he finished, Cerrillo reminded the judge that there was a plea bargain, and that Jon Jr. wouldn't be eligible for parole until he's 62 years old. When asked, Jon Jr. declined to address the Court. Before imposing a sentence, Judge Jackson spoke about his decision.

"I think the Court's primary concern at this point has to be the protection of society to try to ensure that Mr. Mareska does not in the future pose a threat to society," he said. "With that in mind, I've decided to follow the recommendations of the State and the plea agreement."

Jackson sentenced Jon Jr. to life in prison on the charges of first-degree murder and aggravated kidnapping and 10 years to life on the charges of rape and aggravated criminal sodomy. He added that the sentences were to be served consecutively and consecutively to any sentences from the Douglas County cases.

Debenham asked the judge to include a $2,000 compensation fee in the journal entry, which would cover the costs for the funeral service. Should Jon Jr. be released from prison, he is obligated to pay the fee.

"Well, I frankly trust that he will not be given parole, but you may include that," Judge Jackson said.

With that, the court adjourned. Jon Jr. will be eligible for parole on Aug. 23, 2031. At the time, the Kellers were content with the sentence, specifically holding Jon Jr. accountable on each charge.

"For that, we are satisfied," Bob told Fry after the proceeding. "There's no sense of happiness about it, no joy. There is no sense of victory. It's more the feeling of a funeral for us."

Nearly 30 years later, though, age 62 didn't seem as old to the Kellers as it did in 1991.

"We're about 63, and that'd be the earliest age he could get out," Bob said in 2017. "I feel like I'm still strong enough that I could hurt somebody. I don't think he should be out. Life should mean life."

CHAPTER FIFTEEN:

JOURNEY FOR JUSTICE

Like her daughter, Tracy absolutely loved being outside. She and Brenda went for thousands of walks and bike rides on the backroads of Dover, enjoying the squirrels, butterflies, chipmunks, and other wildlife skipping and hopping through the lush greenery and trees of southwest Shawnee County.

Tracy continued walking on the dirt roads outside of the community after Brenda died, but those treks were not so much about savoring nature as they were about relieving stress and managing her emotions. Several times a week, she left the family home in the heart of Dover, hitting the dusty roads with an aggressive stride to the places she shared with Brenda. Once she was in the middle of nowhere, with no houses around and only the blustery wind and open spaces surrounding her, Tracy let go.

"I hope nobody heard me, because I had it out with God," she said. "I was angry with Him. The funny thing is, I wasn't as angry with Jon Mareska as I was with God."

For the first time, Tracy felt like God let her and her daughter down. She struggled for years with her faith, trying to understand why God, with all His grace and love, would let such a horrible thing happen to a kind, faithful little girl. For a while, she would not attend church on Sundays. When she did, Tracy often sneaked into the back, where three long rows of pews rest behind pillars on either side of the main rows. It was the perfect spot to hide.

"It was super hard for me without Brenda there," she said. "It was this place where you and this person experienced something special."

Tracy's inner battle was a war of questions that no one, at least in this life, could or will ever answer. When she wasn't asking God those questions, she asked her husband. Time and time again, Tracy sat on the edge of the porcelain as Bob rested in the family's tub while taking a bath, searching for resolution.

"Why did God let this happen?" she asked her husband hundreds of times.

"I don't know," he replied.

"I would ask him hard ones," she said. "Where was God that day? What will she look like when I see her again? Will I know her? What about all these promises from God's words that we memorized together?"

The most common question was one many of Brenda's friends and family ask to this day: Do you think she knew it was her time?

"That's probably the question I badgered Robert with the most," she said.

There were times Tracy felt like God wasn't there, and there were times she felt He was keeping her alive, giving her the strength to keep going. On a particularly rough day, she returned home one afternoon and decided it was time to join her daughter in the next life. Just as she was about to commit suicide, a friend knocked on the door.

"I was very close to doing that, and she showed up," Tracy said. "And I go, 'Hmmm, He must know I'm pretty close.'"

THE STRUGGLE WITH JOHN

Tracy wasn't alone in sorrow, though the rest of the family coped differently. John took to trouble, finding solace in drinking at high school keg parties held almost weekly in the countryside, downing "pity beers." He also stopped going to church.

"I don't know how much they just let slide," John said. "But I got away with a lot. I wasn't doing drugs, but I was doing all sorts of stupid stuff during high school."

Aside from partying, John used his sister's room, which remained untouched for years after she died, as a place to hang out with a girl. It was the same place Tracy used as a refuge when she really missed Brenda.

"Oh my gosh, I came home from work and he had a girl in Brenda's room," Tracy said. "He called one day and said, 'Mom, I am sorry I was such an ass when I was in high school.'"

Pat did as much as he could to distance himself from the tragedy. From grade school through high school, he did not talk about his sister, avoiding conversations about Brenda to prevent people from seeing his vulnerability. The only joy he felt in the months after she died was Jon Jr.'s sentencing. On that rainy day, Pat jumped into Lavella Buchmeier's arms, laughing and smiling.

"He said, 'The guy that killed my sister is never going to get out of jail as long as he lives,'" Buchmeier said. "It breaks my heart to this day. He cried. He would just cry a lot."

Pat spent as much time at the Buchmeiers' house over the next several years as he did his own home. It was his sanctuary from the sorrow. Even there, however, he couldn't escape the fear. It was common for Buchmeier to fall asleep with her children and Pat sleeping on the floor next to her bed.

"Thank God for the Buchmeiers," Tracy said.

Bob and Tracy began attending Parents of Murdered Children (POMC) meetings two hours away in Wichita. Bob went more often, traveling south on Interstate 35 through the heart of the Flint Hills to gather with those who understood the overwhelming pain of losing a child to homicide.

Founded in 1978 by Cincinnati couple Robert and Charlotte Hullinger, whose daughter was beaten to death with a sledgehammer by an ex-boyfriend, POMC branched across the country. Unlike Jon Jr., their daughter's murderer was out of prison in 16 months and convicted of a second murder in 1997.

The group helped Bob realize that he couldn't hold onto anger for the man who killed Brenda. He knew that resentment would eat him alive as the years passed.

"I saw people go through horrible bitterness," Bob said. "I'd see them rage and come to our group and hate and hate and hate, and go on and on. I just felt like they were stuck."

PURSUIT OF JUSTICE

As the Kellers continued to grieve, Jon Jr. was looking for a way out of a life behind bars. Just one day after accepting the sentences he agreed to, he filed an appeal to modify the length of his term. That rankled the Keller family, who agreed to a plea bargain because they wanted closure.

"He wanted to get out because this happened to him when he was so young. He thought he should have more of a chance," Aunt B said. "You took the life out of a girl this young, and you think you need something. Jesus help us."

The district court did not take long to respond to Jon Jr.'s request for a hearing on the motion. Less than two months later, the court replied with a letter saying that the motion served no useful purpose, and the request was denied.

The Kellers weren't done with the legal system, even as Jon Jr.'s first appeal met a quick end. Within weeks of his sentencing hearing, they were meeting with an attorney in Topeka known for fighting voraciously for his clients. Bob and Tracy approached Pedro Irigonegaray, who at 43 years old had a reputation as a tireless advocate for victims and human rights.

Irigonegaray has worked an array of cases and in dozens of lanes in law, ranging from prosecuting triple-murderer Tyrone Baker, to representing former Gov. Joan Finney when the State Senate sued her to prevent Native Americans from opening casinos, to working with the Kansas Department of Education in representing science during a hearing about the study of evolution in the state's curriculum.

"I have represented a variety of causes because of a sense of integrity for the law, a sense of justice, a sense that this is a worthy fight," Irigonegaray said.

Born in Cuba, Irigonegaray came to the United States with his mother as a political refugee at age 12 in 1961. Eventually, his mom found a job in Topeka at the Kansas Neurological Institute, and he attended school in Topeka, then Kemper Military Academy in Boonville, Missouri, where he earned an associate's degree from the academy's junior college. He later received degrees in business administration and economics at Washburn University. Irigonegaray graduated from Washburn's School of Law in 1973 and opened a private practice the same year. When the Kellers contacted him in May 1992, he knew their daughter's case well.

"I remember reading that this terrible tragedy occurred as a result of an inmate being inappropriately released," he said. "It resulted in the loss of a beautiful child. When a child is brutally assassinated like that, it's much like tossing a stone into a still pond and those concentric circles that move out. The consequences were so devastating, and I believed that a remedy should occur."

To get that remedy, the Kellers wanted the state to acknowledge that a mistake was made when Jon Jr. was placed with Gene and Tammy Blake. The Kellers and their attorneys focused on Osage County attorney Cheryl Stewart, but she had prosecutorial immunity and could not be sued, so they chose to pursue compensation from the State of Kansas.

"You cannot replace Brenda. Your money cannot bring her back," Bob and Tracy wrote to legislators. "But you can send a message. Unfortunately, the State of Kansas has granted immunity from prosecution. In principle, we can appreciate the need for this immunity, but it leaves us with no place to go except to you and your colleagues. We wish we could take this matter to court, but we can't. You are our place of last resort."

Irigonegaray and his firm began their work the first week of May in 1992, sending a letter to the Department of Corrections requesting information about Jon Jr.'s incarceration, including what the state's legal responsibility was for him on the day he attacked Brenda. Little did the Kellers know that letter was just the beginning of a long, arduous process.

MIRED IN FEAR

Crystal and Marilee Sievers loved West Ridge Mall. It was the go-to spot for high school and junior high kids in the early 1990s. The two-story shopping palace had dozens of stores, a large food court, a gigantic arcade, and Topeka's main movie theatre. It was the place to hang out, be seen, and meet friends walking from one end in the northeast corner to the other in the southwest.

The Sievers sisters, still reeling from the loss of their friend, hit the mall to get away from their struggling community one Saturday afternoon in the spring of 1992. As Crystal Sievers walked through the building, she spotted a younger man with straggly long hair and a mustache. She flinched immediately, feeling her stomach drop and heart accelerate.

"I thought I saw Jon, and I was freaking out," she said. "I think at that point I was trying to understand what happened. To this day, anytime I walk into that mall, I think about that day and seeing him somehow in my mind."

That paralyzing fear didn't go away for months, and in some cases, years, for many of those who grew up with Brenda. Brooklynd Thomas woke up in the middle of the night screaming for a year. Sometimes, her mother would run into the bedroom and find her daughter pounding the closet door, thinking she was trapped. Misty Lange slept on her grandparents' bedroom floor well into the summer of 1992. Jim and Judy Wilson, who lived on a remote farm half a mile from the highway, made their daughter attach a long orange flag to her bike so they could watch her ride down to the road from their porch.

"We didn't let her do things by herself," Judy Wilson said. "She hated that orange flag."

Jill Wilson felt lost. She had to find a new best friend and obsessed over Brenda's death until she left junior high. Amber McGhee, who lived just a few houses down from the Kellers, didn't feel safe until she left Dover after high school nearly 10 years later. Until she graduated, McGhee would run from the driveway to her house after being dropped off or driving home. The Sievers sisters reacted differently. Crystal was angry, and Marilee became skittish.

"I felt cheated out of my youth," Crystal Sievers said. "I just wanted to grow up and get out of there. You'd hear a noise in the house and get the ball bat out."

Before Brenda died, kids in Dover were free to roam as they pleased. Afterward, Tyrel and Autumn Buchmeier couldn't just leave and walk to the creek behind their house. Even when the town erected street lights in the months after Brenda's murder, parents had a tight grip on the children.

"Everything just kind of stopped," Autumn Buchmeier said.

To make matters worse, the rumor mill of the small town clicked into high gear. Many held the belief that justice was not complete as long as Jon Sr. was free. At that point, however, few knew that Ivan was at the house around the time Brenda disappeared. Another rumor circulating was that Brenda was in the house at the time Tracy walked into the Blakes' and tried to wake Jon Jr.

"My kids were horrified and wanted details, and I didn't have them," Lavella Buchmeier said. "Our son said, 'They said they chopped her head off.'"

Overnight, the innocence Dover coveted was gone. Children didn't walk around or ride their bikes. There weren't any basketball games at the court by the junior high. Kids did not move without their parents watching.

"I don't think a lot of them understood what happened to Brenda until later," Penny Lister said. "Those kids ... their lives will never be the same."

A MOVING DEDICATION

Much of Irigonegaray and his staff's work in 1992 was tracking down documents pertaining to Jon Jr., his court cases, and the details behind his release from the Osage County Jail on Oct. 1. Two days after he sent a letter to the Department of Corrections, Irigonegaray received a letter from Charles Simmons, the chief legal counsel for the organization. It was short and to the point: Jon Jr. was released on parole on Feb. 25, 1991, from a one- to five-year sentence imposed in Dougas County and was on parole for that sentence on the day he murdered Brenda. He also was on probation for the misdemeanor offenses in Coffey and Osage counties.

According to documents provided by the Keller family, Irigonegaray also reached out to David Debenham on May 21, asking to meet with the attorney who prosecuted Jon Jr. Tracking down documents to file a claim for compensation with the state legislature took months. Throughout the process, Irigonegaray met with Bob and Tracy numerous times. While some lawyers manage to keep their emotions out of a case they're working, Irigonegaray did the exact opposite. He connected with the Kellers, noting that one thing stood out when he met with the couple.

"The pain. The unnecessary pain caused by such a senseless loss," he said. "I have been involved in so many similar matters, and no matter on how many occasions, each time it is as if a scab has been ripped off. In law school, we're taught to keep an imaginary wall between us and the emotions that a client was experiencing, but that has never worked for me."

Irigonegaray told Bob and Tracy what he told all of his clients: They were going to share tears and laughter.

"The pain I saw the Kellers go through, the overwhelming grief, that's as fresh today as it was then," he said in 2019. "If it's true for me, I can't begin to imagine what it's like for them."

As the Kellers' pursuit of justice stretched into the fall of 1992, Warren and Susan Wilson worked to honor Brenda in a way she would have appreciated. On Nov. 8, 1992, the Joy 88 radio station dedicated the Topeka Christian Lending Library, with an emphasis on the children's section, and named it the Brenda Keller Memorial Children's Library.

The library was an addition to the first floor of the former home of the late Alf Landon, a former Kansas governor, according to an article in The Topeka CHRISTIAN. The story described the children's section as "cheerfully painted and decorated." Brenda's area of the room featured her artwork, two photos, and a two-page section of an article about her in The Topeka CHRISTIAN, all framed free of charge by the owner of the Ben Franklin store in the capital city.

Like she did at Brenda's funeral, Pam Leptich spoke at the dedication, focusing on the way Brenda thought about life.

"(Brenda's friends and classmates) are doing more than remembering values of the past," she said. "They are in a much greater sense demonstrating what Brenda taught and how they learned her lessons for the future and for now. This memorial is a promise that the children who read the books of this library will grow and learn because the people who love Brenda loved life.

"May this memorial then be not to Brenda's memory. May it be to what she continues to teach the living. For therein lies the future of goodness."

Many of Brenda's friends attended the dedication. The Federated Church's youth group purchased and furnished signs above the door that opened to the children's section, along with one under her picture. Though they were humbled that their daughter was being honored, it was a rough day for Bob and Tracy, who saw a lifetime of memories go by during the event. A photo of the Kellers after the dedication, taken in front of Brenda's drawings, captures the devastation, as it shows a solemn couple with red eyes and tear-stained cheeks posing for the camera.

PROSECUTORIAL IMMUNITY

As Irigonegaray and his firm prepared to file a compensation claim for the spring of 1993 when the Kansas Legislature was back in session, Bob and Tracy agreed to forego civil litigation against Jon Jr., in exchange for him agreeing to provide access to records such as psychological evaluations, presentencing reports, sentencing reports, and photographs and videos pertaining to Brenda's murder. In doing so, that allowed Irigonegaray to demonstrate that releasing Jon Jr. while he should have been at the Osawatomie Correctional Facility presented a danger to society.

Irigonegaray's staff also obtained the court documents, including the journal entry on Jon Jr.'s sentence modification in Osage County, and the letter from parole officer Devon Knoll about sending him to Osawatomie for the final three months of his sentence. Four days before Christmas in 1992, the Kellers' attorney mailed a letter to Judge James Smith asking him for any details he remembered about the case.

On Dec. 30, 1992, Elizabeth Herbert, an attorney at the firm, spoke with Delton Gilliland, the counselor for Osage County. Herbert explained to Gilliland that they were attempting to determine who made the decision to release Jon Jr. In a memo, Herbert wrote that Gilliland agreed with her assumption that Judge Smith "may not have understood that there was a problem in getting Mareska a space at the Osawatomie program and indicated that I was probably reasonable in assuming that Cheryl Stewart had something to do with the release of Mareska, although he did not specifically verify that."

A week later, on Jan. 6, 1993, Judge Smith replied to Irigonegaray's letter, writing, "With respect to what I authorized or intended to authorize, the hearing and journal entry speak for themselves." The journal entry, from Sept. 24, stated that the judge agreed to modify Jon Jr.'s sentence, as long as he stayed in the Osawatomie facility for the remainder of his sentence. Smith, who retired in 2007 after 27 years on the bench, declined to comment on the case when reached by telephone.

At the beginning of March, just a week before what would have been Brenda's 14th birthday, Irigonegaray spoke with Steve Pigg, an attorney whose firm represented Osage County. During their conversation, Pigg confirmed that Stewart authorized the release of Jon Jr. on Oct. 1, 1991, according to a letter Irigonegaray sent to the Kellers. In the correspondence with Bob and Tracy, he reminded the Kellers that Stewart could not be sued due to prosecutorial immunity and that his firm would focus on filing for compensation with the Joint Legislative Committee on Special Claims Against the State.

"It's important that prosecutors have immunity. They have a difficult job, and we don't want to prosecute either civilly or criminally those civil servants working as prosecutors for an honest mistake," Irigonegaray said. "On the other hand, if their behavior as a prosecutor can be proven to be outside the scope of their authority or grossly negligent to the point of being either reckless or intentional, then they may be held culpable. This just didn't rise to that level."

With the Legislature scheduled to wrap up at the end of the spring in 1993, Irigonegaray planned to file the required paperwork in the fall of that year, anticipating that the Legislature would act on the claim in January 1994. In April of 1993, the Kellers crafted a letter to submit to the Joint Committee on Special Claims.

"What deeply angers us is the realization that this need not have happened!" the Kellers wrote. "It should not have happened! Her murderer was supposed to be in jail!"

APPEAL DENIED

As the Kellers fought for justice through filing a compensation claim, Jon Jr. continued to fight for a reduced sentence. A year after the court system denied an appeal, chief appellant defender Jessica Kunen argued that the district court "abused its discretion by refusing to modify the sentence without a consideration," according to the Supreme Court of Kansas transcript on the appeal. On July 9, 1993, Kunen cited two previous court cases in her argument, both of which the Court said did not support Jon Jr's position.

An article in the July 10 edition of the Topeka Capital-Journal noted that two of the factors that Kunen said should be considered in a requested modification "are whether the State Reception and Diagnostic Center recommended modification and whether significant new or additional information helpful to a defendant has arisen since the original sentencing."

In remarks written by longtime justice Donald Allegrucci, the Kansas Supreme Court stated that the Topeka Correctional Facility report contained no significant or new additional information beneficial to Jon Jr.

"We do not find that the district court abused its discretion in denying the defendant's motion for modification of sentence," the Court said.

A month later, on Aug. 27, Jon Jr. filed a motion in district court for another hearing on his sentencing under the Kansas Sentencing Guidelines Act. According to the Supreme Court's transcript on the motion, Kunen and assistant appellate defender Rick Kittel contended that the district court erred in denying the motion for the conversion of his sentence. As part of the sentencing guidelines, individuals sentenced before July 1, 1993, could receive modifications if their crimes were classified in a "presumptive nonimprisonment grid block" (the intersection where the crime seriousness ranking and the criminal history classification meet).

However, the Court stated that none of the four crimes Jon Jr. pleaded guilty to would be classified in that grid block. First-degree murder is an off-grid felony, and aggravated kidnapping, rape, and aggravated criminal sodomy are more severe convictions than those on the grid. Even though he agreed to the sentences he received, Jon Jr. appealed several times. The August 1993 appeal wasn't the last, and the court proceedings stretched into late 1994.

Meanwhile, the Kellers' battle with the State of Kansas was just beginning in the summer and fall of 1993. Not only did they have Irigonegaray in their corner, but also the state attorney general's office. On Aug. 23, John Campbell, the state's deputy attorney general, responded to a letter from the Legislative Research Department, stating that although Kansas had no legal obligation to compensate the Kellers, his office said compensation would be in the public interest and recommended they receive at least $100,000.

In his letter, Campbell detailed why the office supported compensation, including "at the time of the murder, Mareska should have been in the Osage County Jail. However, Mareska was released from jail contrary to a court order. The release of a known violent predator like Mareska, without even the hint of legal process, is so outrageous as to shock the conscience." Campbell continued, describing Jon Jr.'s release as "devoid of any justification or logic" and writing that the

$100,000 was based on a non-pecuniary loss cap found in the Kansas Wrongful Death Act.

RECOMMENDED AND DENIED

Initially, it seemed like a slam dunk claim for Bob and Tracy. On Nov. 9, 1993, the Joint Committee on Claims Against the State recommended that the Kellers receive $100,000. However, the committee did not agree on the $500,000 that Irigonegaray sought. The couple's attorney also knew that the Legislature had to approve the decision.

"We hope we can put closure to this," Irigonegaray told The Associate Press' Matt Truell.

At the time, Stewart was not involved in the claim, but did speak to Truell, denying a statement by Irigonegaray that she acted as a judge when she ordered Jon Jr. to be released.

"I take strong exception to what Mr. Irigonegaray said," Stewart said, telling the reporter that Jon Jr. was released to his parole officer, who placed him with the Blakes.

The committee ultimately voted 5-4 to compensate the Kellers. According to The Associated Press, one member of the committee, Rep. Rex Crowell, a Republican, voted against the claim because he thought it wasn't enough, while a fellow Republican, Sen. Al Ramirez, said that 40% of the amount would go to Irigonegaray.

Stewart did not speak to the committee before it voted to recommend $100,000 in compensation, but she immediately got involved when it became clear that she was being blamed for Jon Jr.'s release.

"They said I was responsible, it was my fault, and the Legislature said Cheryl Stewart did it," Stewart said. "I said, 'Oh hell, no.' I wasn't going to go down like that, and I didn't go down like that because someone listened to me."

Stewart said she met with Wint Winters, then a former state senator and chair of the Senate Judiciary Committee. Winters died at age 82 in 2013.

"He showed me his file, and I showed him my file (on the case), and he went, 'Oh (shoot), you really didn't have any information, did you, Ms. Stewart?'" Stewart said. "The medical report that I saw, that Wint Winters let me read ... he had a bunch of different kinds of drugs (at the time he committed Brenda's murder). He had some really bad stuff rolling about his body. It wasn't just he got drunk and smoked some grass. There was no indication, and I told this to Wint Winters, that this guy would go do drugs and do what he did. There's nothing that would have predicted that, in my opinion.

"Even if I'd known about the (prior burglaries) and that he had a couple of assaults on women, there's nothing in that that would say he would go out and commit the kind of (crime) he did. Now, if he had a rape (in his criminal history before the murder), then, yeah, we've got a problem. He didn't have a rape."

Numerous attempts by the author to locate the file and toxicology report, including at the State Capitol, were unsuccessful.

On Dec. 15, just five weeks after the joint committee recommended compensation, Stewart testified before the group at the State Capitol. According to Truell's article in the Capital-Journal, Stewart told the committee she had no choice but to order the release of Jon Jr. because the court did not order him to be in jail.

"We had no authority to hold him," she said. "We had someone in jail we could not legally hold."

Stewart also stated that Jon Jr's record did not show that he was dangerous because he had convictions for theft, burglary, vandalism, and domestic violence, to go along with an addiction to alcohol.

"No one saw the need for him to be held there," she said in the article. "Hindsight is a wonderful thing. No one could have predicted he was going to do this. If you want to blame someone, blame Mareska."

Stewart also said that the state's attorney general, Bob Stephan, had a vendetta against her, pointing to a letter from Assistant Attorney General John Campbell that referred to her conduct as "outrageous."

"They never talked to me. They never asked for my files," Stewart said to The Associated Press. "I believe he's misleading this committee."

The committee reversed its decision that day, deciding not to compensate the Kellers. Irigonegaray did not mince words when Truell asked him about the reversal.

"I think this is outrageous," he said. "The family of this young woman who was so brutally attacked, sexually molested, and murdered by a vicious criminal has suffered enough."

Interviewed in 2019, Irigonegaray still felt the sting of the committee's decision that day.

"I was ashamed of their callousness, and of their coldness," he said. "How dare they. How. Dare. They."

Two days after the joint committee changed its decision, Stephan continued to push the Legislature to approve compensation for the Kellers, writing a letter to Sen. Tim Emert, the chairman of the committee, in which he said he was "shocked" by the decision. Stephan made the letter public on Dec. 22, but for the moment, Bob and Tracy's push for justice was on hold more than two years after their daughter's murder.

CHAPTER SIXTEEN:

A NOBLE FIGHT

At first glance, Bill Lucero and Bob seem like an odd pair. Lucero, a self-described Unitarian, is a leftist whose politics are the opposite of many of the longtime Dover pastor's beliefs. But they share a common bond: the murder of a loved one.

Lucero was 26 years old when his stepmother shot and killed his father in 1972. Per Lucero, his stepmother said she was about to commit suicide and was holding a gun when Rubel Lucero walked into the kitchen of their home in New Mexico.

Rubel saw his wife point the gun at her head and tried to distract her by throwing a cup of hot coffee at her. She turned, pointed the gun at him, and fired, hitting him in the stomach and killing him. Though she was arrested and tried for manslaughter, a jury found the woman not guilty by temporary insanity. She spent two years in a state hospital before being released.

"I've never had any conversation with this woman," Lucero said. "I've never met her. I don't have any desire to. Some murder victim's families feel like if they don't want revenge that they need some type of closure by meeting. That never appealed to me."

In the months after his father's death, Lucero watched as hatred ate his grandfather alive. A year later, battling depression and the devastation of losing his son, he died.

"It killed him," Lucero said. "He was never the same. So, I not only lost a father, but I lost a grandfather."

In the same year that Lucero's father died, the U.S. Supreme Court invalidated all death penalty sentences in the landmark case Furman v. Georgia, reducing all of those sentences to life in prison. From 1972 to 1976, no one was sentenced to death or executed. That changed in 1976 when Georgia sentenced Troy Leon Gregg to death for the murder of two men during a robbery. Georgia, like several other states, had been working since 1972 to establish a list of circumstances sufficient for capital punishment.

During that span, Lucero did not spend much time thinking about his stance on the death penalty. He was far more concerned with such issues as the Vietnam War, until he realized that the death of his father and grandfather gave him insight others might not have about capital punishment.

"That fact that my dad had been murdered ... the irony hit me," he said. "Everybody knows what they would do, and I was the one who encountered it. I'd seen what it'd done to my grandfather."

Lucero began to dig into the topic and said his research showed that victims did not receive the closure some think they would with a death sentence or execution. By 1978, he was so invested in fighting against the death penalty that he testified before the Kansas Legislature, which was considering reinstating capital punishment.

"I gave various reasons why it didn't seem like it would be very effective," he said. "I said, 'My father was murdered. I don't see how this is going to do anything for me.' You could have heard a pin drop at that point."

When Lucero left the Statehouse that day, a mob of reporters gathered around him, taking pictures and asking him dozens of questions. The next day, he was on the front page of several newspapers. Shortly thereafter, he became a founding member of the Coalition to Keep Kansas Free of the Death Penalty, now known as the Kansas Coalition Against the Death Penalty. For decades, he was one of the staunchest advocates of abolishing capital punishment in the state, testifying several times, lobbying against it through multiple governors, and staging protests at the Capitol.

In early 1994, the death penalty was a polarizing issue in Kansas politics, with a governor, Joan Finney, who was against it. However, several lawmakers pushed to reinstate capital punishment during that legislative session. Lucero organized an effort to sway the votes of senators and representatives, in hopes of preventing it. As part of that effort, he asked Sister Helen Prejean to speak to various politicians. Immortalized in the Academy Award-winning movie "Dead Man Walking," Prejean wrote a bestselling book about the impact of the death penalty that served as the basis for the film.

"It was in the newspapers that we were bringing back Helen Prejean, and I got a call from Bob Keller," Lucero said. "He said, 'I'm quite interested to hear Sister Prejean.' I said, 'I know of you. You're that little girl's father.'"

Lucero not only invited Bob to the meeting, but also asked if he could attend a meeting of Parents of Murdered Children (POMC) with Bob.

SPEAKING TO THE SENATE

Bob met Sister Prejean at the meeting, but he was more taken by the speaker before her, a woman named Sue Norton from Arkansas City, a town of about 12,000 people in south central Kansas. Four years earlier, Norton's father and stepmother were murdered in a small Oklahoma town about an hour from Arkansas City.

The killer, Robert Knighton, escaped from a halfway house in Kansas City in January 1990, embarking on a crime spree with two accomplices – Knighton's girlfriend, Ruth Williams, and a friend,

Lawrence Brittain. As the trio drove through rural Oklahoma low on gas, they spotted a secluded farmhouse near the tiny town of Tonkawa. Before robbing Richard and Virginia Denney of $61 and an old pickup truck, Knighton shot the couple, killing both. Brittain received a life sentence, Williams 30 years, and Knighton the death penalty.

Even though Knighton murdered her father, Norton forgave and befriended him. In a Wichita Eagle article in 2000, Norton said she found no peace in Knighton being sentenced to die.

"I didn't understand why I had this turmoil in my mind," she said. "Why wasn't I glad that we were winning? And why wasn't I glad that it was almost over? ... I prayed, and I did forgive him."

Shortly after his sentencing, Knighton agreed to meet with Norton. During their conversation, she told Knighton she didn't hate him.

"If you're guilty, I forgive you," she said before taking his hand in prayer.

Norton's message impacted Bob, who was wrestling with his stance on capital punishment. Bob and Lucero met a few times, including the latter attending a POMC meeting, before Bob said he thought he opposed the death penalty. Lucero asked Bob if he would speak to the Legislature about the matter.

On Feb. 18, 1994, as the debate over capital punishment raged in the Statehouse, Bob stood before the Senate Judiciary Committee and said:

"On a Saturday afternoon, in October 1991, my 12-year-old daughter, Brenda, decided to go on a bike ride. She never came home. Less than a mile from her home, in broad daylight, Brenda was grabbed from behind, pulled off the road, and forced to go to a secluded area, where she was raped. Throughout this process, she was savagely beaten. Then, after her attacker was through with her, he strangled her, and tossed her body into a shed. The man is now serving what will be a minimum of 40 years in prison. If the death penalty had been Kansas law that day, he would probably be on death row at this very moment.

"I was thinking about that the other day. I've asked myself how would I feel if this man were to be executed? What would it be like to know that someday in the near future he would be strapped to a table and killed? This man who destroyed my daughter's very precious life. To be honest with you, there are times when I find that idea very appealing.

"But then I think of Brenda. Not how she died, but how she lived. The little girl who announced when she was 5 that she thought maybe God put her in the world to love bugs. And all through her very short time in this world she was dedicated to saving and protecting bugs and worms and spiders and snakes and things most people would just as soon step on. And I think—no—I know, she would be horrified if a man, not a bug, not a snake, not a beast, but a human being, were to be killed in her name.

"The one thing that I can't get away from, the one thing that keeps me from joining others in calling for capital punishment is the very thing that losing Brenda has taught me. Once somebody is dead, there is no getting up again. After a life is taken, you can't give it back. Death is final. As Brenda's daddy, I know that all too well. My arms ache to hold her. And nothing you do will give her back to our family. Not anything, not even killing her killer.

"And what if, in our zeal to get tough on crime, an innocent man is executed? Mistakes can still be made. To err is human. Once he's dead, all you can say to his parents is 'Oops! I'm sorry. We made a mistake.' But you can never give him back his life. And for me, life is too precious to take that chance.'"

Unfortunately for anti-death penalty advocates, Bob's powerful message that day lost some of its thunder, Lucero said, when Gov. Finney also made a statement at that Capitol building opposing death sentences.

An article in the Topeka Capital-Journal the next morning stated that Finney told the Senate Judiciary Committee, "Please let us not send a message of violence and retaliation to our children, but rather work to cure the resentment that is festering within their hearts."

During her statement, Finney faced several questions from Dick Bond, a Republican who opposed the death penalty and pushed the governor to veto a capital punishment bill. But Finney said that she would keep her promise, made in 1993, to let the bill pass without her signature. Bond pushed Finney, saying that she had a constitutional duty to sign or veto the measure, not "pass" on the issues, according to the Capital-Journal.

"Finney got into an immediate argument with Bond," Lucero said. "Once they got done, she walked off in a huff, and that was right before Bob testified."

Reporters listening to the statement followed Finney out of the courtroom and didn't hear Bob speak.

MURDER FUELS REINSTATEMENT

The death penalty was a polarizing issue in the Legislature that year in large part due to a brutal murder in the summer of 1993. In July of that year, Stephanie Schmidt, a 19-year-old student at Pittsburg State University in southeast Kansas, was raped and murdered by a coworker, Donald Ray Gideon. The killer was a convicted rapist paroled after serving 10 years for rape and sodomy.

That murder led to Stephanie's Law, a bill allowing the state to keep those convicted of sex crimes confined after they complete their sentences, if professionals deem that they should not be released. The measure went all the way to the U.S. Supreme Court, which upheld the law.

Gideon received 100 years in prison, but many, including some legislators, felt the death penalty should have been applied, just as many individuals felt like Jon Jr. should have been sentenced to death for killing Brenda. After more than 20 years of debate, Schmidt's death at the hands of a convicted sex offender on parole was a tipping point to get capital punishment reinstated.

The day before Finney and Bob spoke to the Senate Judiciary Committee in opposition of the death penalty, Schmidt's parents spoke at the Statehouse, asking them to reinstate it. During that hearing, Schmidt's mother, Peggy, said she wasn't asking for justice for her daughter.

"If that were the case, Don Gideon should be made to suffer like he made Stephanie suffer," she said. "The death penalty is more humane, considerate, and compassionate than any criminal act these animals impose on their victims."

According to the Topeka Capital-Journal, Schmidt's father, Gene, said the risk of executing an innocent person shouldn't prevent legislatures from passing the law.

"My daughter was executed," he said. "My daughter was innocent. The death penalty is in the hands of the criminals. And by voting no on the death penalty, you are voting to definitely execute innocent lives in the largest of numbers."

The Kansas House of Representatives had already passed a capital punishment bill allowing juries to impose the penalty on murderers of police officers, prosecutors, jailers, corrections officers, judges, court officers, parole officers, and inmates. That measure also allowed the penalty to be imposed for a homicide during a kidnapping, sexually violent crime, or premeditated murder.

The day after the Schmidts testified, Lucero was fuming when Gov. Finney told the committee she wouldn't veto the bill and would allow it to pass without signing it.

"I was really livid," he said. "That's not what she told me in private."

However, Lucero and others opposing capital punishment caught a bit of a reprieve a month later when the House rejected the death penalty bill passed by the Senate on March 19. Representatives voted 69-54 against, partly because many of the members of the House didn't think it was stringent enough.

In addition, according to the Capital-Journal, the vote may have been the result of political posturing. An article on March 19 stated that Bob Miller, the House speaker, said some representatives wanted to keep the capital punishment bill alive to assist their candidate for the upcoming gubernatorial election.

CRIME AND PUNISHMENT

Ultimately, on April 8, the Kansas Legislature passed a bill to reinstate capital punishment. Before it passed, Tim Emert, the senator from Independence, Kansas, spoke before the final vote on the measure, telling his fellow lawmakers how much of an impact Bob's testimony had on him, Lucero said.

"Emert was knocked off his feet by Bob's testimony," he said. "When they did the final vote on the floor, which passed 21-19, Emert stood up and said, 'I don't know if any of you attended the committee hearing other than the committee members, but I was particularly impressed by the testimony of the Rev. Bob Keller.' That was the voice he heard."

After the Senate passed the bill, the House voted 67-58 to approve the death penalty, in part because the adjusted bill applied to more individuals convicted of first-degree murder. Once it passed, Lucero and the Kansas Coalition Against the Death Penalty promised to protest with a fast outside of Finney's office in the Statehouse.

"We're not asking her to break her word," Lucero said of Finney's statement about allowing a capital punishment bill to pass without her signature. "We're asking her to do what's best for Kansas, and that's what she said she wanted to do. We're not trying to pester her. We're trying to support her."

Ironically, the day the Legislature passed the bill was the day of one of the most notorious crimes in Topeka history. Just hours before the House voted, Robert Lewis Jackson shot and murdered three people in Shanghi Lil's, a gentlemen's club in the south part of town and across the street from Gene and Tammy Blake's salon.

A court released Jackson, then 23, three months earlier because of a retroactive release clause in the state's sentencing guidelines. He was in jail in Shawnee County 11 times and sentenced to five to 20 years in prison for aggravated burglary and one to two years for theft. But he was placed on supervised probation for five years and, after several months of legal haggling, ended up being released on Jan. 13, 1994.

On the night of the triple murder, Jackson was at Shanghi Lil's earlier in the evening and made sexual remarks to a waitress, which made her uncomfortable. According to the Capital-Journal, Jackson's actions also prompted complaints by other waitresses and dancers, and bouncer Matt Fabry, the same man who fought Jon Mareska Sr. at a bar in 1990, asked him to leave.

Jackson returned at closing time (2 a.m.), getting into a shoving match with Fabry, who fell to the ground. Jackson then drew a handgun and shot Fabry in the face, killing him. Another employee, Daniel Rutherford, rushed to help Fabry and was shot in the face. Jackson also murdered customer Jon Stratton, who was shot eight times while trying to help Fabry.

Police arrested Jackson the same day at an acquaintance's house and charged him with three counts of premeditated murder, two counts of aggravated battery, one count each of felony unlawful possession of a firearm, misdemeanor criminal damage to property, and misdemeanor criminal trespassing.

Within the next week, the families of Rutherford, Stratton, and Fabry buried each man. Fabry, who was 33, left behind two daughters, and more than 300 mourners attended his funeral service, according to the Capital-Journal. On April 14, 1994, the newspaper ran a story about the bouncer with the headline, "Victim had 'finally found his way.'"

The article described Fabry as a large man who had long hair and tattoos, drove a motorcycle, and had a heart as big as his stature, even though he struggled with alcohol and drugs.

"He said, 'Mom, I think I've really matured, and I think I need to start accepting responsibility for things,'" his mother, Linda, told the paper. "We had noticed a change in him in his last few visits."

His daughters remembered their father for the toys, phone calls, and $2 bills he gave them.

"I'm never going to cry over this man (Jackson) because he's hard and cold," the youngest daughter told her grandmother. "My daddy is soft and warm."

Less than a year later, Jackson received nearly 70 years in prison on several convictions. He won't be eligible for parole until 2062, when he's 93 years old.

THIS, TOO, SHALL PASS

By April 18, 1994, the death penalty bill passed by the Kansas Legislature was just four days away from becoming a law. According to state law, a bill must remain with a governor for 10 days once he or she receives it. Due to a slew of measures being passed on April 8, Finney did not receive it until later the following week. Without her signature, Kansas would reinstate capital punishment at midnight on April 23.

Leading up to the deadline, Capital-Journal reporter Tim Hrenchir wrote an article about the death penalty and the impact it would have had on several people in Shawnee County convicted of murder. That list, which features nine of the 80 people convicted of homicide in the county during the 1990s, included Jon Jr. and Jackson.

Of the nine inmates Hrenchir wrote about, one died in prison, one committed suicide on the day of his crime, one died at age 93, just two weeks after being released, and six remain incarcerated. As of 2024, the remaining six are still in Kansas prisons, and while Jon Jr. wasn't eligible for the death penalty, Lucero expects him to be behind bars the rest of this life.

"He's not ever getting out," he said. "There's no parole board that would ever release him."

The State of Kansas officially reinstated the death penalty, via lethal injection, on the Friday after Hrenchir's article, as, true to her word, Gov. Finney allowed the bill to pass without signing it. The governor issued a short statement regarding her decision, saying she didn't veto capital punishment because she believed most Kansans supported it.

In the nearly 30 years since the bill took effect on July 1, 1994, only 13 men received the death penalty in Kansas, and nine of those still face capital punishment. Their crimes are extreme, ranging from several murders by brothers Jonathan and Reginald Carr during the "Wichita Massacre," to serial killer John Robinson Sr., to Justin Thurber, who slaughtered Cowley County Community College dance team member Jodi Sanderholm in 2007. One of the men, James Kraig Kahler, murdered his estranged wife, two daughters, and his wife's grandmother in Burlingame in 2009.

The first person to receive the death sentence in Kansas since the 1960s was Gary Kleypas, who raped and killed Pittsburg State student Carrie Williams in 1996. More than 25 years later, Kleypas still awaits execution.

"Some feel so much better that justice has been done once we put that death collar on them," Lucero said. "But there's no demand for it anymore. The courts aren't real excited about doing it. They're fearful of executing the wrong person. There's lots of good legal reasons not to do it. Nobody considers all the problems that go with it."

DENIED AGAIN

Represented by Topeka attorney Pedro Irigonegaray, Bob and Tracy continued to pursue compensation from the State of Kansas in the fall of 1994. Despite the support of Attorney General Bob Stephan, who told the Joint Committee on Special Claims Against the State that Osage County Attorney Cheryl Stewart "acted without lawful authority" in releasing Jon Jr. to a parole officer in October 1991, the result was the same.

For the second time in a year, the committee voted 6-5 on Nov. 15 against recommending a payment to the Kellers. Stewart, who spoke to the same group in December 1993, didn't appear and said she would let her previous statement that Judge James Smith never said Mareska was to stay in jail stand, according to the Topeka Capital-Journal.

"I think she was doing what she believed the law to be," Sen. Tim Emert said. "It's a horrible tragedy."

In an attempt to sway the committee before the vote, the Kellers' team, which included Irigonegaray's firm and Lucero, put together a two-page document with the following topics: Who is Jon Mareska? Why is he free? What did the Kansas attorney general say? What are we asking you to do?

Under "Why is he free," they pointed to the fateful sentence modification hearing, quoting the court transcript from the day Judge Smith asked Stewart to confirm that Jon Jr. would be moved to the Osawatomie facility. When answering "What are we asking you to do?" they made it clear that the Kellers were far more interested in justice than money.

"The judicial system failed miserably, and we ask you to recognize this failure by compensating the Keller family $100,000, as requested by the attorney general," the document read. "We believe this would send a message to all officials who are responsible for the care and keeping of dangerous criminals. It would say to them that we in Kansas do not take lightly the careless release of criminals before their time."

Some of the remarks of the legislators who voted against compensation hit a nerve with Irigonegaray.

"The main problem was that, unlike John Campbell, who looked at this from a perspective of what is right, the legislators we were dealing with were concerned with what was politically advantageous," Irigonegaray said. "Some had the incredible opinion, in my opinion, that somehow denying payment was the right political decision. I could not get over that. It was uncontroverted that he had been released prior to the sentence being completed, and that as a consequence, he had the ability to commit this heinous murder."

As if that wasn't enough to cope with, the Kellers also had to endure a last-ditch effort by Jon Jr. to modify his sentence at the end of the year. Represented by appellate defenders Jessica Kunen and Rick Kittel again during his final appeal, Jon Jr. challenged the points from the courts on his previous appeals. The Kansas Supreme Court, however, affirmed the previous judgment, ending his court battles to get out of prison any earlier than 2031.

Despite a second denial from the legislative committee, the Kellers' drive for justice continued into spring 1995, beginning with a letter Bob wrote to Sen. Alicia Salisbury, a Republican who served four terms from 1984 to 2000. He wrote, "Senate Bill 95 is stuck in committee. Bill Lucero tells me they are hung up primarily over payment of lawyer fees, and who knows what just might happen to our claim in the process. I was wondering if there's anything you could do to help us."

The Kellers also made handouts with a photo of Brenda not long before she died, wearing a pretty blue dress with her distinctive bright red hair resting on both shoulders, along with a poem she wrote and the Bible verse from Corinthians 15:53: "For our earthly bodies, the ones we have now that can die, must be transformed into heavenly bodies that cannot perish, but will live forever."

Along with that, on the day before what would have been his daughter's 16th birthday, Bob wrote a two-page letter to the committee, telling them that a day that should be a celebration was now one of pain. He also referenced a quote by a legislator who opposed compensation, agreeing that the state didn't kill Brenda, but writing "if this representative of the state had followed proper procedure, this disturbed man would not have been able to kill anyone."

In his closing paragraph, Bob wrote: "There were times, especially at first, when I would think, 'Maybe this is a bad dream, and in the morning, I'll wake up and she will be alive.' But it's not a dream. You cannot replace Brenda. Your money cannot bring her back. But you can send a message. I believe a positive response from you would send a message to all officials who are responsible for the care and keeping of dangerous criminals that the citizens of Kansas do not take lightly the careless release of dangerous prisoners onto the streets before they have served their time."

Bob's plea for justice, however, would have to wait another two years.

CHAPTER SEVENTEEN:

JUSTICE DELAYED BUT SERVED

Once the Legislature declined compensation for the Kellers during the 1995 session, Bob and Tracy tried to move on. After struggling to find his way while getting into plenty of trouble throughout high school, Brenda's big brother John graduated from Mission Valley just weeks after the claim didn't pass. During high school, John connected with a high school English teacher who helped him navigate the years after his sister's death.

"Mr. Cound was the reason that I went to KU (the University of Kansas)," he said. "I loved the way he taught and loved the way he encouraged people to think."

John Cound, a longtime English and theater teacher, inspired John to initially pursue a career in teaching, but life has a way of altering plans. John, who met his future wife during high school, started his own family just as he graduated from college.

"When I was about to graduate, my wife got pregnant," John said. "I decided I needed to get a job that actually pays something. So, I'd been doing web coding for a small startup company. They went under during the dot-com boom, but I found a job in Kansas City doing front-end coding for an advertising company."

As John was leaving for college, Pat was in junior high and adjusting to a completely different life than the one he knew for nine years with his sister. As his parents endured their grief, Pat spent much of his time with the Buchmeiers.

"He was more quiet for a long time," Autumn Buchmeier said. "He stayed the night at our house, and it was always the three of us together (along with her brother Tyrel), but it would be a pretty somber occasion."

Pat continued to avoid conversations about Brenda as he grew into adolescence, though there were constant reminders about her, especially when visiting his grandmother. Jean always had pictures of Brenda and items her granddaughter made, including a magnet on the refrigerator.

"My grandma would always talk about her," he said. "Years ago, it would be emotional, and I wouldn't want to deal with it. When I would hear things, it would sting, and I developed ways to avoid conversations."

It hurt Pat to even think about his sister for a long time.

"It was like I didn't want to be reminded at all ... I wanted to forget her entire memory," he said. "Because I was selfish, I guess."

Tracy described the years after Brenda died as a "fog." It did help that the community embraced her. One local farmer gave her a horse, and another supplied the Kellers with hay for several years. Tracy spent many an afternoon riding her horse across the countryside. It was common to see her riding down the highway before turning off onto dirt roads and fields around Dover.

Several of Brenda's friends spent significant amounts of time with Tracy into their high school years. Amy Best dove into 4-H, working with Tracy to build giant gingerbread houses, while Jill Wilson rode horses in a pasture with her. Amber McGhee rode with Tracy for two or three hours at a time. They didn't talk much, but Tracy taught McGhee several things she didn't know about handling a horse.

"I don't think we ever talked about Brenda," McGhee said.

Brooklynd Thomas visited Bob and Tracy as often as she could, helping Tracy clean the Kellers' house, with the exception of one room.

"I remember never touching Brenda's room," Thomas said.

Though there weren't many people in the community who weren't understanding, those who embraced them even more after the murder were quick to defend the Kellers. Lavella Buchmeier remembers sitting in the town café a few years after the tragedy and hearing a local farmer refer to Tracy as "half-daft" and saying, "She needs to get over it."

"I looked at him and said, 'I'd be completely (expletive) daft,'" Lavella Buchmeier said. "You don't ever get over something like that."

A GROWING FAMILY

One day several years after Brenda's murder, Jean and Roy visited Bob, and the mother and son ended up driving down Douglas Road, passing the cemetery where Brenda is buried and the spot where she went missing. The next structure on that route is the Blakes' house, which had been repainted a few years earlier. Back behind the house, across the pond, was the barren land where the boathouse, which Gene Blake bulldozed not long after the murder, once rested. As Bob and Jean drove past the house, Jean asked Bob if that was where her granddaughter died.

"He just said, 'How did we get on this subject anyway?'" Jean said.

There were and are constant reminders in Dover and elsewhere, especially on a road Bob and Tracy drive virtually every day. In a rare moment when Bob displayed his grief publicly after his daughter's death, he spoke at a family reunion after Brenda died and struggled to finish a speech. Aunt B spoke to Bob after the get-together, giving him a copy of the poem "This is a Child's Grave" by Marion Cohen, which reads in part:

"This is a child's grave. You may dig a hole, build a castle. You may pick the flowers, pull up the grass. You may leave your toys, clutter the path. ... This is a child's grave. There are no rules. No rules, please. Please, no rules."

Aunt B said Bob took to the poem, reading it on difficult days.

"He liked it," she said. "He said, 'That's what has helped me so much.'"

It also helped that Roy and Jean stayed in Topeka for several years. In 1995, however, they moved back to Wichita, where Roy served as the visitation pastor at Crestway Free Methodist Church in Wichita. After two years there, they moved to Hillsboro, where Roy was visitation pastor at the Parkview Mennonite Brethren Church.

Along the way, the family patriarch and matriarch watched as their family continued to grow. Beverly and Janice had more children, and Beverly adopted several more. Roy and Jean had six grandchildren during their time in Hillsboro. Janice said she thought of Brenda every time one of the girls in the family celebrated her 12th birthday.

"I was always glad when that year was over," she said. "I had three girls. My sister had five girls. We had lots of girls. When each of them turned 12, I couldn't wait for that year to be over. I was scared."

Meanwhile, as John found a niche in web work and advertising, his brother discovered his passion through the Explorers, a group of teenage and younger boys working with and learning from the Dover Fire Department.

"I liked driving trucks. I thought it was really cool I could drive them," Pat said. "There was a lot of good people who were really encouraging. I had an interest in it, and they noticed it. Me and a couple of kids got involved, and that's what started it."

By the late 1990s, Pat was off to Hutchinson Community College to study fire science in the city where he was born.

FINALLY, COMPENSATION

By 1997, the Kellers' compensation claim with the state had gone back and forth between the Kansas Senate and House of Representatives for several years. Represented by Pedro Irigonegaray and his firm, Bob and Tracy first submitted their claim in 1993. Two years later, the House and Senate both approved different versions of the claims bill, according to the Topeka Capital-Journal, but couldn't agree on a compromise. In 1996, the House approved the claim, but the Senate removed it from the final bill.

On Thursday, April 3, 1997, just a month before Brenda would have graduated from high school, the House adopted a report authorizing payment to the Kellers in the amount of $100,000. Within a few weeks, Gov. Bill Graves approved the claim.

"No amount of money can bring Brenda back," Bob told the Capital-Journal. "But we're glad the state is finally owning up to its responsibility. Basically, we wanted to get some kind of statement from the state that it recognizes its responsibility."

The approval came as a bit of a surprise to the Kellers, who had given up on it being passed, even when Sen. Greg Packer, a Republican representing Shawnee County, said he was going to push for it during the 1997 session.

"That kind of got things going again," Bob said.

Still, the Kellers endured nearly five years of wrangling in the Legislature, including some quotes and comments they'll never forget. Among those was Sen. "Roadblock" Sherman Jones, a former major league pitcher, who said, "The State of Kansas cannot give away money based on tragedy. If you are exonerated, the committee cannot make the award."

Another legislator, David Adkins, said that the claim shouldn't be approved because the State did not murder Brenda.

"I would have liked to have seen the Legislature embrace the Kellers from the beginning," Irigonegaray said. "It took a long time to get this matter resolved, and that only added insult to the injury."

MOVING ON AND OUT

Justice. That was the goal for the Kellers from the first day they met with Irigonegaray in the spring of 1992. That was just one of Irigonegaray's objectives. The attorney also wanted to do all he could to prevent another family from having to endure the pain the Kellers did when their daughter was murdered by a man who shouldn't have been free when it happened.

"I believe what they did brought a spotlight to shine on the process which had occurred and that light made it clear that errors had been committed," Irigonegaray said. "I am confident that lessons were learned, and in that regard, they achieved a sense of justice."

Despite putting countless hours and an abundance of energy into the claim, Irigonegaray's firm worked the case pro bono.

"You know, Pedro didn't charge us a penny for all the work he did," Bob said. "He's a good man."

For Irigonegaray, it was never a matter of money. It was a matter of doing the right thing.

"You notice I hadn't said a word about that," he said. "My goal wasn't compensation. My goal was their justice. I knew that the right thing was to let them decide what to do with their funds."

What the Kellers eventually did with the money was use a portion of it to move into a new home. In the late 1990s, while Pat was in high school, they moved from the parsonage across from the Dover Federated Church to a small farm in the country. The road leading past the farm is one of the same ones Brenda traveled during her last ride.

The property was large enough for Tracy to care for a throng of animals. In the years since the move, the Kellers have had a large barn with horses, cows, and pigs; a fenced-in pasture with goats and sheep; and a house full of dogs, cats, and other pets, just as Brenda would have liked it.

As one enters the house on the land, wading through several pets, a photo of Brenda rests on the wall. It's a photo Pam Leptich took not long before Brenda died.

WHAT'S IN THE HEART OF A MAN?

Cheryl Stewart served as the Osage County attorney for several years before leaving the area in the late 1990s to work as an attorney in the Kansas City area. Though Brenda's case wasn't prevalent as the years passed, Stewart did hear about it from time to time.

"When you're a prosecutor, you learn to take hits, people blame you. It's one of those poignant, haunting things that occurred because of the way everything works that settled on my desk, settled on me," Stewart said. "I definitely feel for the family because that's a very tragic thing. Nothing can take that back. Nothing can change what that man did."

Stewart also reiterated that nobody could have foreseen Jon Jr. committing such a terrible crime, pointing to another case involving a man she knew from her days as a correctional officer in Topeka. Howard Steven Borders spent a significant amount of time in county jail on misdemeanors, but never struck Stewart as a dangerous individual. Just a month after Brenda's murder, Borders broke into his estranged girlfriend's house, sexually molesting her and her daughters and stabbing them to death. Borders, now in his 60s and serving time in the same facility as Jon Jr., won't be eligible for parole until he's 77 years old.

"Who could have predicted that? Nobody that I know worked with him or was around him ever thought he would have been capable of anything like that," Stewart said. "Nobody knows what's in the heart or mind of a man. No one knows that but him and God."

While Stewart feels singled out, life in Osage County wasn't necessarily easy for others involved in the case, according to the law enforcement officer who transported Jon Jr. from Burlington to Lyndon in June 1991. Eldon Croucher, who worked for the Osage County Sheriff's Department for years, remembers running into one of the attorneys who represented Jon Jr.

"I told her, 'You can't have a conscience,'" Croucher said. "And she said, 'Why's that?' I said, 'You got that (expletive) released, and then he rapes and kills a little girl.' And she goes, 'Well, he was an abused child. His father broke his arm,' and all this other stuff. I said, 'Well, I'll tell you what: I don't care if he had his arm broke. I don't care if he was abused. He knew the difference between right and wrong. If he was abused, why don't you go tell that minister and his wife that? Maybe it'll make them feel a lot better.' She didn't have anything to say."

THE DEATH PENALTY AND THE HEALING PROCESS

Bob continued to work with Lucero into 1998, advocating against the death penalty. By early 1998, only one person in Kansas was on death row. On Feb. 10, 1998, he spoke to the Kansas Legislature in opposition of capital punishment. As he stood before lawmakers in the State Capitol, Bob spoke about his family: "I am a father. I have two sons, one who is 21 and in college, the other who is 16 and in high school. I also have a daughter. She is now living on the other side. That's how I like to describe her current situation. Living on the other side. My daughter's name is Brenda."

Bob talked about his daughter's murder, saying he had six years to think about the death penalty and why he was against it. He said politics shouldn't play a role in capital punishment.

"This is not a matter of conservative or liberal," he said. "It is not Republican vs. Democrat. Nor is it necessarily a matter of spiritual vs. unspiritual."

Bob told the members of the House and Senate about his experiences in Parents of Murdered Children, sitting and listening to people who express their rage, frustration, and fear. Then, he spoke about the role of the death penalty in the healing process and how destructive murder is to a family.

"There's rarely, if ever, time to say goodbye," he said. "There's the horror of thinking of those last violent moments."

Bob also detailed how hurtful the court proceedings can be, which he experienced not only in hearing what happened to Brenda, but also in comments such as "death is death," by defense attorney Byron Cerrillo during the sentencing hearing in 1992. He told legislators that Jon Jr.'s plea bargain saved his family some grief.

"If the laws were the same then as now, it is very, very possible that this man could be on death row," he said. "Because of the plea, our time in court was very limited. There was no trial. There was no day-after-day grind."

Bob noted that a drawn-out trial is anything but comforting to family members.

"I just don't see how healing for the family can occur," he said.

As he finished his speech, Bob said people asked him how he was satisfied that the man who murdered his daughter could be paroled after 40 years. He admitted thinking about ways to make Jon Jr. suffer, but came to the conclusion that no punishment could equal the crime.

"I face the hard reality that his crime is so heinous, so depraved, there is no way he can pay for what he has done to Brenda, to my wife, to me, to my sons, to her grandparents, to her friends, to our community," he said. "I am convinced that the only way for healing to begin is for me to give up the urge to make him suffer and to begin taking steps toward forgiveness."

In his final statement, Bob asked the Legislature to give those who murder children life in prison.

BREAK IN THE HANRAHAN CASE

Nearly a decade after the disappearance and murder of Topekan Jack Hanrahan, a counselor listened as one of his patients, Thomas Berberich, made a shocking revelation: He was the man who murdered the pre-teen.

Dr. Don Strong was counseling Berberich, a 35-year-old from the capital city, less than two years after the latter received a prison sentence on an aggravated incest conviction. Berberich served 17 months for the offense, which he committed in 1987. According to an article in the Topeka Capital-Journal, Berberich confessed to Strong during a session on Jan. 24, 1989.

Strong later told a Court that Berberich said to him: "He had killed him. I said did he mean Jack Hanrahan, and he said yes," according to the Capital Journal. The newspaper also stated that Strong, a certified mental health counselor, notified Shawnee County Judge William Carpenter of the confession the day after it happened. However, that information was lost in the shuffle for nearly eight years. It didn't resurface until late 1996 when the Kansas Bureau of Investigation revisited Hanrahan's case.

Berberich filed a motion asking Shawnee County District Judge Charles Andrews to throw out statements by Strong. Berberich's attorneys argued that Strong violated the psychologist-patient privilege.

Judge Andrews ruled that it applied only to a licensed psychologist and patient and that Berberich "did not form a reasonable belief that Dr. Strong was a licensed psychologist." Andrews wrote that Strong advertised himself as a counselor, his office sign said he was a counselor, certificates on his walls indicated he was a counselor, and Strong testified he always held himself out as a counselor, adding that Berberich's claims that he thought Strong was a psychologist because his defense attorney said he was were "less than credible."

Behind the scenes, the Hanrahans, who divorced after their son's murder, worked diligently for justice. John and Carol Hanrahan met separately with Shawnee County District Attorney JoAn Hamilton and other officials a few days before officers arrested Berberich.

"I would get asked 100 times a day why something hadn't been done," John Hanrahan said.

On Jan. 30, 1998, Hamilton charged Berberich, who also faced two counts of drug possession and one count of possession of drug paraphernalia in an unrelated case, with first-degree murder in Osage County.

Berberich's bond was set at $500,000, and he faced 15 years to life on the murder charge, but that was just the beginning of a yearlong battle about his confession. By April 1999, the argument made it all the way to the Kansas Supreme Court, which ruled that Berberich's statements to Strong were not protected communications. Within hours, Hamilton filed a motion to revoke Berberich's bond.

"At least we have a start of justice for the Hanrahan family," Hamilton said. "I'm glad we can go forth."

IVAN'S DECLINE

After Brenda's murder, diabetes further eroded the life of Ivan. Even as he endured regular treatments on his foot because of the disease, Ivan continued to live the way he wanted.

"He drank whiskey. He wouldn't quit drinking," said Terry Wright, a cousin of Ivan's. "He drank when he shouldn't have."

During the 1990s, Ivan changed careers. He ended up running trailer parks with his fiancée, who declined to comment on her relationship with him or his life after Brenda's death. At one point, Ivan and his fiancée moved to Texas to manage a trailer park before moving back to Kansas. The couple also lived in a trailer on the Blakes' property for a while. By then, his health had declined to the point that he had to be fed through a tube in his stomach.

"Ivan didn't want to listen," Wright said. "His body shut down on him and killed him."

Ivan died at age 54 on Oct. 4, 1998, 15 days shy of the seventh anniversary of Brenda's murder. At the time of his death and for years after, few people outside of law enforcement knew that he was a person of interest until the Shawnee County Sheriff's Department cleared him. Many of those close to him, including his stepsisters and cousins, did not know his name was attached to the case.

"I cannot believe that he would have anything to do with it," said Terry Theole, Ivan's stepbrother. "That doesn't seem like anything Ivan would have done or been a part of. He just wasn't that type of person."

"He had a bad attitude about his wife after they divorced," Theole added. "But I don't think Ivan was a pedophile."

The other person of interest in the case, Jon Sr., spent the rest of the 1990s at a Topeka nursing home. As the years passed, he moved further into dementia. His sister assumed guardianship of him in the early 1990s, and she and Gene Blake saw Jon Sr. as often as they could. But Jon Sr.'s mental capacity deteriorated to the point that he had to rely on his sister to order for him when they went out to eat.

"He was hard to talk to because sometimes he didn't know what you were talking about," Tammy Blake said of her brother. "We'd take him to lunch, and I'd have to watch him because he would be acting silly. He'd start laughing and carrying on."

The Blakes also checked Jon Sr. out of the home and brought him back to their house in Dover several times. Crystal and Marilee Sievers remembered seeing him in the years after the murder.

"It's very uncomfortable to see him, very uncomfortable," Crystal Sievers said.

Meanwhile, Jon Jr.'s stay at the Lansing Correctional Facility was a rocky one. From 1996 to 1999, he had 12 disciplinary reports and 14 violations. Those transgressions included violating published orders, possession of dangerous contraband, unauthorized presence in the restroom area, unauthorized dealing or trading, threatening a fellow inmate, theft, using stimulants, and avoiding an officer.

TRYING TO MOVE ON

By the mid-1990s, Brenda's schoolmates were attending Mission Valley High School. Though time healed some of the wounds, many still struggled until the day they graduated and beyond. Crystal Sievers said she drove recklessly down dirt roads hoping she would lose control, and she developed body dysmorphic disorder, a mental health illness defined by an obsession with one's perceived flaws in appearance.

"I think that's where the survivor's guilt started," she said. "Why wasn't it me? Why wasn't it us? He had such an opportunity to do it to us."

The Sievers sisters fought often throughout high school. Marilee referred to their scraps as "all-out brawls" over minute things like who was going to drive home. Meanwhile, after getting into several dust-ups with his schoolmates during grade school and junior high, Sam Bays had a better experience in high school.

"We all grow up. The boys and girls got more mature, and there was a bigger crowd," Bays said. "I got along a lot better with my classmates after middle school. Things evolved."

While Brenda impacted Bays' life with her kindness, Bob impacted it spiritually. During middle school, his parents invited Bob to their house to talk to him about God. He spoke to Bays several times and gave him the book "Mere Christianity," by theologian C.S. Lewis.

"It planted the seed that led me to knowing Christ," Bays said.

Though the pain of losing their friend eased as they transitioned from adolescence to adulthood, the loss was heavy for many of Brenda's schoolmates through high school. Julie Gomez wasn't comfortable walking from her house outside of town to Dover for five years. Brooklynd Thomas tried to manage the pain by writing prolifically in her diary, but was still a self-described "problem child."

"When she died, it brought up a lot of stuff that happened to me as a child," Thomas said. "I wondered why it was her and not me."

Things never completely got back to normal for most of those close to Brenda. Amy Best was melancholy in March and October for a long time and worried that Brenda might be forgotten as little as people talked about her in the years after the murder.

"Those of us in her class, we were overanalyzing every decision or comment we made," she said. "You didn't want to talk about it because everyone would be worried about you. So, we didn't say anything."

CHAPTER EIGHTEEN:

SCHOOL IS OUT OF SESSION

In 1998 and as his father aged, longtime music teacher Ted Lassen wanted to move closer to home in Colorado. He ended up teaching piano at a fine arts school in the Denver area. Years after leaving Dover for a school in the large metropolitan area, Brenda impacted Lassen's work life. Lassen kept a book of jokes she bought for him in his desk. Every time he opened the drawer holding the book, he thought of her.

"Some kid got in there and started to grab at it, and I said, 'You leave that alone,'" he said. "They asked about it. It had a pink cover and the clean joke title on it."

When they asked, Lassen told them Brenda's story, from being a good student to her murder.

"Their eyes would get big and their mouths would drop open," Lassen said. "This came up every couple of years or so. It will always be on my mind because of what a horrible experience it was. People will ask me sometimes what the best things and worst things were in my job … of course, the worst thing was losing Brenda."

Lassen left the Dover schools not long before they closed due to consolidation. With dwindling numbers at dozens of schools in the state, many began to combine. The junior high moved to Harveyville in 2002, which was the last year the grade school was open. In 2003, kindergarten through eighth graders attended school at a newly built wing attached to Mission Valley High School.

That marked the end of an era for a number of educators who worked tirelessly at the schools in Dover, including Allen Zordel. He taught there from 1983 until the junior high closed in 2001. Like Lassen, Zordel thinks of Brenda often.

"I think of her pretty much every day," Zordel said. "I have a little kindergarten girl this year with red hair. It's not as red as Brenda's, but I see her smile and I think of Brenda."

Brenda's murder also affected Zordel as a parent. He remembered losing track of his daughter at the swimming pool in his apartment complex. He left for only a few minutes, but she wasn't there when he got back.

"It took me 10 minutes to find her," he said. "My heart was pounding. I thought about Brenda."

The longest tenured teacher of the group, Jim Ediger, retired when the grade school closed its doors, capping three decades in the district, including four years in Harveyville early in his career.

"That was perfect timing," Ediger said. "I was ready to retire."

Ediger still lives in Kansas with his family but doesn't travel through Dover that often. When he and his wife do stop by the café in town, the memories come back.

"It's something that was always on your mind when you were teaching, and it always will be," he said.

Pam Leptich became a jack of all trades at the Dover schools through the years. In the mid-1990s, after Teri Anderson left to become a principal in Topeka, Leptich was the principal and interim superintendent for a few years. She finished her career teaching from 1996 to 1999 before retiring.

"All the time," she said about Brenda. "I've never stopped thinking about her. Ever."

BERBERICH'S DAY IN COURT

As the end neared for the Dover schools, things heated up in the Jack Hanrahan case. On the last day of January in 2000, Thomas Berberich's trial began at the Osage County Courthouse in Lyndon. In the afternoon, Shawnee County District Attorney JoAn Hamilton and defense attorney William Rork examined Sgt. Danny Hay, the lead detective in the murder investigation for the Topeka Police Department. On the second day of the trial, a Tuesday, John and Carol Hanrahan took the stand, telling the jury about the last time they saw their son.

"He left by himself," Carol Hanrahan said. "It was only the second time he had gone anywhere by himself."

Additional testimony included law enforcement officers, one of whom testified that, even though officers thought the boy might have been molested, a rape kit wasn't used and X-rays weren't taken.

Over the next several days, those taking the witness stand included Don Strong, the doctor who said Berberich confessed to the murder, and an inmate who told the jury that Berberich admitted killing Hanrahan while they were both in the Osage County Jail. Just nine days after the trial started, the case went to the jury.

On Feb. 10, after 20 hours of deliberations over three days, the jury found Berberich not guilty. Several women in the Hanrahan family gasped, and others cried. Carol and John Hanrahan were expressionless when Judge James Smith, the same man who presided over Jon Jr.'s case in Osage County in 1991, read the verdict.

"Thanks, man," Berberich told Rork after hugging him and leaving the courtroom.

One juror, Teri Graham, told reporters that the jury wanted evidence of a direct connection between Jack Hanrahan and Berberich. Despite the testimony of a family member that the two attended the same wedding dance several months before the murder, jurors felt the direct connection didn't happen.

"Jurors looked at all the evidence, examining it from different angles, and finally, there was a unanimous vote to acquit," Graham said. "It was physically and emotionally draining."

Jack Hanrahan's case remains unsolved to this day. From time to time, Tim Hrenchir, the longtime reporter who wrote the first stories in the coverage of Brenda's case, includes the case in update pieces about the most notorious cold cases in Shawnee County.

Berberich died at age 57 in 2011.

'SOME SORT OF CLOSURE'

Like it did to many, the night of Oct. 19, 1991, and early morning of Oct. 20, 1991, shook Paul Meek to the core. Then a 31-year-old who was at the beginning of a long career in emergency management and health care, Meek had the daunting responsibility to videotape Brenda's body in the boatshed. Interviewed more than 25 years later, the memory of that duty brought tears.

But Meek, who served in Desert Storm and worked as the chief of the fire department in Soldier, Kansas, as a registered nurse, and as the director of the hospital and public health preparedness program for the Kansas Department of Health and Environment, tried to make the best of an awful event.

In 1994, he founded the Kansas Search and Rescue Dog Association, an organization that continues to operate to this day. In the nearly 30 years since the KSARDA started, it has assisted in hundreds of searches, including working in Greensburg, Kansas, after an EF-5 tornado obliterated the small community in the south central part of the state.

"My thought was (Brenda) did love animals, and we focus on canines because they say one dog is worth 50 foot-searchers," Meek said. "I was looking for a more positive outlet, and it helped me to learn to deal with what I'd witnessed. It was a real drive for me to take the pain away."

That pain stayed with Crystal Sievers well into college, where she studied criminal justice at Washburn University, partly because of what happened to her friend.

"From that day forward, I've been trying to right the wrong," she said.

While at Washburn, Sievers began to research Brenda's case, asking questions and trying to get more information from her parents. She wanted to see the Shawnee County Sheriff Department's reports and the evidence from the crime scene.

"I always felt kept in the dark from a lot of this," she said. "I wanted to get some sort of closure because I think everybody was trying to protect the kids."

One of her assignments at Washburn was to interview an inmate for a corrections class. Sievers said she wanted to interview Jon Jr. for that project but wasn't ready emotionally. She eventually interviewed a female inmate in Topeka but continued taking as many classes about criminal law as she could. After graduating, Sievers moved away from Topeka and started a career in electronic surveillance for several years before working in law enforcement and at a law firm.

"I moved out of town alone, and that (Brenda's murder) was a big part of it," she said. "Small towns creep me out. I was so ready to get out."

A few of Brenda's schoolmates went into education. Jana Blodgett went to Emporia State University, then became a counselor at a middle school. Amy Best was an elementary teacher for years before moving into administration as a principal. Two others, Misty Lange and Marilee Sievers, went into nursing. The former's career put her face-to-face with inmates nearly every day.

"I've seen the other side of criminals," Lange said. "The biggest example I can give you is a gun store shooting with four guys. One of those, I didn't get to know. The other three were in infirmary with us. They made one split terrible decision, and it ruined their lives."

Despite seeing the better side of people who have committed some awful crimes, Lange doesn't have compassion for the man who killed her friend.

"I have nothing for him," she said. "I'm sure there are people who think he made this dumb decision. I don't see him that way. I do struggle because I know deep down he can't be a terrible, awful human being … somewhere something has to be decent. But I'm on the other end with him."

Sam Bays attended Kansas State University after graduating from Mission Valley. After receiving a bachelor's degree in mechanical and nuclear engineering, he earned a master's degree and doctorate in the latter. It was during college that he became more invested in God.

"I had a roommate and he said something that was interesting: that everyone's relationship with God is personal,'" Bays said. "So that made me start thinking about Him, that He is somebody I could relate to directly. Over the years, it grew on me. I started going to a First Presbyterian church. I never had one of those "I'm a Christian today" moments. After a while, it was one of those things, 'Yeah, I'm a Christian. I know it.'"

Perhaps the most telling anecdote about the impact Brenda's murder had on her friends is that of Tyrel Buchmeier, whom she babysat for several years. Buchmeier went into law enforcement after high school, working as a deputy in Wabaunsee County. He served in that role for several years before beginning a new career, but still is a reserve officer. For decades now, Buchmeier has kept a picture of Brenda locked in his gun safe and a note in his wallet that includes Jon Jr.'s inmate information.

"I keep it tucked in the back with my hunting license and medical license," he said. "It's got the case number, his Kansas Department of Corrections number, his date of birth, and his earliest release date."

All these years later, Buchmeier looks at the piece of paper often.

"More than I should," he said. "Probably monthly."

THE KELLERS THROUGH THE YEARS

Bob went to dozens of meetings for Parents of Murdered Children through the years, but some cases stuck with him. He remembers a husband and wife who would not attend a meeting at Denny's restaurant in Topeka because it was located across the street from HyperMart, now Walmart. The couple's daughter was walking home from a Walmart, where she worked, when she was abducted and murdered. The mother and father's tale of their grief hit close to home.

"They couldn't even go by Walmart," Bob said. "And here, if we want to go anywhere, we have to drive by (the Blakes') every day."

As much as the support group helped for several years, it began to wear on the Kellers, especially Bob, who struggled to see people go through horrible bitterness. Eventually, they stopped attending meetings.

"Robert said they have meetings and all that and he said, 'I can't do that. I can't do that forever,'" Aunt B said. "I think he realized it was time. It was healing time."

Bob served as the pastor at the Dover Federated Church until 2009, when he needed a break from the ministry. He worked as a hospice chaplain in Topeka for several years before returning to the church in 2013, much to the relief of many of the longtime churchgoers in the community.

"We had another man in (as pastor), but he wasn't Bob," Dottie Wendland said. "It was awfully hard for us to accept him. I think he would have been all right, but we were so glad to get Bob back. He's just part of Dover."

As is Tracy. While a few of the folks in Dover were surprised Bob and Tracy remained in the community after Brenda died, most figured they would. The Kellers entertained moving just one time in the mid-1990s when Bob considered pastoring at another church. But they weren't going to leave their daughter alone.

"Early, because she's here, that might have been (why we stayed)," Tracy said. "But the older we get ... I love Dover. I just do. I love the people."

Tracy has worked at an animal clinic in Shawnee County for 25 years, caring for dogs, cats, horses, goats, and dozens of other animals that her daughter loved as much as life itself.

John's career also has spanned 25 years, as he's worked his way up in advertising. He used his expertise to build the website for his mother's horseriding business, which lasted for three years in the early 2000s. John and his wife have two children, the oldest of which is Brenda's namesake, Brendan.

Pat also started a family, raising two boys, giving Bob and Tracy four grandchildren. Unlike John, Pat took a career path that he planned to follow since his early days of volunteering with the Explorers. After earning his degree in fire science from Hutchinson Community College, he became a full-time fireman. He also works a part-time job in woodcrafting.

"I was a volunteer in Auburn, and there was a fire a couple houses away," Pat said. "There was a father outside saying his son and potentially daughter were in the house. We had to break a window and do some resuscitation. It really was like, 'Oh, that was awesome.' It really sparked my drive, and that was like, 'I really want to do this.'"

ALL IN THE FAMILY

When Bob left the Federated Church in 2009, he and Tracy were in their mid-50s and had been empty-nesters for a decade. Then, the couple adopted two children, a brother and sister who were growing up in a difficult situation that included a father who was in prison.

The challenge was a different one than raising their biological children, but both thoroughly enjoyed having kids in the house again. It was particularly helpful to Tracy during the holiday season.

"Adopting them did take my focus off of missing Brenda at Christmas, so that helped," Tracy said. "I've become so invested in the adopted kids that I don't spend a whole lot of time thinking about it. I'll think about her when I put her ornaments on the Christmas tree, or something like that."

Like Brenda, the Kellers' adopted daughter sat next to Tracy at church as she grew into a young woman, sometimes singing with her mother. Bob and Tracy's patience helped the brother and sister through high school, and both moved out and began their adult lives by 2021.

Roy and Jean were the family patriarch and matriarch well into their late 80s. Roy retired after more than 50 years at the pulpit, though he occasionally delivered a message, including at the Dover Federated Church when the couple visited town.

"I absolutely love hearing Dad give the message," Bob said. "He's still great at it."

Living in a small house with Roy in Valley Center, Jean fell and hit her head in mid-October of 2019. After a few days in the hospital, she died just six weeks short of celebrating her 88th birthday. Held on Oct. 19, 2019, her funeral was exactly 28 years after her granddaughter died. That seemed fitting given how close Jean and Brenda were, and Brenda is mentioned prominently in Jean's obituary.

"Her hardest loss was October 19, 1991 … her precious, red-haired granddaughter Brenda Michelle Keller, taken from this life way too early, whom she forever loved," the obituary reads.

After 69 years of marriage, Roy struggled without his wife. He moved out of their home not long after she passed because he didn't want to live there without Jean. He gardened almost daily after moving in with Janice and enjoyed time with his grandchildren and praying for his family, but he often was sad.

"He just misses mom so much," Janice said.

Roy celebrated his 91st and final birthday on Oct. 4, 2020. He died on March 20, 2021, survived by 17 grandchildren and 27 great-grandchildren.

A TALE OF TRAGEDY

Gene and Tammy Blake retired as hairdressers in their 60s, splitting their time between their home in Dover and their lake cabin in Burlington. Gene Blake was trucking right along in his early 70s when he was diagnosed with prostate cancer in 2010. The side effects of radiation therapy, combined with surgery, began several years of deteriorating health.

Three years before that diagnosis, the Blakes suffered another loss. In August 2007, their youngest son, Darrin Blake, died at age 42, leaving behind two young daughters and a successful auto upholstery business.

"He had problems the night before, and he called here and talked to Gene, and Gene said, 'Well, relax, and you'll get over it,'" Tammy Blake said. "His birthday was on August 18, and that's when he took his life, early in the morning. We'd planned a big party that night, and they went over there and found him. That was devastating."

The Blakes struggled mightily and started going to counseling. In the span of 21 years, they lost one son to a debilitating disease, the other to suicide, and endured the agonizing pain of their nephew murdering a 12-year-old on their property.

"Gene and Tammy, they've had loss, too," Bob said. "They're not immune to pain."

Not long after Gene Blake's health began to decline, Bob decided to stop by and speak to the couple on his way home. During his visit, he told the Blakes that he and Tracy did not blame them for what happened to Brenda.

"I had never been in their house. They'd been coming to church, and they hadn't been in awhile and I knew he was sick, so I just turned in there to visit with them," Bob said. "It was weird because I hadn't been in there. I knew Jon Mareska had probably been sitting in the chair that I was sitting in. I was sitting in the same room. We had a talk, and I told them, 'We don't hold a grudge against you guys.' And we just started talking about it."

Bob's empathy, available even to a family many blamed for Brenda's death, lifted a massive weight off the shoulders of the Blakes. They resumed attending the Federated Church and helped the Kellers when they could. Gene Blake would drive to their house and use a Bobcat to move hay or sod on their property.

"It made me feel better," Tammy Blake said. "Gene thought a lot of Bob. I think that was one of the reasons we decided to go to church."

Jon Sr.'s health also continued to decline. Bob nearly encountered him during his work as a hospice chaplain. He was working in a nursing home Jon Sr. lived in, though he didn't realize it at the time, and came across his name while he was checking in one day.

"That really caught me off guard, seeing the name Jon Mareska," he said. "Then I realized it was the dad."

Jon Sr. died at age 72 on Sept. 4, 2017, at CountrySide Health Center. Dozens of family members and friends, including many of the colorful characters he rode his Harley-Davidson with for more than 20 years, attended the service. All of the individuals contacted declined requests for an interview, including the daughter of a man who was one of Jon Sr.'s best friends. She referred to him as "Brother Jon" and said all of the bikers who hung out with her father were like uncles and sweet to kids.

His death left unanswered questions about Brenda's last moments, questions he wasn't capable of answering due to brain damage and dementia.

Gene Blake also struggled mentally, and his physical health continued to decline. Tammy Blake remembered her husband saying he was going hunting for rabbits, which made little sense to her at the time. Hours later, he ended up on a dirt road on the outskirts of Dover, without a clue how to get home. A couple in the community picked him up and brought him back to the farm.

Gene Blake died at age 81 on March 8, 2019, the day that would have been Brenda's 40th birthday. Tammy Blake asked Bob to officiate the service, but he already was committed to working another funeral out of town on the same day.

"I felt bad about that," Bob said. "It meant a lot that she asked."

'THERE WAS NO DEMON'

Jon Jr. moved from the Lansing Correctional Facility, where he was for seven years, to the Hutchinson Correctional Facility in December 2002. He's been in that prison for two decades now. For several years, his experience in Hutchinson was much like it was in the other prisons: Turbulent. From 2000 through 2014, he was disciplined for 20 violations, including tobacco contraband, dangerous contraband, use of stimulants, misuse of state property, work performance, debt adjustments, sexual activity, and disobeying orders. In the years since, he has had more than a dozen violations, including several in 2024.

For several years, he did not have a relationship with his mother, who wasn't aware he was arrested for Brenda's murder until he contacted her. Despite his conviction, Jon Jr. did maintain a connection with several friends, including his ex-girlfriend from Lawrence High.

"I would ask him, 'Did you do this?' He always denied it," Becky Taylor said. "He always signed the letters 'Love, Jon.'"

He told several people, including his mother, that he was framed for the crime. He also asked Taylor to come visit him, but that never happened.

"I never got the courage to go," she said. "I remember being petrified that he was not going to make it, but I remember him telling me at some point that his dad and uncles had been in jail. They've got to know somebody that's in prison, and he'd be OK."

Taylor communicated with Jon Jr. for several years. The exchanges were little more than chit-chat. He asked how she was doing and about her daughter. One year, she received a Christmas card. He even sent a picture with one letter and told her he "found God" in another.

"Everybody does that (finds God) in prison," she said. "There was never anything in there about why he was there."

Many of those who had been close to Jon Jr. did not learn about his conviction until years after it happened, including his stepsister, Teresa Benson. She had not seen or spoken to him for more than a decade when they finally reconnected, and didn't know he was convicted of killing a 12-year-old girl. Jon Jr. told Benson that he killed a man during a cocaine deal gone bad outside of a bar and blacked out, so he didn't remember what happened.

"He said all they had was a footprint or a shoe print, and he said his father framed him," she said. "Lois Dentis was the closest with Jon after I left, and we were trying to find out what happened with Jon, and she informed me and told me how to get in contact with him. She didn't tell me exactly what happened."

That Jon Jr. went to prison shocked Benson, who never saw a dark side of him while they were growing up. They slept in the same bed as young children and were together all the time until she left to live with her mother in Arkansas.

"I've racked my brain trying to find that demon," she said. "I would sit around and think there had to have been something. I can truly say it's not there. He was as normal a teenager as I could possibly say."

Even though two of his friends from Tulsa, Di'Anna and Stephanie Dentis, each had a run-in with Jon Jr., they didn't think he was capable of the heinous crime he committed. Like everyone in the Brookside group, they learned he was in prison years later. Still, they were not aware he was incarcerated for murder until interviewing for this book. Di'Anna Dentis even mailed him a couple of pictures after he asked for one years ago.

"I was talking to one of my coworkers about you contacting me and said, 'Why is this guy trying to contact me?'" she said. "(Jon Jr.) tried to rape me and burned me when he didn't succeed. And my coworker said, 'Maybe you should find out.' When I found out, I said, 'You have got to be kidding me.'"

TAKE CAUTION

As she did every day, Brooklynd Thomas walked to the end of the block, waiting at the corner to be there when her daughter got off the school bus. For the first time, however, her daughter did not walk off the bus. Thomas was frantic.

"My daughter was just instantly hysterical and screaming and bawling," said Kaiden Barraclough, Thomas' mother. "She had the bus driver searching the bus, she called the school. I'm scared to death, trying to stay calm, trying to get Brooklynd to stay calm and figure out where (the daughter) is."

As Thomas drove off to search for her daughter, Barraclough stayed in the house, where the entire family lived, and as she looked out the window, a voice ran through her head.

"It was Bob saying, 'My little Rosebud (the name she'd given her granddaughter) is gone,'" Barraclough said. "What a horrible thing. People have suffered from that that weren't even born at the time."

As it turns out, Thomas' daughter jumped off the bus on the wrong stop and was found after a few terrifying hours. That day and the panic that came with it is a symbol of just how much Brenda's murder has impacted her friends and schoolmates.

"My cousin calls me a hovering parent," Thomas said. "I'm always there."

Over-protection is a common theme among those who knew Brenda. Crystal Sievers wouldn't let her girls ride their bikes in the park and remembers what happened to her friend every time she sees an Amber Alert. Marilee Sievers, who has a boy and a girl, would not allow them to play in the front yard as they grew up.

"I probably remind them too much you can't trust people," she said. "I still freak out when they walk home from school by themselves."

Their children riding bikes is a trigger for many, including Brenda's brother. John tries to be rational about letting his daughter ride her bike in the neighborhood, but it's on his mind when she asks, and he makes her take her cell phone so that he and his wife can track her whereabouts. Julie Gomez won't let her kids go for a run unless they agree to check in with her after every lap of the track near their home.

"I'm very vocal with my kids about what happens if someone comes and grabs you," Gomez said.

During an interview with Tyrel Buchmeier in a small town close to Dover, he repeatedly looked over his shoulder as two small children rode their bikes around a nearby park. He said he still has a difficult time 30 years later seeing young girls riding their bicycles and with parents letting them do so by themselves.

"My daughter knows that when I was a kid, my best friend's sister was murdered," he said. "It has affected my daughter's life. We're at Walmart, and she says, 'I'm going to get stuff over here,' and I say, 'Oh, no you're not. You're staying with me.'"

Knowing when to let go also has been difficult. Tyrel's sister Autumn admits that she has "overeducated" her children about safety and said, "I kind of assume everybody is a potential pedophile," going as far as to follow her children in her car as they ride their bikes.

All of them share one thing in common: They talk to their kids about Brenda. They don't go into the gory details, but their children are aware that their friend was murdered when she was 12 years old. Many of Brenda's friends struggle as parents, determining when the time is right to give their kids more freedom.

"As a teacher, I see kids in Mareska's situation and it unnerves me," Best said. "I think that was shaped by this experience. As a parent, when you tell your kid, I want her to know to be cautious, but I don't want her to be afraid of the world. How much do I tell her?"

Bays studied the numbers. He knows that child abduction and murder by a stranger is incredibly rare. But he also was among those traumatized by such a crime and religiously locks the doors at night and stresses safety as a Boy Scout leader.

"I've talked to my older child about Brenda," said Bays, a father of two. "I let him know that it's personal because of what happened to Brenda."

CHAPTER NINETEEN:

WHAT REALLY HAPPENED?

"*They. Were. There.*"

Penny Lister says it with emphasis when she talks about a fateful drive and what she saw at 5:30 p.m. on Saturday, Oct. 19. For more than 30 years, that evening and the tragic death of their daughter's friend has gnawed at Lister and her husband, Larry. They are adamant that Jon Jr. isn't the only one who should be held accountable for Brenda's murder, enough so that they only agreed to an interview with one stipulation.

"If we're going to open this up again," Larry Lister said at his family's kitchen table in February 2017, "it needs to be finished this time. It needs to be right, because it wasn't right the first time. There were more people involved."

The Listers aren't alone in the belief that Jon Sr. participated in the crime, and many maintain that Ivan was, as well. It's a theory based on Penny Lister's account of the drive from her home just outside of Dover to the grade school that rests to the east of Douglas Road and seven-tenths of a mile north of Gene and Tammy Blake's house.

The image of Jon Jr., Jon Sr., and Ivan sitting at the picnic table in the front yard of the Blakes' home, talking and laughing, haunts Penny Lister. Seconds later, she cruised by Brenda pushing her bike near the pasture north of the Blakes'. A few minutes later, as Penny Lister and her daughter returned from dropping off pies for the Ladies Aid banquet, Brenda was gone. So were the Mareskas and Ivan.

"You pay attention to these things when you have girls," Penny Lister said. "They were all three involved in the kidnapping. Beyond that, to me, you're guilty by association. They knew."

Even those closest to the Blakes believe Jon Sr. and Ivan knew what happened that night.

"I think all three were involved," Mary Sievers said.

"My personal opinion … I think the kid's dad (Jon Sr.) was in on it," Leon Sievers added.

"I think Cousin Ivan was, too, at least as an observer," Mary Sievers said.

To add to the consternation, many in the community said Jon Jr.'s confession isn't the complete truth. Some of that stems from the fact that Larry Lister and several others searching the property hours before Clinton Lambotte found Brenda's body maintain that she was not in the boatshed during the first part of the search.

"I was there from here to your car (about 30 feet) and there was nothing in it," Larry Lister said. "She was not there."

Larry Lister, along with Leon Sievers, Jim Wilson, and several others, searched the Blakes' property as midnight approached on Oct. 19. Lister, Sievers, and Wilson each said Brenda was not in the boatshed at that time, leading many to think that Jon Jr., and possibly Jon Sr., moved Brenda as the search was heating up.

Is it possible both Mareskas were attempting to conceal the murder? A shovel on the property points to a dubious prospect.

Several deputies, officers, and attorneys noted that Jon Jr.'s attorney, Byron Cerrillo, had access to the files and evidence. They said if

Cerrillo found any indication that Jon Jr. wasn't solely responsible, he would have used that to prove reasonable doubt.

UNANSWERED QUESTIONS

Many in Dover believe a portion of the assault took place in one of two barns just north of the Blakes' house. Larry Lister said he found bicycle tracks from the pond toward the barns and house in a south-easterly direction. One of the reasons some think Brenda was in one of those two buildings is the short period of time Jon Jr. had to get her from Douglas Road to an out-of-sight location on the property.

"Right next to the road there was a scale house, a building with scales," said Allen Moran, the deputy who assisted in the search. "It's gone now, but behind it there was a barn. Part of the story that I heard was he'd first taken her into the barn to fix the bicycle, or whatever the case was. Where he took her, we never did know, other than where we found her."

Others don't believe the part of Jon Jr.'s confession that he walked behind Brenda and grabbed her hair before forcing her to the fence lining the east side of Blakes' pasture. Several of the Dover residents interviewed insisted Brenda would have fought her attacker, pointing out that she wasn't a meek, timid little girl and that cycling thousands of miles made her strong and athletic.

A popular theory is Jon Jr. lured Brenda into a dangerous situation, perhaps offering to help her fix her bike. That would have been easier than pushing her and her bike across the pavement, making her crawl through the barbed wire, and throwing the Schwinn over the fence, all while risking being seen by someone driving on Douglas Road or a neighbor in one of three houses less than 100 yards north of where Brenda disappeared.

"I do not believe in the length of time Penny was gone he could have successfully drug her off without some sign of something," Lavella Buchmeier said. "She's a very tall girl, lanky. She was not docile. She had two siblings that were boys, and she would have fought tooth and nail."

However, Jon Jr. wasn't a weakling. At 6-foot-2 and with a slim, muscular build, he could have overpowered Brenda quickly.

"If he wanted, and she wasn't screaming and kicking up a major fuss, there's no way he would have had problems with her," said Capital-Journal reporter Steve Fry, who was less than 10 feet away from Jon Jr. several times during court appearances. "He could carry her, pick her up by the waist."

Several individuals investigating and working the case concede that it's possible Jon Jr. didn't act alone that night. Some even say it's possible that his confession wasn't the complete truth. But, to a person, they all agree on an important point: None of the evidence discovered during the investigation and search points to anyone other than Jon Jr. assaulting, raping, and murdering Brenda.

"What we have is what he gave us. There's no third witness," Debenham said. "There's no, 'This is what I saw him do.' In that situation, you're left with his story."

That's not to say Jon Sr. wasn't a person of interest. After all, it appears he lied or because of his brain injury was confused early in the search when he told Tracy that he was working on the roof the day of the crime and saw a boy and a girl walking south along Douglas Road. He also referred to Jon Jr. as his nephew when Tracy asked if anyone else was in the Blakes' house.

Is it possible Jon Sr. was trying to cover for his son? Or was Jon Sr., as many deputies and detectives said, mentally disabled to the point that he had no idea what was going on or was incoherent? The officer who spent the most time with Jon Jr. that day, Myron Stucky, instinctually thought the elder Mareska was responsible for the crime, at least initially.

"I always thought the old man was just as guilty as Jon, but maybe not," Stucky said.

The department determined that Jon Sr. wasn't involved in the rape and murder based on the evidence collected and his interview. It should be noted that his hair and blood were not collected after that determination, so there was no evidence to compare against the material gathered at the scene. This remains a point of contention among some who reason that if Jon Jr. was a non-secretor, his father may have been, as well.

Some of the officials interviewed believe Jon Sr. was involved after the crime, possibly as Jon Jr. attempted to conceal what he'd done, a prospect seemingly supported by not only the discovery of the shovel, but also volunteer Sandy Mitchell's account of hearing voices around a barn on the property, including one that she thought said, "Oh God," during the search.

"Just because he was there with him doesn't necessarily mean involved, but he knew about it and maybe didn't do anything," Stucky said. "He didn't stop it. That's a feeling I've always had."

Several involved in the case take exception to any belief that they didn't take a close look at Senior and his possible involvement in the crime. While they say he could have helped Jon Jr. after the rape and murder, no evidence pointed to that.

"We would have looked at it to make sure that, if there were other people involved, that we had them, too," Debenham said. "When I say other people, they could have been involved in the coverup later on."

As for Ivan, he voluntarily provided the Sheriff's Department with his hair and blood, which did not match trace evidence procured by officers. Still, some in Dover say he should have been charged because he had to know what happened that night.

Aside from a questionable timeline he gave Baer and Metz a few days after the murder, there's nothing to implicate Ivan. The majority of the officers didn't even remember him when interviewed.

Ivan may not have helped Jon Jr., but he was there to monitor the Mareskas. Why did he leave town that night, if the Blakes tasked him with watching Jon Jr. and Jon Sr.? Also, a local child witness stated that he or she saw Jon Jr. at about 6:05 p.m. driving TAMSTOY slowly to the south on Douglas Road. In 2019, that child, now an adult in his/her 40s, exchanged texts with the author of this book. In the texts, the individual said as he or she played in the woods just off the road, he or she watched Jon Jr. turn into 69th Street before turning around when Jon Jr. realized he'd been seen.

Did Ivan allow Jon Jr. to drive the car when he wasn't supposed to do so? Did he really doze off and not know Jon Jr. took the car? Those are questions, along with numerous other ones, that likely won't ever be answered.

Ultimately, only four people know what happened that night, and three of them – Brenda, Jon Sr., and Ivan – are no longer alive. The one person left, Jon Jr., isn't talking.

CHAPTER TWENTY:

REMEMBERING BRENDA

Several of the people who knew Brenda wonder if she put herself in God's hands the moment she realized Jon Jr. was going to kill her. How else can you explain that she didn't scream, at least based on what her murderer said, and that no one heard any noises during the period of time Jon Jr. attacked her?

"I think Brenda probably fought back and resisted up to a point," Tyrel Buchmeier said. "I think Brenda had a 'Jesus take the wheel' moment."

While many struggle with how God could let something so awful happen, Bob wonders if his daughter was a martyr. Is it possible Brenda died the way she did so that her testimony to the Lord would last for decades beyond her untimely death?

Every person who knew Brenda mentioned God when asked how she should be remembered. Longtime teacher and coach Allen Zordel said she should be remembered as "God's gift." Brenda always was kind, but her life changed when she committed to God at a summer camp the year before she died. In the final 16 months she lived, she was even more kind and empathetic, never judging people who did not share her faith.

"When she really woke up to the Lord, it was a little bit scary, because she was way past me," Tracy said.

Sweet. Smart. Creative. Beautiful. Those adjectives came up time and time again as friends and family spoke about Brenda. In addition to her faith, Brenda's love for animals is what people remember. She wouldn't kill a fly or bug, going so far as to cup a wasp in her hands and carry it outside, risking a sting to protect one of God's creatures.

"She was a very sweet, precious little girl that loved, loved, loved so deeply," Jean said.

Brenda is remembered as an artist, good enough to win awards and have her work displayed in the library dedicated in her memory. Until the day she died, Jean kept much of her granddaughter's art. When Beverly and Janice cleaned out their mother's house after her death, they found an area devoted to Brenda, including pictures she drew and a small doll she made out of peanuts.

"She was special, just a joy," Beverly said. "She did seem like she was going to be a really neat adult. You were just starting to get a glimpse of what she was going to grow into. If I have a grandkid that likes bugs or something like that, I think of her."

Jean's keepsakes stretched beyond the Kellers' house. Janice found even more memorabilia, including paintings, drawings, and a photo of Brenda, when she cleaned out a storage unit belonging to her parents.

"We were trying to get rid of stuff, and I thought, 'I can't throw it away' because we all love her so much," Janice said. "We were just tender toward her. We talk about what she would have been doing. I'd want her to be remembered as a precious girl who loved the Lord. Through all of this, she would have wanted us to get closer to Christ."

IF SHE WAS ALIVE TODAY ...

Who would Brenda Keller be today? It's a question many of her friends think about now that they've grown up and moved on to their own careers. The answer to that question, at least to those who knew her, has an almost-universal answer.

"Any time we played, I chose teacher and she chose veterinarian," Amy Best said.

Jill Wilson said she often thinks about what Brenda would be like as an adult.

"I wonder what she would have become," she said. "Probably a veterinarian because she always had pets – dogs, turtles, rats. I think that's probably what I would have picked for her."

Another common response to that question is that she would have been as she lived: a lovely person, full of life.

"If she was alive today, people would have a hard time saying anything negative about her," Amber McGhee said. "She was just amazing."

One person who doesn't play the "what if" game is her mother. She and Brenda shared so many traits, from the love of animals, God, and nature, to singing, exercising, and art, and Tracy tries not to dwell.

"I try not to think about what (she'd be like)," she said. "I don't spend a lot of time looking at what I want to have and more at what I do have."

Brenda, however, is never far from her thoughts, nor the thoughts of many people in Dover. Some, like Allen Moran, think of her when visiting family in the cemetery just outside of town. Moran makes a point of stopping by to see her on Memorial Day when he's honoring his brother and others. Lavella Buchmeier can't help but think of her any time she's at the Dover Community Center, once the grade school.

For others, it's an image or a day that brings Brenda's memory back. Brooklynd Thomas can't watch "The Little Mermaid," Brenda's favorite movie. Zordel thought of her when he had a red-headed girl in class. Pam Leptich can't look at one of Brenda's classmates without thinking about her. For many, March 8, her birthday, and Oct. 19 are sad, difficult days.

"I ask myself every day why God would allow (her murder)," Wilson said. "It was fate, but she was an amazing person and didn't deserve it."

Perhaps Bob was right: Brenda's death had a purpose. While losing her was devastating, her legacy endures, be it in a scrapbook Jean made for her daughter-in-law a few years after Brenda died, or in artwork many of her friends, family members, and teachers either still have or remember.

Most of her friends and classmates talk to their children about Brenda, not only as a cautionary tale, but also as an example of how to be generous and thoughtful. Sam Bays refers to her as "the kindest person I've ever met and probably ever will meet."

Brenda would have taken comfort in that fact that some, like Terri Anderson, the principal who cared about her deeply, became more devout after her death.

"One thing it definitely did is it brought me to my knees," Anderson said. "I could not do it myself, and it led me to a life that is a lot more religious. That, in itself, is a major thing. I started going to church and Sunday school."

LIKE A BUTTERFLY

Though some things have changed during the past 33 years in Dover, the church has the same homey look and feel. As patrons walk up concrete stairs and into the nearly century-old building, tables flank the left and right side of the entrance. Resting on the table to the left are CDs of Bob's recent sermons, Dover Federated Church business cards, programs for the day's service, and prayer lists.

The table on the right holds a guest book, which confirms that almost all of the people visiting the church are there week in and week out. Red carpet lines the floor on the first level of the church, with eight rows of stained wooden pews on either side of the center aisle. Behind the main rows of pews lie short pews less than 10 feet long and three rows deep. A steep set of stairs inside the entrance leads to four more rows of pews on either side behind a balcony 15 feet above the first floor.

A nursery stocked with decades-old toys is at the back of the second floor. The balcony overlooking the church is the technology hub of the building, with an impressive sound system and projector – the product of a long fundraising campaign – providing booming vocals as Bob, Tracy, and members sing, as well as vibrant imagery for PowerPoint presentations during Bob's sermons.

Stained glass windows shine on the east and west walls, which lead to a beautiful varnished wood stage featuring an aging pulpit at the center. Two flags, including an American flag, sit on either side of the stage, with several microphones and an organ on the left side. A large wooden cross at the back of the stage dominates the south end of the church.

For 40 years, Bob has delivered God's message in the church, weaving personal stories and humor into passages from the Bible. On Jan. 29, 2017, as part of an ongoing series, his sermon was about the book of Genesis, particularly the story of brothers Cain and Abel.

"Today, the beginning of sin as it gets out of control, the tragic story of Cain," he said. "Starting in verse one, now the man had relations with his wife, Eve, this is right after the fall and sin, they've been kicked out of paradise. And she conceived and gave birth to Cain. Again, she gave birth, to his brother Abel. Now, here is this beautiful moment in Adam and Eve's life, they've had their first baby. Imagine the joy, and they think on God's promise to send a deliverer. … Great hopes. That's the point I'm trying to get to. There's always great hopes when you have a child."

As Bob commonly does, he used a personal anecdote to enhance the sermon: "I'll never forget working nights at a Kwik Shop in Wichita. When I say nights, I mean midnight to eight in the morning. That was a crazy place, crazy time to work. Weird people come out in the night time. I'll never forget this huge man comes walking in, tall, big, and he buys something, and I click on the register, and he hit it! 'I'm sorry, I'm looking for nickels,' he said. 'I said, OK,'" as the church erupted in laughter.

Bob continued, telling the congregation that he eventually became friends with the man, sharing with him the joy he was experiencing after the birth of his first son in 1976.

"Soon, there was Abel," he said. "But I think the joy was brief. And you start to think about it, the first baby born grew up to be a murderer. And the second born grew up to be the first victim. Think about that."

Bob paused after that statement, scanning the church, where Gene and Tammy Blake sat in the back row and the author of this book sat 15 feet to the left of them.

"I thought about that when I was giving the sermon, how fitting it was that you were there," Bob said later.

Bob continued to tell the story of Cain, who murdered his brother out of jealously. In the Bible, Cain, a farmer, and Abel, a shepherd, each offered sacrifices of their produce to God, and God favored the younger brother.

"The Lord had regard for Abel and his offering, but for Cain he had no regard for his offering," Bob said. "Why did he prefer one over the other? I think it was faith. At the heart of it, one was offering by faith. So, Cain was very angry, his countenance fell. He became depressed. And the Lord God said to Cain, 'Why are you angry? And why has your countenance fallen? If you do well, will not your countenance be lifted up? And if you do not do well, sin is crouching at the door, and it desires for you.'"

Not long after, Cain killed Abel.

"So here, we see the terrible effects of sin, as it's allowed to just grow along to the bitter end," Bob said. "Sin begins in the human heart, and if unchecked, it works its way out, in our thoughts, in our words, and ultimately in our deeds. If you let it go, it gets the upper hand, and it results in terrible, terrible destruction."

Bob couldn't help but think about Brenda during this sermon, though he didn't mention his daughter. He concluded the 30-minute message by saying, "Sin is like an acorn. It falls from an oak tree, and there it is laying on the ground. While it's there and hasn't taken root, a child can pick it up, but if it's allowed to take root, eventually it becomes so large. God has his part to deal with sin. He gave us Jesus. He gave us the Spirit, and then we have our part to walk in independence on the Spirit, to walk in faith with God. So, don't flirt with it, don't dabble with it. Throw the bum out. Even here in this terrible, terrible story, we find hope. And that hope is through your life and through Jesus Christ."

Brenda's tragic death devastated the community for years, but, as Bob said, in this terrible story, there is hope. Hope in her memory, whether it's Paul Meek establishing the state's first dog search and rescue organization, Anderson digging into her faith more, or in the smiles and laughter from friends when they talk about her.

While the Kellers don't invest much time thinking about the man who killed their daughter, Bob acknowledged that he occasionally checks with a friend to see what Jon Jr. has been up to in prison.

"I think that because I believe what I preach on, that I can put Jon Mareska in God's hands and know that if he doesn't repent, it's going to be a horrible thing for him," Bob said. "But I also know that the grace of God is available for him, too."

Tracy added, "I think Brenda would have wanted someone to explain the grace of God to Jon Mareska."

Above all, the Kellers want their daughter to be remembered as a person of faith who devoted her life to God at an early age. Perhaps the best way to illustrate Brenda Keller's short, but impactful life is to borrow from a short story she wrote, "The Little Boy and His Butterfly," which is displayed on her gravestone:

"Once upon a time, there was a boy. The boy had a very favorite spot under a tree. One day, he was sitting under his tree when he saw a very pretty caterpillar. It had a yellow stripe down his back and was all green. The boy took the caterpillar home and put it in a cage. The boy fed his caterpillar leaves every day. One morning, the caterpillar was not in the cage, but there was a little oval-shaped ball. The boy took the cage downstairs and showed it to his mother. His mother said that it was a cocoon. The boy put it back up in his room and went outside to his favorite tree. He sat and thought about his caterpillar. How he wished he could play with his caterpillar under his tree. He lay in the leaves and thought of all the different caterpillars. Soon, his mom called, and it was time to eat. After supper, he went to bed and dreamed about caterpillars. He waited several weeks, and the caterpillar didn't come out. One day, the boy was sitting in the pile of leaves under the tree, and the cocoon began to wiggle. The boy watched, and soon he saw a little bit of cocoon start to split open. Soon, he was looking at a very beautiful butterfly. The boy opened the cage door, and the beautiful butterfly flew away. The boy shouted, 'Goodbye!'"

EPILOGUE

Of the more than 75 interviews done for this book, the words of one person are missing. Aside from his confession to Shawnee County Sheriff's Department, television reports, and minimal spoken words taken from court transcripts, there are no words from Jon Mareska Jr.

During nearly six years of research, writing, and editing, I attempted to contact Jon Jr. numerous times, including several letters sent from 2017 through 2022. On only one occasion did he respond. In April 2019, Jon Jr. mailed a handwritten letter from the Hutchinson Correctional Facility. Pulling that letter out of the mailbox was one of the most exciting days of the journey of a lifetime learning about Brenda Keller, her family and friends, Dover, and the man who ended her life.

In that letter, Jon Jr. wrote that he decided to respond because I got his attention after tracking down and contacting several of his family members, including two sisters and his mother.

"First, let me start out apologizing," he wrote. "For not showing the proper respect in giving some kind of response to you before now. I also hope you understand my hesitancy. Here I got this gentleman that is writing a story about what took place almost 28 years ago. I do have a lot of questions about things such as what is the purpose in writing this story and what are your motivation (sic)."

Motivation. It's a common question almost everybody involved in the case asks. "Why do you want to write about this? What story are you telling?"

When I started working on this, the thought of writing a book about Brenda Keller seemed like a dream, one that would be incredibly difficult to realize. The story began years ago when Brenda died. Two of her schoolmates and friends were two of my best friends in high school. Brenda's murder hit close and hit hard. Several years later, Brenda's name came up again, in of all places, the City Hall building in Burlingame, Kansas.

On a cold day in February 1996, a friend's parents asked me to testify on their behalf in an ongoing disagreement about their neighbor's dogs at a local hearing. During that proceeding, the father of my friend randomly, or so I thought at the time, referred to the Brenda Keller case.

The comment struck a chord. Two days later, I drove from our house in Burlingame to Dover. I had no idea why I was there, other than I couldn't stop thinking about Brenda. I drove down Douglas Road, not knowing where she died or rode her bike that fateful day in 1991.

After driving around for a few hours, I ended up in the cemetery. I knew from conversations with our mutual friends that her headstone would be easy to find. It took no more than five minutes. I got out of my well-used blue 1991 Ford Thunderbird and stood at Brenda's resting place for quite a while. For the next 20 years, even when I worked out of state in the newspaper business, I stopped by to visit Brenda at least once a year.

Not until graduate school, however, did I realize I kept coming to see her because a greater power was imploring me to tell her story. By January 2017, I had one semester left before receiving my master's degree, and I needed a final project to graduate. After weighing the options, I decided to write about Brenda.

After some hesitation, Bob and Tracy granted me permission to work on a story about their daughter. The goal at that point was to finish a 30-page story in five months. After 20 interviews and hours of research, I wrote 80 pages. By the time I was finished, I knew I had to write a book.

'I AM A LITTLE SKEPTICAL'

The work over the next few years went slowly. My father was diagnosed with cancer in August 2017, I changed jobs, and my family and I moved. By the beginning of 2019, I'd barely scratched the surface. Two things served as a kick in the pants: First, Bob called and asked how the book was going. Second, my father, who was dying by that point, asked me to finish what I started.

I dug in for several months, pausing during the summer once my father declined and joined Brenda in the afterlife. It was mid-August 2019, and my father had left us two weeks earlier. I had interviewed dozens of people in Brenda's life, but I knew virtually nothing about Jon Jr. beyond what I read in newspaper articles and reports. I was stuck, and I wrestled with the thought "would I betray the story by spending time telling his story?"

My wife, a driving force in this work, looked at me and said, "Brenda would want you to tell Jon's story." That reminded me of something Tracy told me during our first interview: "Brenda would have wanted to help Jon. She would have talked to him."

Even with the decision to tell his story, I needed to catch a break in the form of a name or phone number. I knew nothing about his family, beyond his aunt and uncle, and his mother, at the time, would not talk. So, I asked my father and Brenda for help on a sizzling hot day as I sat next to my father's headstone. Within a few weeks, there was a comment on one of my blogs about Brenda from Jon Jr.'s step-sister. After interviewing her, I had dozens of potential contacts like Stephanie and Di'Anna Dentis.

I suspect one of the reasons Jon Jr. responded after contacting his family is that many of the people close to him heard different stories in the years after he went to prison. Some said he told them he was framed. Some said they were told he wasn't involved. Some don't believe he killed Brenda, believing he took the blame for his father.

"Let you know that I am a little skeptical about all this," he wrote in his letter. "My family are also skeptical, some are against it all together. I discussed it with them several times. I have even discussed it with someone that I consider an advisor. I told them all that you do deserve the respect to get some kind of input from me."

I completed the paperwork to meet Jon Jr. and submitted it within a few weeks. I have not heard from him since, despite sending several letters. Unfortunately, the COVID pandemic would have prevented us from meeting from 2020 to 2021. Nonetheless, the interviews about his upbringing, early addictions, and lifelong struggles by age 22 shed some light on what led to the crime he committed, though it obviously does not excuse it.

For the time being, Jon Jr. is still in the Hutchinson Correctional Facility, where he'll be until at least Aug. 13, 2031, when he is eligible for parole. Most of Brenda's family and friends promise they'll be at the parole hearing in a joint effort to keep him behind bars. Others, like Judge Fred Jackson, who sentenced Jon Jr., and Bill Lucero, who fought against the death penalty for decades, don't think he'll ever be released.

As for the possibility Jon Jr. was framed, there's overwhelming evidence he was involved in Brenda's murder. The Sheriff's Department still has a brown bag of evidence, including blood and semen. Because the case happened in 1991, the KBI did not run DNA tests. More than 30 years later, they could test the evidence and possibly determine how many of the three men at the Blake house on Oct. 19, 1991, were involved.

FROM BRENDA TO BRENNA

As Scott Wanamaker walked down an embankment off a gravel road north of Topeka in May 2012, he didn't realize how similar the journey he was on was to that of his father's 20 years earlier. It was after 7 p.m. on May 25, and nightfall was a little more than an hour away as he made his way down to an isolated area with a creek off of 6600 Huxman Road.

In 1991, Wanamaker's dad, Mark, took a comparable walk from a rural country road, through a field, and across a pond, where he saw Brenda's body after Clinton Lambotte discovered it hours earlier. Scott Wanamaker, a sergeant with the Shawnee County Sheriff's Office, was responding to a call from the department's helicopter pilot, who said he located what appeared to be a body.

When Scott Wanamaker arrived at the creek, he found Brenna Morgart, an 18-year-old who graduated summa cum laude from Seaman High School five days earlier. Like Brenda, Morgart was a devout, driven young woman. Like Brenda, she was brutally murdered.

According to an article written by Steve Fry in the Topeka Capital-Journal, Morgart was running near her home in north Topeka on the morning of May 25 when 20-year-old Dustin Leftwich hit her with his car, forced her into the trunk, and drove her to the creek four miles away. There, he hit her with a tire iron and attempted to rape her, before dragging her to the creek, where she drowned.

"I'm telling you, that one made me think of Brenda, especially when we were all done with it that day," Scott Wanamaker said. "When my brain is on track of doing something, it's on getting the job done, and that's the way most law enforcement are. But, the aftereffects, holy cow, this is kind of like that situation. I even told a couple of the guys that I work with that this brings back some memories of what happened in Dover."

Scott Wanamaker not only discovered Morgart's body, but also walked Leftwich out of his house and to the police car when he was arrested. That brought back memories of Jon Jr.

"He had a 1,000-yard stare on his face, and he just didn't care," Scott Wanamaker said of Leftwich, who is spending life in prison in the Lansing Correctional Facility. "It's pretty crazy to look these people in the eye and see that they don't care for another human life."

Scott Wanamaker said he opted to follow his father into law enforcement after watching him work cases for 18 years as a detective for the Sheriff's Department, as well as hanging out with his father on Take Your Son to Work Day. After retiring from the department in 1999, Mark Wanamaker worked as an officer in the Topeka Public Schools' police unit for 12 years.

"I don't miss the police work," he said. "I miss the people. You wake up one day, and, 'OK, it's just time. I'm done with police work after 40 years at it.'"

Though many of the deputies and officers involved in Brenda's case left the Sheriff's Department during the late 1990s, several remained in law enforcement. Bill Kilian moved from Shawnee County to Wabaunsee County, serving as sheriff. His undersheriff was Jack Metz, who later worked on the security team at the Shawnee County Courthouse. Harry Carpenter retired from the Wabaunsee County Sheriff's Department in 1993. He died in April 2023 at age 81.

Mike Ramirez and Larry Baer, two of the lead detectives working the case, remain friends to this day, 25 years after retiring from the Sheriff's Office. Dave Reser, one of the first people to see Brenda's body, retired and started an excavation business. Myron Stucky, the reserve officer who sat in a squad car with the Mareskas for two hours, worked as a teacher in the Washburn Rural district in Topeka, and at Blue Cross and Blue Shield of Kansas.

"You work all your life and still need that all-important health insurance," Stucky said. "Blue Cross and Blue Shield is my retirement job."

Two of the other officers who worked the case have joined Brenda in the afterlife. Alvin Moran, who lived in Dover his entire life, died at age 66 in 2010, and Ken Smith suffered a stroke in 2019 and died in 2020.

Brenda's death also touched Allen Moran's late daughter, Sandra Moran Pletcher, who died in 2015. Before she succumbed to cancer, Pletcher wrote a novel, "State of Grace," motivated by Brenda's case. According to Bywater Books, the book is about an 11-year-old girl's obsession with finding the killer of her best friend in a small Kansas town in the early 1980s.

"It's about Brenda's situation, but she changed things because she didn't want to get anybody involved in the story," Allen Moran said. "I really think about Sandy (when he thinks of this case). She worked at the Girl Scout camp and would ride her bicycle from west of Dover there to the Girl Scout camp. I think about how, even though it was years later, it could have been her."

FORGING AHEAD

"I kept living, dear. That's what I did. I kept living."

For years afterward, people asked attorney Cheryl Stewart about Brenda's death. Though it wasn't as confrontational as the time a man at a church in Scranton told her that she caused the tragedy, people weren't afraid to approach her about the ordeal.

"I would answer people's questions if they asked me," she said. "If they didn't want to know what happened, I'd just say, 'OK.' I can't make people listen to me."

Stewart was the county attorney in Osage County from 1989 through 1994, then continued to work as a lawyer in the area until 1998. She was a guardian ad litem and judge pro tem in Wyandotte County in Kansas City from 1998 to 2005, according to her LinkedIn profile. She continued to work in law, including as an assistant county attorney, in the Kansas City area until moving elsewhere in Kansas, where she became a defense attorney.

"I think I do more good as a defense attorney," Stewart said. "My position at this point is to make sure the system functions so that you, me, and the rest can breathe and not worry about somebody banging the door in, so it's protecting our rights."

While Stewart remains adamant that she was not at fault for what happened on Oct. 19, 1991, she also has compassion for the Keller family.

"I'm sorry for the parents," she said. "Losing a child is awful. I'm not going to say it doesn't make me feel bad. It does. There's just nothing I could have done."

It's worth noting that while Cheryl Stewart signed the journal entry on the case in which Osage County released Jon Jr. from its custody to the state, she did not make the decision to place him with Gene and Tammy Blake in Dover.

More than 25 years after he represented Bob and Tracy in their compensation case against the state, well-known attorney Pedro Irigonegaray continues to seek justice. Through the years, he has fought for LGBTQ rights, including battles against late Westboro Baptist Church pastor Fred Phelps, and represented pro-evolution scientists during the Kansas Board of Education evolution hearings in 2005. Like the Kellers' case, he did not accept compensation for the latter.

"I was offered thousands of dollars to do that work," Irigonegaray said. "I refused to accept a single penny because those pennies would come from the funds that should have gone to children and their education."

Now in his 70s, Irigonegaray continues to practice law as a partner at Irigonegaray, Turney, & Revenaugh, which is "committed to the same moral objective: helping underserved communities and families in Topeka, Shawnee County, and beyond."

David Debenham retired in 2022 after working as a district court judge, and Maggie Lutes continues to practice law. The latter worked for the Shawnee County District Attorney's Office until 1995, when she left for Wichita to work in the Sedgwick County Office. Lutes is the chief of the charging unit, which determines if cases are charged in the court system. Even after 30 years of working as an attorney, she said Brenda's murder is a case that stands out.

"It was just sad," she said. "The world envelopes the most innocent."

LIVES LIVED ROUGH

Mike Goodenough always was the life of the party. Whether leading the Brookside Breakers or bringing a carload of people to Henthorne Park for a night of drinking, smoking weed, and listening to classic rock, he was the straw that stirred the drink. That continued when he joined the Marines after high school and when he returned to the Tulsa area.

For a time, Goodenough tried to help Jon Jr. while he was in prison, fellow Breaker Tim Livermore said.

"Jon was calling a lot, and he was sending money when he could, but it got to the point where it was too much for him on the phone bills," he said. "My understanding is that he (Jon Jr.) told him he was accused of rape, and that's all it was. Mike said he lost track of him, and that was hard on him because he was close to Jon."

The party never left Goodenough. He battled an addiction to alcohol his entire life and died at age 49 in 2018. Goodenough, who lived on a boat on Lake Keystone, tried to swim across the lake one night and drowned.

"They believe he jumped into the water and went into cardiac arrest," Di'Anna Dentis said.

Goodenough's death hit the Brookside crew hard, but it wasn't the only loss the group has suffered through the years. A handful of people Jon Jr. grew up with have died. Many of those who made it through some turbulent years have had difficult lives.

The death of Livermore's sister to a car accident when he was a teen sent him down a path of addiction that spanned decades. In 2020, he was diagnosed with cirrhosis of the liver.

"I've put my time in; I'm a half century old," said Livermore, who died at age 51 in 2021. "I'm not in any hurry to leave. I've got three boys and three beautiful granddaughters."

Lois Dentis' run as a bondswoman and drug dealer lasted for several years. She ended up spending more than two years in an Oklahoma prison for trafficking in children, a crime that might be confused for sex trafficking. According to the Oklahoma Count of Criminal Appeals, trafficking in children is defined as receiving money for adoption without disclosure to other persons.

She left prison in June 2003 and relied on Di'Anna Dentis for most of the rest of her life to survive. Lois Dentis died in a house fire in her early 60s.

"Di'Anna and my mom were close," Stephanie Dentis said. "They were the only two that were close."

Despite growing up in dysfunction, two of the Dentis sisters have had productive lives. Di'Anna Dentis has been a long-haul truck driver for more than 20 years, winning an award from her company for recruiting the most drivers in 2018. Stephanie Dentis began working at a small restaurant in Tulsa in 1988 and never left. She manages it today.

"This was my first job when I turned 16," Stephanie Dentis said. "I like people. It's different every single day. You never get bored. It's perfect for me. I can still gab a lot and get paid for it."

Jon Jr.'s former girlfriends have had varied lives. Becky Taylor and Sharron Jenkins have families and work in Kansas and Oklahoma, respectively. Kim Hardesty, on the other hand, has endured an extremely difficult life that includes time behind bars, overcoming addiction, and surviving rape.

"I've been raped four times, attempted three times, since I was 20. I've been through a hell of a lot," Hardesty said. "I'm one hell of a survivor, I can tell you that."

Time has moved on for Jon Jr.'s family. His stepsisters Teresa and Debbie live in different states and haven't spoken to him in decades. LaDonna Thomas, his mother, recently left Arkansas, where she lived for more than 20 years, to live near her sister in another state. His uncle Chip retired a few years ago and moved out of Kansas.

MAKING PEACE WITH THE WOODS

Marilee Sievers just couldn't bring herself to walk to the pond behind Gene and Tammy Blake's house and barns. For decades after Brenda's murder, she walked to the barn east of the pond and stopped.

"I remember Gene trying to go back there with me, and he said, 'She's gone, there's nothing there. Everything is OK. You can go back there,'" Sievers said. "I just couldn't. There's nothing we could possibly see that would help."

At one time, Sievers and her sister, Crystal, spent hours swimming in the pond and exploring the timber around the boatshed. But, the wooded playground ceased to exist for the Sievers sisters after the crime. For decades, they would not go near the pond or shed. Thirty years after losing their friend, Marilee Sievers finally ventured to the other side of the pond.

"I've been back to the woods a few times now," she said. "I've made my peace with the woods and have been able to enjoy the trails and area that Crystal and I used to love and play at as children. It really is a beautiful place."

The Sievers have done well. Crystal Sievers works in law, and her sister has worked as a graphic designer and nurse. Mary Sievers retired as a nurse and goes bowling with Tammy Blake almost weekly. Leon Sievers, who was among those near the boathouse when Clinton

Lambotte found Brenda's body, died in 2018, about a year after being interviewed for this book.

Many of the friends and schoolmates Brenda grew up with are enjoying successful lives, including Jill Wilson. She works as a business analyst and purchasing agent. Wilson's father Jim, also among those who found Brenda that fateful night, died in 2022 at age 84.

Like many professionals, Kristi Osburn and Julie Gomez worked from home during the COVID-19 pandemic. Lavella Buchmeier has been cutting hair for 40 years now, while her daughter, Autumn, is a nurse practitioner and her son, Tyrel, continues to work as a reserve officer outside of his full-time job. He still carries the note with Jon Jr.'s prison information in his wallet.

All of the teachers at the Dover Junior High and Dover Grade School have retired. Ted Lassen still has the book of jokes Brenda gave him. Terri Anderson was a principal in Topeka for several years before retiring. Pam Leptich moved away from Kansas, teaching a few classes at a small college and performing in plays. Allen Zordel retired after teaching for 40 years.

The reporters who covered Brenda's case worked in newspapers for many years afterward. Tim Hrenchir passed the 40-year mark at the Topeka Capital-Journal. Roberta Peterson worked her way up to editor-in-chief at a large chain before leaving the business. She still works as a writer and editor at a nonprofit organization. Steve Fry left the Capital-Journal after 40-plus years and worked for WIBW-TV for three years before retiring in 2020.

BOB'S CHAMPION

The loss of both of his parents hit Bob hard. In the span of 17 months, he lost his biggest fans. Bob spoke about his father during a message in January 2022 at the Federated Church.

During the sermon, he told a story about playing basketball in the seventh grade, largely because Roy made him play. Though he rarely saw the court, Bob got into a game at the end of the season and played several minutes.

"So, somehow, I ended up underneath the basket all by myself and shot a layup," Bob told the congregation. "And I missed. But the ball ended up in my hands again … so, I shot again. And I missed again. And, somehow, the ball ended up in my hands again. So, I shot again. And I missed again."

With the entire church laughing, Bob paused for a moment, then continued telling the story. After the game, one of the starters came up to Bob, slapped him on the back and said, "Keller, I've never seen anything like that." Bob replied, "I've never seen anything like that, either."

"No, I'm talking about your dad," the teammate said.

As Bob misfired several times, Roy was hooting and hollering, cheering on his son wildly to make a shot, the teammate said. As the message that Sunday continued, Bob spoke about his father and how much he missed his dad, who was always there to support him.

"What I'm saying is he was my champion," he said. "And I miss that."

Bob and Tracy's lives remain much the same as they have for years. Bob still does chaplain work, and Tracy continues to treat animals. They still have dozens of critters at their pseudo-zoo. They raised their adopted kids until both left home to begin their adult lives in recent years.

As time has passed, John and Pat's spiritual lives have changed. Though they respect their parents' beliefs, they are not religious and can be described as agnostic.

"I'm not really big on labels," Pat said. "There's a transactionalism that comes with a religious person, and it becomes a situation where they're able to cancel everything."

John's belief system changed in college, when he began researching science and evolution. When asked if he forgave Jon Jr., he said, "I don't have a biblical need to forgive. Probably not. I don't harbor any anger at the guy. I don't know what his story is, and I really don't want to know that much."

In the years since, John said he has enjoyed debating religion and evolution with his father and uncles at family get-togethers. Both brothers deny that Brenda's death is the reason for their beliefs.

"I don't believe in religion," said Pat, "but I don't know if it's because of that. I feel like some religious viewpoints hamper your ability to absorb things from a different angle."

Brenda's memory continues to endure in the family, regardless of differences in faith. During one of my visits to Dover in 2022, I pulled up to her headstone near the east end of the cemetery. It was a warm, sunny day, with a gentle breeze making a plastic flower next to the monument sway from side to side. There were fresh daisies next to the marker, likely left by one of the dozens of steady visitors who will never forget Brenda Michelle Keller. To the south, birds swooped in and out of trees, where squirrels played, racing up and down the branches. Below Brenda's name, a ladybug crawled across the marble. As I reached down to wipe a few blades of grass from the concrete under the heart-shaped marker, the ladybug flew off. I smiled and said "Goodbye."